Nomadic Art of the Eastern Eurasian Steppes

The Eugene V. Thaw and Other New York Collections

EMMA C. BUNKER

with contributions by

James C.Y. Watt   Zhixin Sun

The Metropolitan Museum of Art, New York
Yale University Press, New Haven and London

This publication is issued in conjunction with the exhibition "Nomadic Art of the Eastern Eurasian Steppes: The Eugene V. Thaw and Other New York Collections," held at The Metropolitan Museum of Art, New York, October 1, 2002–January 5, 2003.

The exhibition is made possible in part by the William Randolph Hearst Foundation.

This publication is made possible by The Adelaide Milton de Groot Fund, in memory of the de Groot and Hawley families.

Published by The Metropolitan Museum of Art, New York

John P. O'Neill, Editor in Chief
Emily Walter, Editor, with the assistance of Elizabeth Powers
Bruce Campbell, Designer
Peter Antony and Megan Arney, Production
Robert Weisberg, Desktop Publishing
Jean Wagner, Bibliographic Editor

Photography of objects in the exhibition by Oi-Cheong Lee and Joseph Coscia Jr., The Photograph Studio, The Metropolitan Museum of Art

Maps designed by Adam Hart, The Metropolitan Museum of Art

Objects in the following catalogue entries were scientifically examined by Pieter Meyers, Conservator, Los Angeles County Museum of Art: 10, 16, 22, 23, 26, 27, 30, 37, 46, 47, 54, 64, 65, 69, 70, 71, 78, 80, 82, 83, 86, 105, 109, 110, 113, 131, 156, 157, 160, 169, 176.

Typeset in Perpetua by Professional Graphics Inc., Rockford, Illinois
Color separations by Professional Graphics Inc., Rockford, Illinois
Printed on 130 gsm Lumisilk
Printed and bound by CS Graphics PTE Ltd., Singapore

Library of Congress Cataloging-in-Publication Data

Bunker, Emma C.
    Nomadic art of the eastern Eurasian steppes : the Eugene V. Thaw and other New York collections / Emma C. Bunker; with contributions by James C.Y. Watt, Zhixin Sun.
        p. cm.
    Catalog of an exhibition held at the Metropolitan Museum of Art, Oct. 1, 2002–Jan. 5, 2003.
    Includes bibliographical references and index.
    ISBN 1-58839-066-7 (hc) — ISBN 0-300-09688-7 (Yale University Press)
    1. Metal-work, Nomadic—Eurasia—Exhibitions. 2. Decoration and ornament—Animal forms—Eurasia—Exhibitions. 3. Thaw, Eugene Victor—Art collections—Exhibitions. 4. Metalwork—Private collections—New York (State)—New York—Exhibitions. I. Watt, James C.Y. II. Sun, Zhixin, 1951– III. Metropolitan Museum of Art (New York, N.Y.). IV. Title

NK6407.25.B86 2002
732'086'91—dc21   2002075328

Jacket illustration: Harness jingle with stag, Northeast China, 7th–6th century B.C. (cat. no. 29)

Frontispiece: Finial with standing ibex, North China, 7th–6th century B.C. (cat. no. 25)

TABLE OF CONTENTS

DIRECTOR'S FOREWORD

This exhibition, *Nomadic Art of the Eastern Eurasian Steppes*, has been staged to celebrate the gift by Eugene V. Thaw of his extensive collection of bronze, silver, and gold objects from the steppes of Eurasia. The qualifier "eastern" in the title of the exhibition reflects the preponderance of objects from Mongolia and North China, although there are not a few pieces in the collection that originated from as far as west of the Black Sea. In this exhibition, the Thaw collection is augmented by a few objects each from several collectors in the New York area and from the Museum's own holdings.

Works of art from the steppe zone of the Eurasian continent are not strange to the Metropolitan Museum. Over the years, the Museum has mounted a number of exhibitions of the art of the steppes, including, in 1975, *From the Lands of the Scythians* and, as recently as 2000, *The Golden Deer of Eurasia*. All of these have been loan exhibitions from countries in which the objects were found, and most of the exhibits have related to the western part of the Eurasian steppes and to cultures associated with the Scythians and the Sarmatians, with the inclusion of some objects from Siberia and the Altai Mountains. The present exhibition is the first at the Metropolitan Museum that comprises mainly objects that are now in the permanent collection of the Museum and shows predominantly articles from the eastern part of the Eurasian steppes.

The gift of the Thaw collection increases measurably the Museum's holdings in the art of the early nomads of the Eurasian steppes dating from the first millennium B.C. to the early centuries of our era. Hitherto, early nomadic art has been represented by small groups of objects in the departments of Greek and Roman, ancient Near Eastern, and Asian art. The Museum will now be able to put on permanent display a large selection of artifacts from the Eurasian steppes, representing in its galleries a major branch of the arts of the ancient world. The art of the steppes, characterized by powerful animal imagery and dynamic designs, is visually compelling to us today, as it must have been in ancient times to the peoples in sedentary societies who came into contact with the pastoral nomads. Art historians are increasingly turning to the study of this tradition as an important source for the decorative arts in Eurasia in subsequent periods. The Thaw collection at the Metropolitan Museum will facilitate this study.

The name of Eugene V. Thaw has long been associated with Western art, particularly old master drawings, of which he is a well-known collector and connoisseur. Some know him also as a major collector of Native American art. Few know of his long-standing interest in the art of the ancient nomads. We are grateful that he has seen fit to donate this collection, which he has formed over the years, to the Metropolitan Museum. His gift will benefit both the visitors to the Museum and the scholarly community. I would like also to extend my thanks to Katherine and George Fan and to Shelby White and Leon Levy, as well as to those who have chosen to lend anonymously, for further enriching this exhibition.

The exhibition and this catalogue would not have been possible without the wide-ranging participation of Emma C. Bunker, Research Consultant in the Asian Art Department of the Denver Art Museum, whose vast knowledge of the art and culture of the nomadic peoples of the Eurasian steppes has earned her the reputation of preeminent scholar in the field. The exhibition was organized by the Department of Asian Art, under the direction of James C.Y. Watt, Brooke Russell Astor Chairman of the department, who was assisted in this effort by Zhixin Sun, Associate Curator. I wish to extend my deepest thanks both to Mrs. Bunker and to the Department of Asian Art for the excellent results of their study of the Thaw collection and the planning of the exhibition.

The Metropolitan Museum is indebted to the generous support of the William Randolph Hearst Foundation toward this exhibition. It was through funding from The Adelaide Milton de Groot Fund, in memory of the de Groot and Hawley families, that this exhibition catalogue was made possible.

Philippe de Montebello
Director
The Metropolitan Museum of Art

ACKNOWLEDGMENTS

I am both thrilled and honored to have been invited by Eugene V. Thaw to help form and research his landmark collection of steppe art, for which I owe him an enormous debt of gratitude. It is rare that one finds a collector as knowledgeable and discerning as Gene, and our work together has proved to be not only a magical collaborative effort but a delightful pleasure. Both Gene and I live in the West, ride horses, and herd cattle. We can therefore be said to have firsthand experience in the lifestyle of the pastoral world and a special insight, crucial to the writing of this book, into the mentality of people involved with animals.

Gene's vision in forming this collection and in presenting it to The Metropolitan Museum of Art demonstrates his perceptive recognition of an aesthetic that has long been overlooked. The pastoral peoples of the Eurasian steppes made a significant contribution in antiquity to the artistic and technological development of both Asia and Europe, a contribution that is now highlighted by a rich representation of their art in this great museum.

I am particularly grateful to Philippe de Montebello, Director of the Metropolitan Museum, and to James C.Y. Watt, Brooke Russell Astor Chairman of the Department of Asian Art, for entrusting me with the presentation in this catalogue of Eugene Thaw's generous gift. The publication, which is both timely and scholarly, is the result of a collaboration between many people of diverse backgrounds. Who else but James Watt, one of the leading scholars in the field of Chinese art today, could better present China's urban point of view toward its northern nomadic neighbors. By contrast, Eugene Thaw is one of the great dealers in old master paintings and drawings. Known for his "eye" and connoisseurship, he has collected instinctively, with an intuition for rarity and beauty.

At the Metropolitan Museum, I would like to thank John P. O'Neill, Editor in Chief, for his support of this project and for his faith that Emily Walter, Senior Editor, and I could successfully organize this complex publication. Without her resourcefulness and fascination with the subject, this catalogue could not have been produced. Whenever I was stymied or at a loss for words, Emily would provide just the right solution. My colleague Zhixin Sun, Associate Curator in the Department of Asian Art and a contributor to this volume, was enormously helpful throughout the cataloguing process. I am most appreciative of the scientific information provided by Richard Stone, Conservator. My heartfelt thanks goes to Judith Smith, Administrator of the Department of Asian Art, who coordinated all the activities and personalities involved, and did it with diplomatic panache. When things seemed overwhelming, she was always available to solve problems.

Last, but not least, I wish to thank the Metropolitan Museum colleagues involved with the production of this catalogue for their diligence and encouragement. Bruce Campbell created the sensitive and refined design. Oi-Cheong Lee and Joseph Coscia Jr. brilliantly photographed the objects, making them sparkle and showing them to their best advantage. Peter Antony, Chief Production Manager, and Megan Arney, Production Manager, ensured that the photographs were well produced, both in clarity and color. Jean Wagner, bibliographic editor, with unflappable attention to detail, made sure that my references were correct. Adam Hart designed the handsome maps. Elizabeth Powers worked as research editor, and Shi-yee Liu translated the Chinese titles in the bibliography.

The variety of objects presented here also required help and advice from many other colleagues, both in China and in Russia, as well as in the United States. Foremost are Han Rubin and Wu En, both of whom traveled with me throughout China, helping me to gain access to many excavated examples and to understand how they were produced. Without their advice this publication could never have been written. I am grateful to Sergei Miniaev and to my late colleagues Yevgeny Lubo-Lesnichenko, Eleanora Novgorodova, and Maria Zavitukhina. I am especially thankful to Jenny F. So and Katheryn M. Linduff, both of whom read parts of the text, made constructive suggestions, and generously shared with me all their resources. Additional scientific examination by Pieter Meyers, Conservator at the Los Angeles County Museum of Art, of many pieces before they were acquired by Eugene

Thaw was crucial to confirmation of their authenticity and to my understanding of how they were manufactured. I am also appreciative of John Stevenson's helpful advice in the initial writing of my essays.

Obscure references and publications were acquired through inter-library loan by Nancy Simon, librarian at the Denver Art Museum, and by John Stucky, at the Asian Art Museum of San Francisco. Helpful advice and information were also provided by Robert H. Ellsworth, Joseph G. Gerena, Catherine Simon Geventer, James J. Lally, Bo Lawergren, Judith Lerner, Karen Rubinson, and the staffs of Ariadne Gallery, Inc., Eskenazi Ltd., and Ward & Company, Inc. Invaluable help in reading references in Chinese was always available from my friend Ranyin Wu, and endless xeroxes were happily provided by Joyce and Bob Noyces, often working after hours.

I would like to thank in particular William Watson, Keeper of the Chinese Collection at the British Museum and my professor at the Institute of Fine Arts in New York City, who first introduced me to the art of the steppes and guided me north through the Great Wall.

To Katherine and George Fan, to Shelby White and Leon Levy, and to those who who have lent anonymously to this exhibition, I am pleased for having been given the opportunity to study their collections and grateful for their generosity, help, and advice.

Finally, I wish to thank my husband, John Bunker, for his support and his goodwill, enabling me to spend the many hours necessary to complete this project.

Emma C. Bunker

For the organization and installation of the exhibition, my colleague Zhixin Sun, Associate Curator in the Department of Asian Art, has served as coordinator. The imaginative exhibition design is by Michael Batista, the elegant graphics is the work of Jill Hammarberg, and the brilliant lighting is directed by Zack Zanolli. The installation team of Jeffrey Perhacs, Nancy Reynolds, Frederick Sager, and Alexandra Walcott mounted, in their magical way, the many small objects in the exhibition. Linda Sylling oversaw all practical aspects of the installation, and Taylor Miller supervised the construction work.

My own participation has been ably ordered and assisted by Judith Smith, who also worked with Emma C. Bunker and Zhixin Sun in pulling together all the illustrative material for the catalogue and acted as liaison for the Department of Asian Art with Emma Bunker during its preparation. Yangming Chu and Hwai-ling Yeh-Lewis spent hour upon hour organizing and reorganizing the list of exhibits and the many images in the course of the preparation of the exhibition.

Bruce Campbell, as usual, has designed the catalogue in a style that is appropriate to the content. The handsome volume is also enhanced by the expert and sympathetic photography of Oi-Cheong Lee and Joseph Coscia Jr. of the Museum's Photograph Studio.

The scientific authentication of antiquities in metal, especially those in precious metals, is always difficult after the objects have been in collections and handled for a number of years. Special thanks are due to Pieter Meyers, of the Los Angeles County Museum of Art, who reexamined many pieces in the Eugene V. Thaw collection after they had been deposited at the Metropolitan Museum.

In the course of learning about the subject of steppe art, I benefited from discussions with Eugene Thaw, Karen Rubinson, and, of course, Emma Bunker. Esther Jacobson read what I wrote for this catalogue and corrected some mistakes—those that remain are mine alone.

Finally, I acknowledge Emily Walter, the editor of this catalogue, who improved my writing and whose patience and good sense turned a chore into a pleasure.

James C.Y. Watt

COLLECTOR'S FOREWORD

As an art dealer for nearly half a century, I had the vivid experience of having thousands of works of art pass through my hands. Each one required that I learn something about it, judge how much I liked or disliked it, and rank it against others of its kind. Being in the presence of the object itself, rather than looking at a slide or photograph—or today, a computer image—provokes this kind of intense inquiry, especially if one is risking one's scarce resources to own it. It was this striving for discipline and the instinct for putting objects into some sort of order that led me to become a collector.

Throughout my career as a dealer I collected master drawings, which I continue to do. This collection, destined for the Pierpont Morgan Library in New York, has been published and widely exhibited. It has certainly been my principal focus as a collector, and is by some measure my life's work.

Some fifteen years ago, I began the gradual process of retirement from art dealing—but not from my involvement with art. My wife, Clare, and I moved to Santa Fe, New Mexico, far removed from any temptation on my part to commute from our home in the suburbs to my Manhattan office. Santa Fe has lots of art but few old master drawings, and it soon became clear that I would have to find a new outlet for my passion to collect. With the greatest help from Ralph T. Coe, former Director of the Nelson-Atkins Museum of Art in Kansas City,[1] who had also retired to Santa Fe, I began a collection of North American Indian art, which is now housed in the new wing of the Fenimore Art Museum, in Cooperstown, New York.

Just as I add a drawing or two every so often to the substantial collection already in the Morgan Library, so, too, do I occasionally add a work of American Indian art, if it is outstanding and fills a gap, to the Cooperstown museum. But filling in gaps was not enough of a challenge to someone who was possessed by the desire to collect—indeed, far more intensely than even I had ever suspected.

Quite simply, I had a craving—to hold objects in my hands, to learn about them, to make judgments about their quality. Also, I needed a subject that was relatively unexplored, objects not already collected by worldwide competitors, such as Rembrandt etchings or Tang dynasty ceramics. Something not too fashionable would also be more affordable, especially for a collection that I tended to think of as therapy for an obsession I could not control.

Years ago, I knew the late Bruce Chatwin when he worked at Sotheby's as a very young man and, like him and others mad about objects, I often dropped in to visit the London private dealer and guru of ancient objects John Hewett. Somehow, in that circle I became aware of the so-called Ordos bronzes and purchased a few, just to establish an acquaintance. I also aquired Alfred Salmony's seminal book, in which were published the large group he called Sino-Siberian, which had been assembled before 1930 by the great dealer C. T. Loo in Paris.[2] A few years later, in 1970, I saw and was intrigued by the pioneering exhibition at Asia Society, New York, "Animal Style Art from East to West," organized and catalogued by Emma C. Bunker. Bruce Chatwin collaborated with Emmy on that exhibition, writing an essay extolling the culture of nomadism, a subject that would become a leitmotif in his subsequent career as a novelist and travel writer (*In Patagonia, The Songlines*, etc.).

I traded away a few pieces from that early group, and when the American Indian collection left our house for the Fenimore Art Museum, I had two Ordos pieces remaining in my possession—one a very fine bronze deer with folded legs and the other a belt plaque that I had learned was a forgery. After I had made a fairly substantial reentry into this field, I discovered that my longtime associate at E. V. Thaw and Co., Patricia Tang, knew Emmy Bunker, who had over the years become the most highly respected authority on the art of the Asian steppes. I, of course, contrived to meet her, and the rest of that story is revealed in this catalogue of the collection she helped me to assemble.

Again through Patty Tang, I got to meet James C.Y. Watt, just as he was about to assume the chairmanship of the Department of Asian Art at the Metropolitan Museum. Philippe de Montebello had heard via the grapevine—which great museum directors invariably have access to—that I was now collecting Ordos bronzes. He maneuvered James and me to seats around his grand table in the director's office, and suddenly there was talk of an exhibition of nomadic art that would be held in about two years' time. I then set about to expand and refine the collection, with the advice and encouragement that I had come to depend on from Emmy Bunker. Luck and serendipity of course play a role in such activities. One day James and Emmy were meeting with me in my office for an early discussion of the Met's plans, when a private collector-dealer from Kyoto walked in carrying—wrapped in a towel—a rare Ordos bronze helmet. Of course, it was immediately acquired.

Emmy Bunker, as well as being the brilliant cataloguer of the collection, has become a good friend to Clare and to me, and we three are very gratified that the works will remain always in the Metropolitan. For there it will surely shed light on the movement of styles across the vast steppes of Eurasia during the first millennium B.C., as the nomadic peoples bridged the great spaces between the high civilizations of China and the Mediterranean.

Eugene Victor Thaw
February 2002

1. Ted Coe curated the great bicentennial exhibition "Sacred Circles" for London and Kansas City in 1976. The catalogue he wrote is the "bible" for collectors of North American Indian art.
2. Alfred Salmony was Professor of Art History at the Institute of Fine Arts, New York University, and his book was an early essay in English on this new field of research.

The World of the Eurasian Nomads

A

SIBERIA

• Szidorova

Ob River

• Arzhan

Minusinsk •   *SAYAN MOUNTAINS*

Pazyryk •   Irkutsk •   *LAKE BAIKAL*

ALTAI MOUNTAINS   **TUVA**   • Ulan Ude

Amur River

• Chilikta

KE BALKHASH

Ulaan Baatar •

MONGOLIA

YSTAN   **ISSYK-KUL**

• Ürümqi   *GOBI DESERT*

TIAN SHAN MOUNTAINS

N

TAKLA MAKAN DESERT

Beijing •

AMIR MNTS

ORDOS

CHINA

Nomadic Art of the
Eastern Eurasian Steppes

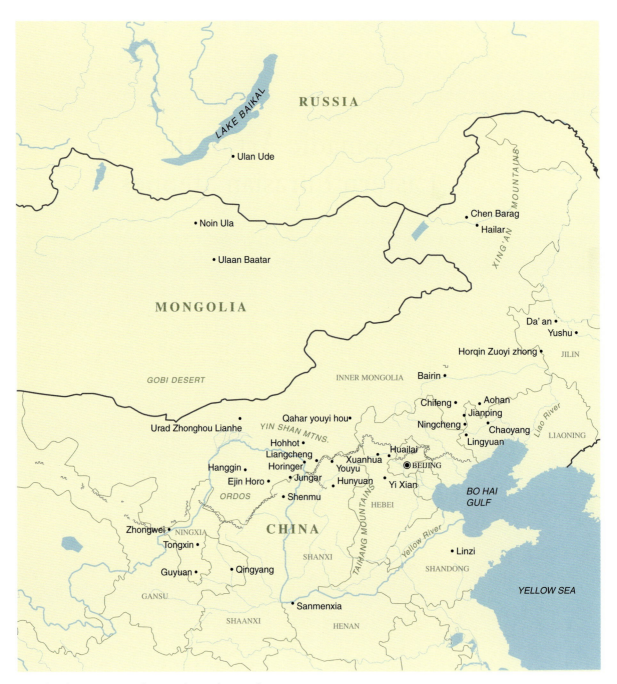

North China, Mongolia, and Southern Siberia

INTRODUCTION

JAMES C.Y. WATT

There is a major source of artistic styles and motifs that has so far not featured in the general writing on the visual arts of Europe and Asia. This is the art of the pastoral nomads who roamed the Eurasian steppes for most of the first millennium before our era. Over the vast expanse of grasslands stretching from Siberia to Scythia, there are no natural boundaries, and the cultural artifacts of the horse-riding nomads display a remarkable homogeneity—perhaps reflecting similarities in their way of life and in their natural environments. This was particularly the case in the early part of the millennium, when pastoral nomadism began to spread among the peoples who inhabited the steppes of Eurasia. By the fifth century B.C., the nomads had achieved a high degree of material prosperity as a result of economic success in livestock herding and trading—peacefully or by force of arms—as evidenced by the rich archaeological remains from this period. Prosperity also brought about the flourishing of an artistic style that was to leave an indelible impression on the arts of nomadic societies in Eurasia through all subsequent periods and that was absorbed into the decorative vocabulary of works of art in agrarian societies whose domains bordered their lands.

Present-day knowledge concerning the arts of the nomadic world is insufficient for a systematic art-historical exposition. However, it is hoped that the present exhibition, drawn mainly from one collection, will serve to illustrate some of the salient features of a neglected artistic tradition and draw attention to the exhibits as works of art rather than as archaeological objects. Nevertheless, in the catalogue entries, by Emma C. Bunker, reference to cognate material found in archaeological context will be included.

PASTORAL NOMADISM

The economy of the pastoral nomads was based on livestock herding and involved a constant search for pastures. The extent of their migration differed from group to group, and there was no universal pattern. For some it may have involved only transit between summer and winter habitats, although the distances separating the two locations varied greatly, while others were constantly on the move. The composition of the herds—sheep, goats, horses, camels, and cattle—also varied with natural conditions.

Before the onset of nomadism, steppe peoples depended on hunting and animal husbandry; some agriculture was practiced, but only where soil, water, and climate permitted. The exact causes for the shift to nomadism is still a matter of scholarly debate. The academic discourse on this subject can reach a degree of verbal and technical complexity that defies any attempt at comprehension by the ordinary reader.[1] The most common conjectures advanced as explanations for the origin of nomadism are based on climatic change, ecological adaptation, and social organization—each of these possibly being a factor in the cause.

Our knowledge of the early nomads derives from two sources. The first is the writings of ancient authors, notably those of Greece, Achaemenid Persia, and China. The second comes from archaeological work, mainly the excavation of kurgans—ancient graves covered by earth and stone mounds, the largest of which can reach nearly sixty feet in height and two hundred feet in diameter. The names by which nomadic peoples are known are taken from early writings. The fifth-century B.C. Greek historian Herodotus referred to nomads as Scythians, because they inhabited the northern shores of the Black Sea—known as Scythia—and came into close contact with the Greeks. Achaemenid Iranian inscriptions give us the appellation Saka, the name by which the Iranians called the nomads they encountered. And early Chinese texts recorded the names of various nomadic tribes on China's northern borders (some different names may refer to the same people). But it was not until the second century B.C. that the historian Sima Qian gave an account of the Xiongnu (formerly romanized as Hsiung-nu), the people—or a confederation of tribes—who had amassed along the line demarcated by the Great Wall.

Archaeologists (both the field and the armchair varieties) use names such as those mentioned above to refer to nomads in the description and discussion of archaeological data and artifacts identified as associated with nomadic peoples. However, the names of tribes or confederations that appear in the historical records of literate sedentary societies relate to specific events and locations in border areas. The application of these names to peoples active in different times and places far from the recorded events can, and does, cause confusion for nonspecialists. Some authors use the name Scythian in the more restricted sense to refer to the peoples in the north Pontic (Black Sea) area—as recorded by Herodotus—while others designate all nomadic peoples as Scythians, sometimes making a distinction between European Scythians and Asian Scythians. Yet others use the term Scytho-Siberian as the designation for all early nomadic peoples. In the East, the records of the Xiongnu in Chinese historical writings have also caused this appellation to be applied rather loosely to most sites and artifacts found in the eastern part of the Eurasian steppes that display a nomadic flavor, particularly sites and artifacts judged to date from the third century B.C. and later. Thus, the period from the third century B.C. to the sixth century A.D. in the "Asiatic" part of the nomadic world is sometimes known as the Hunnic period, on the assumption that the Huns, or their predecessors the Xiongnu (pronounced hūn-nu in antiquity), were the dominant power in the Asiatic steppes at this time.

THE ART OF THE NOMADS

The material culture of the nomads is known to us from archaeological remains, mostly recovered from burials and, in later periods, from settlement sites such as those in the Transbaikal area associated with the Xiongnu.[2] Unfortunately, most kurgans, especially the more prominent ones, were pillaged in antiquity. The few undisturbed graves hold a wealth of objects, mostly of gold and bronze. Other objects fashioned from wood, leather, birch bark, felt, and other perishable materials survive to varying extent depending on local conditions.

The salient feature of the art of the nomads is the prevalence of animal motifs. This has given rise to the term "animal style" in the literature. The animals, both wild and domestic, are represented either realistically or in degrees of stylization, achieving at times a hieratic aspect. Irrespective of the degree of stylization, the images are imbued with a power and vitality that are most striking, especially in the motif of the animal combat, which began to appear by about the eighth century B.C. This animal art can be studied in several ways, from anthropological approaches, including the search for the symbolic and religious significance of the motifs, to the purely art-historical. At the most basic and practical level, the species of animals represented on objects from different areas also provide clues to the general direction of the migration of peoples over time, as opposed to movements within seasonal confines. It has been pointed out, for example, that the images of the birds, felines, and deer seen on objects from Scythian burials in Ukraine find close parallels in the fauna that still inhabit the Altai Mountain region in southern Siberia. This observation, together with the typological study of artifacts found in the Altai and in Ukraine, has given rise to the hypothesis that the Scythians in Ukraine may have originated in the Altai and moved westward into the Pontic region early in the nomadic period, about the eighth century B.C.[3]

Up to the present, the study of the artistic aspect of the material remains of the early nomads has been incorporated into a search for a cultural context for the interpretation of the entire archaeological record. However, no consensus has been reached as to a standard model for the "cultural ecology" of the nomads. The chief difficulty in this study is the lack of written records by the nomads themselves. One attempt to overcome this difficulty is to find parallels in the cultural traits of ancient civilizations of sedentary peoples who are supposed to have been related to the nomads in some way and who did leave written texts regarding their systems of beliefs—and, to a certain extent, their history. Based in part on the physiological study of the human remains in nomadic burials and in part on the writing of peoples who had early contact with the nomads, it has been generally assumed that the early nomads were Indo-Europeans, and Indo-Iranians in particular, with some allowance for the intrusion of Mongoloids in the eastern part of the Eurasian steppes during the Hunnic period. The terms Indo-European and Indo-Iranian originated in nineteenth-century linguistic studies and have been extrapolated to designate racial or ethnic groupings. The system of religious beliefs and the practices of early Indo-Iranians who developed urban civilizations, as recorded in the Iranian *Avesta* and the Indian Vedic texts, is then applied to the interpretation of archaeological finds associated with the nomads. Thus, for example, "the deer is considered a totemic vestige occasionally substituted for the horse; the horse referred to kingship, and its sacrifices to the renewal of cosmic order; and gold referred primarily, though not exclusively, to solar values or to the solar-warrior."[4] This approach is open to certain objections, as has been pointed out by Esther Jacobson, whose own study is based on the internal evidence offered by the art of the nomads from its earliest manifestation in the beginning of the first millennium B.C., paying heed to the "cultural integrity" of the nomads themselves.[5]

Respect for the cultural integrity of the nomads does not obviate the study of cultural and artistic exchanges between nomads and the sedentary societies with which they came in contact. These exchanges became more prevalent from about the fifth century onward—the Scythians with the Greeks, the Saka with the Iranians, and the Siberian-Mongolian nomads with the Chinese. It is not proposed here to enter into a theoretical debate as to the symbolic significance of nomadic art at any stage of its history or the mode of cultural exchange between early nomads and sedentary populations—particularly in the consideration of precedence, that is, the questions of who influenced whom and in what respect. There is already a considerable body of literature on these questions.[6] Rather, it is proposed, in the concluding essay of this volume, to sketch an outline of the later history of nomadic art, beginning at the end of the first millennium B.C., a time generally considered too late for the study of nomadic art proper. As the great majority of the objects in this exhibition are from the northern border regions of China, and as there is a wealth of material in later Chinese art that lends itself to analytical study, our discussion will be concerned mainly with the aftermath of the intense contact between the nomadic tribes and the settled populations in North China from about the second century A.D. onward. Also discussed will be the survival of certain styles in the arts of eastern Central Asia in the medieval period that can be attributed to an origin in the world of the Eurasian steppes.

In the next two essays, Emma C. Bunker gives a broader description of the ecology of the steppes and the peoples who inhabited it, followed by a detailed account of the archaeological record of the different regions from which the objects in this exhibition are likely to have been found. Her encyclopedic knowledge of the archaeology of this area provides the basis for attributions as to dating and regional association and for the discussions in the catalogue entries.

The catalogue is ordered by types of objects rather than by dates, regional styles, or association with particular cultures or groups of people. Nevertheless, it may be pointed out that there are certain types of objects that can be associated with particular tribes or confederations of tribes. For example, the helmets (cat. nos. 46, 47), short sword (cat. no. 45), and knife (cat. no. 41) are attributed by Chinese archaeologists to the Donghu group, early inhabitants of Northeast China. Belt plaques and buckles representing animals in combat (cat. nos. 68, 72, 94, 97, 104), and the silver recumbent horse (cat. no. 101) are considered to be typical of the Xiongnu.[7] The gold and gold-wrapped plaques with three deer (cat. nos. 152, 154) and the pair of horse plaques in gilded bronze (cat. no. 85) can be firmly attributed to the Xianbei group, who replaced the Xiongnu in Mongolia in the first century B.C. More detailed identification of objects by regional style and by association with specific groups of people will have to await further study. It is hoped that the solid information provided in the catalogue entries will be a major step toward this exploration.

1. See, for example Tosi 1992.
2. Davydova 1995; Davydova, 1996; Miniaev 1998.
3. Reeder 1999, p. 38.
4. Jacobson 1992, p. 3.
5. Jacobson 1992; Jacobson 1999.
6. See, for example, Bunker 1983–85; Jacobson 1988; and So 1995a.
7. Personal communication, Huang Xueyin, Curator, Museum of Inner Mongolia, November 2001.

Figure 1. View of the grasslands from Binder Uul, Hentii aimag, eastern Mongolia, June 1996. Photo: Emma C. Bunker

THE LAND AND THE PEOPLE

EMMA C. BUNKER

Diogenes the Cynic said that man first crowded into cities to escape the fury of those outside. Locked within their walls, they committed every outrage against one another as if this were the sole object of their coming together. [Beyond the city walls, a different approach to life developed,] the Nomadic Alternative.

C. Bruce Chatwin, "The Nomadic Alternative," in Bunker, Chatwin, and Farkas 1970, pp. 176, 177

The word "steppe," meaning grassy plain in Russian, has become synonymous with the vast belt of Eurasian grasslands that extends west for thousands of miles from the Great Wall of China into central Europe (figs. 1, 2).[1] During the first millennium B.C., it was inhabited by groups of pastoral peoples whose economies were based on a combination of stock raising, herding, hunting, and agriculture, depending on the regional ecology. The steppe peoples have often been portrayed as wandering barbarians more intent on raiding and stealing goods from their settled neighbors than trading with them, but today scholars are gaining a more accurate picture of nomadic life. Organized around prescribed seasonal migrations over long-established routes from home camps to known destinations, which provided water, pasture, and hunting grounds, their lives were in fact highly structured. In many regions, these routes are still in use today and comprise the only roads available across the vast expanse of the steppe (fig. 3). The Eurasian pastoral peoples were integral parts of larger regional systems that included settled communities. Over time, both groups developed strong, mutually beneficial ties, and the exchanges between them infused both cultures with a remarkable hybrid vigor that resulted in an explosion of artistic productivity.

The pastoral peoples of the Eurasian steppes left no written legacy, but the artifacts that remain provide clues to their

Figure 2. The Great Wall, North China, begun in the 1st millennium B.C. Photo: Emma C. Bunker

7

history and cultural beliefs. Beautifully crafted objects made of metal, bone, wood, and fabric designed to accommodate a mobile lifestyle, they include personal ornaments, belt accessories, horse gear, tools, weapons, mirrors, and small vessels, often richly decorated with intricate motifs—animals, birds, reptiles, and human figures—visual representations of the natural and the supernatural worlds.

Traditionally relegated to the periphery of art history, these splendid artifacts have the distinction of being among the most misunderstood objects in Eurasian history. Known primarily through chance finds, they have until recently remained archaeological orphans, without cultural context, and have been described in a bewildering array of ambiguous terms that have little historical or archaeological basis: animal style, Ordos, Sino-Siberian, Scytho-Siberian, and Scytho-Thracian.[2] Today, the artifacts from the Eurasian steppes can be compared with finds from archaeologically excavated sites, making it possible to attribute them to regional styles described in terminology based on fact rather than fiction.

The steppe zone of Eurasia has played a major role in Eurasian history, although its importance is often overlooked. In antiquity, it served as an important information highway, connecting east with west and opening up transregional trade routes that would be used for centuries, such as the famous Silk Road through the deserts of Central Asia and the later Tea Road spanning north and west from Beijing to St. Petersburg. The nomadic groups that lived on the steppes were intermediaries in the transmission of many innovations from one place to another. Wheeled transport, for example, was introduced into China in the late second millennium B.C. through contact with neighboring pastoral peoples,[3] and some four hundred years later horseback riding was brought into China the same way.

The vast Eurasian land mass is not ecologically homogeneous, although its grassland belt runs for thousands of miles, almost from the Pacific Ocean to the North Sea, part of a beautiful mosaic of deserts, forests, lakes, mountains, rivers, and seas (figs. 4, 5). In the distant past, these areas were not defined by political boundaries. Today, the main body of the steppe lies within the borders of the former Soviet Union.[4] To the east it extends into Mongolia and Northeast China, while to the west it reaches as far as the Carpathian Mountain range in central Europe. The ancient pastoral peoples inhabited not only the grasslands of the steppe belt but also territory adjacent to the north and south (see the map on pp. XII–XIII).

The steppe zone is further subdivided by mountains and rivers into smaller geographic areas. The Urals and the Sayano-Altai Mountains effectively separate three major regions: the Black Sea steppe, the Kazakh steppe, and the Mongolian steppe, each of which has a distinctive terrain and ecology. Its many rivers include the Dnieper, the Volga, and

Figure 3. Roads across eastern Mongolia, following the ancient migration routes, June 1996. Photo: Emma C. Bunker

Figure 4. Ordos Desert, southwestern Inner Mongolia, June 1996.
Photo: Emma C. Bunker

Figure 5. Lake Baikal, Buryat Autonomous Republic, eastern Siberia,
May 1995. Photo: Emma C. Bunker

the Don, which flow southward into the Black and Caspian Seas in the west, and the Ob, the Yenisei, and the Lena in the east, which flow northward into the Arctic Ocean.

China's northern frontier zone, in the southern region of the Mongolian steppes, is divided by the Taihang Mountains, which run north to south along the western border of Hebei Province (fig. 6). West of the Taihang, the land is characterized by grasslands conducive to large-scale herding. East of the Taihang, the mountainous, forested land is more suited to hunting, trapping, and fur trading, while farther east, in the Dongbei region, the fertile soil of the Liao River valley could sustain limited agriculture, hunting, fishing, and

settled stock breeding. Each of these regions influenced the economic development of the local inhabitants and is reflected in their material culture.

The early inhabitants of the Eurasian grasslands were true environmentalists. They strove for harmony with nature and exploited only those natural resources essential to their survival and well-being. Land was carefully conserved, and water was considered sacred. Today, tragically, outsiders are encroaching upon the terrain, polluting the waters and destroying the delicate ecological balance of the land.

Until the end of the second millennium B.C., the pastoral peoples lived in basically sedentary communities, with some

Figure 6. Taihang Mountains,
Hebei Province, May 1995.
Photo: Emma C. Bunker

Figure 7. Nomads herding in Hentii aimag, eastern Mongolia, May 1996. Photo: Emma C. Bunker

Figure 8. Bazaar in Kashgar, Xinjiang Uyghur Autonomous Region, 1989. Photo: Joan Hartman-Goldsmith

agriculture and animal husbandry, producing only a limited range of artifacts, mainly small weapons and tools but few personal ornaments. By the first millennium B.C., many groups had turned increasingly to large-scale livestock breeding, herding, and hunting (fig. 7). The development of a more mobile lifestyle was the result of different factors in each geographic region—climatic and environmental changes, economic pressure from other groups, and the need for more pasture to sustain larger herds. This shift was made possible by the introduction of horseback riding, which occurred sometime during the second millennium B.C.[5] In some areas, grain and other necessities were obtained by force or by barter—for animal products—with settled communities, and as pastoral groups became more mobile, commercial ventures expanded, resulting in consumer networks and seasonal trading centers that have prevailed for centuries (fig. 8).

Pastoral economies went hand in hand with cultural values. Animals, both wild and domesticated, provided the most essential resources for sustenance: wool, leather, and fur for clothing and for the coverings of portable dwellings; dung for fuel; meat, butter, milk, and cheese for food. Horses were used as pack animals and for riding and provided fermented mare's milk, or *kumiss,* a favorite alcoholic beverage (fig. 9).[6] In the pastoral world, animals were partners with humans in a mutually beneficial relationship that ensured the survival of both.

The lives of the pastoral peoples were by necessity guided by the seasonal demands of herding, hunting, the raising of livestock, and the ecology of their environment. In the spring and summer, mounted herders, highly sophisticated in their knowledge of livestock management, followed the seasonal routes that had been established over the centuries to find pasture and water. At the approach of winter, they returned to home camps for shelter and for fodder for their herds.

The steppe peoples did not exist in isolation. Often they formed confederations that included peoples taken in conquest or that were formed by alliances with other ethnic

Figure 9. Painting, by T.S. Battuya, of a mare being milked to make *kumiss.*

Figure 10. Erecting a framework for a *ger*, Xinjiang Uyghur Autonomous Region, June 1996. Photo: Emma C. Bunker

Figure 11. A *ger* in Hentii aimag, eastern Mongolia, June 1995. Photo: Emma C. Bunker

groups. As a result of seasonal migrations, trade, intermarriage, and, occasionally, warfare, they were also in contact with civilizations on their southern and western frontiers. In the Near East, there was intercourse with the Assyrians, Urartians, Medes, Achaemenids, and Parthians, and, in the Black Sea area, the Greeks. In the Far East, they interacted with the dynastic Chinese (hereafter referred to as the Chinese). And although they left no written records themselves, references to these groups and to their customs are frequent in the ancient literature of neighboring cultures.

Tales of the "Scythians" by the fifth-century B.C. Greek historian Herodotus (on this term, see the essay by James C. Y. Watt in this volume)[7] are matched by those of the first-century B.C. Chinese historian Sima Qian, who devoted an entire chapter of the *Shiji* (Records of the Grand Historian) to the Xiongnu, whom he described as tent dwellers who "wandered from place to place pasturing their animals" on the northern borders of China.[8] "The animals they raised consist mainly of horses, cattle and sheep, but include such rare beasts as camels. They move about in search of water and pasture. In burials, the Xiongnu use accessories of gold, silver, clothing and fur, but they do not construct grave mounds."[9] Also in the first century B.C., the Greek author Strabo wrote that the Roxolani, a branch of the Sarmatians, had "tents made of [felt] that were fastened to wagons in which they spent their lives. Round about the tents were the herds which afforded milk, cheese, and meat on which they lived. They followed the grazing herds, from time to time, moving to other places that had grass."[10] The prowess of the steppe peoples in warfare is described by many ancient writers. Herodotus speaks of the great fighting ability of the Scythians[11] and the Thracians,[12] while Sima Qian notes the mounted archers whose skill would inspire King Wuling of the state of Zhao to adopt—in an edict traditionally dated to 307 B.C.[13]—horse gear, riding clothes, and all the accoutrements associated with horses and horseback riding to improve the efficacy of his mounted troops.

The first-century Chinese historian Huan Kuan wrote in the *Yan tie lun* (On Salt and Iron) that the Xiongnu lived in *qionglu* (dome-shaped) tents.[14] *Qionglu* refers to an early type of *ger,* the typical steppe trellis tent that has a round, felt-covered, portable framework of wooden poles (fig. 10); it is also called a *yurt* (a Russian word borrowed from Turkish that means "home territory" or "campsite").[15] As noted by Strabo, this type of portable dwelling was on occasion mounted on a wheeled cart similar to the covered wagons of the American West to transport the belongings of the herdsmen. The *ger* is so well suited to pastoral mobility that it continues in use today (fig. 11).[16]

Felt, one of the most ingenious products of the north,[17] was used by the Scythians[18] and the Xiongnu,[19] and has been found in the frozen fourth-century tombs of Pazyryk in the Altai Mountains of Siberia (fig. 12).[20] Made by beating, spreading, wetting, and then rolling large quantities of wool to produce a fabric of matted wool, felt still is used for clothing and to cover *ger* frames (fig. 13).

The major economic asset and prize possession in the steppe world was the horse, and remains so today. Ready mounts are always available, tied next to every *ger,* like a parked car (fig. 14). Gas stations in the steppes are few and far between (and most often closed), so that the use of horses continues to be of paramount importance, even in the twenty-first century. Displays of horsemanship still are featured at yearly festivals, especially horse racing and local versions of

Figure 12. Reconstruction of a horse caparisoned with felt, from kurgan 1, Pazyryk, Altai Mountains, 4th century B.C. Photo courtesy of Yevgeny Lubo-Lesnichenko

Figure 13. Painting, by T.S. Battuya, of wool being rolled for felt.

Figure 14. Ponies tied near a *ger*, Xinjiang Uyghur Autonomous Region, June 1996. Photo: Emma C. Bunker

buzkashi, the wild equestrian sport of "goat-grabbing," in which mounted riders skirmish over an animal carcass and try to place it in a designated goal or scoring circle.[21]

Also popular as a sport and display of male prowess was wrestling, which appeared as early as the third century B.C.[22] It is still practiced at annual festivals, such as the Mongolian *naadam,* throughout the steppes. The winner of such a contest today is frequently awarded a fine horse (figs. 15, 16).

Despite all the references in ancient sources to the various pastoral groups, the early historians' main concerns were the regions these groups inhabited and the political alliances they established with their neighbors rather than with their values and beliefs.[23] Little about their material culture appears to have been of interest. To learn about their cultural achievements, relationships with nearby settlements, and contacts with other, more distant Eurasian cultures, we must turn to the artifacts themselves.

1. This identification derives from the landmark study by Karl Jettmar, *Die frühen Steppenvölker* (1964), translated into English as *Art of the Steppes* in 1967. Some regions are not true steppe, but taiga (forest) and desert steppe. The term "pastoral" is used here to refer to dependence on domesticated herd animals held as property; see Chang and Koster 1986,

Figure 15. Wrestling contest at the *naadam* festival, Hovsgöl aimag, Mongolia, July 1995. Photo: Robert McCracken Peck

Figure 16. Wrestlers with a prize horse at the *naadam* festival, Hovsgöl aimag, Mongolia, July 1995. Photo: Robert McCracken Peck

p. 99. The term "nomad" is used to refer to those peoples whose lifestyle was more mobile than that of their more sedentary urban neighbors.

2. See Bunker et al. 1997, pp. 7–8, for a discussion of these obsolete terms.

3. So and Bunker 1995, pp. 26–27.

4. Masson and Taylor 1989, pp. 780–82. The Moldavian ASSR, the Ukrainian SSR, the Volga and Kuban River regions, the Kalmyk ASSR (Kalmykia), the Kazakh SSR (Kazakhstan) with the Uzbek SSR (Uzbekistan) to its south, the Altai regions, the Tuva ASSR (Tuva), the Buryat ASSR, the Amur River, and, on the Pacific seaboard, the Khabarovsk regions.

5. Kuzmina (2000) and Bokovenko (2000) have convincingly shown that mounted herding developed in the steppe zone in the second millennium B.C., not in the fourth millennium B.C., as has been suggested by some scholars in the past.

6. Fermented mare's milk was the popular alcoholic drink among the Xiongnu; see Watson 1993, vol. 2, p. 143. *Kumiss* is still consumed in the steppes today. Known as *airag* in Mongolian, *rujiu* in Chinese, *kumis* in Turkish, and *oxygaia* in Greek, fermented mare's milk was also a favorite beverage of the Scythians, as noted by Herodotus.

7. Herodotus bk. 4; for burial customs, see ibid., chaps. 71–75.

8. B. Watson 1961, chap. 110.

9. Ibid.

10. Strabo quoted in Sulimirsky 1963, p. 294.

11. Herodotus bk. 4.

12. Ibid., 5.3.

13. So and Bunker 1995, p. 29.

14. McGovern 1939, pp. 44–45. For the *Yan tie lun*, see Loewe 1993.

15. Andrews 1979.

16. Yü 1967, p. 40. See also Kriukov and Kurylev 1992.

17. Burkett 1979, pp. 7–8. The earliest extant examples of felt have been found at the neolithic site of Catalhüyük in Turkey.

18. Herodotus 4.74.

19. B. Watson 1961, p. 156.

20. Rudenko 1970, passim; So and Bunker 1995, p. 28, fig. 8.

21. Azoy 1982.

22. For a discussion of wrestling among the steppe peoples, see Bunker 1997.

23. For a comprehensive compendium of the historical contacts between ancient China and its northern pastoral neighbors, see Di Cosmo 2002.

ARTIFACTS: REGIONAL STYLES AND METHODS OF PRODUCTION

EMMA C. BUNKER

All the steppe peoples displayed a proficiency in metal-working. They produced small personal weapons with integrally cast hilts; personal ornaments of metal to signify status and clan affiliation; and a distinctive costume consisting of a short jacket, trousers, and a prominent belt, frequently hung with tools and weapons. Although their lifestyles were animal-oriented and their artifacts typologically similar, they did not all belong to one vast cultural continuum, as has frequently been suggested.[1] Rather, each regional group retained its own identity. And although they were culturally and technologically interconnected, their material remains have distinguishing characteristics.

Distinct artistic vocabularies were also developed. Stylistic motifs — derived from myth, local fauna, and domesticated animals — gave visual expression to customs and beliefs, each one imbued with meaning that pertained to spiritual and cultural values.[2] Even today such motifs are emblems of clan, rank, family, and kinship. In a culture in which history, religious beliefs, and codes of ethics were transmitted by oral and pictorial — rather than written — accounts, art served as a powerful binding force.

The flowering of creativity among the Eurasian pastoral peoples during the first millennium B.C. appears to have accompanied the transition from a settled agro-pastoral lifestyle to one that was more mobile and more dependent on herding, hunting, and the marketing of animal products. From their very beginnings, the peoples of the Eurasian steppes placed a greater value on animals than did their sedentary neighbors to the south and imbued their artifacts with a distinctly northern flavor. This quality is recognizable in the type and decoration of the implements and ornaments they designed and that they embellished with zoomorphic motifs that served as status symbols and clan markers.

In the past, pottery and patterns of burial have been the primary factors in distinguishing regional cultures in the Eurasian steppes. More recently, based on results of archaeological excavations — most of which were made in China by the Chinese in the latter half of the twentieth century — these cultures can also be identified by metal artifacts. Many such artifacts have been assigned dates within a relative chronology based on stylistic and metallurgical comparisons with material from sedentary communities, but the accuracy of these dates is questionable. It is hoped that in the future, radiocarbon analysis of excavated material combined with the comparison of artifacts will result in greater accuracy.[3]

Within each geographic region an economic complex was formed which yielded a range of artifacts that met the needs of the peoples in that region. The production of equestrian gear, funerary canopy and cart ornaments, tools, weapons, and personal ornaments is consistent throughout the Eurasian steppes, but the visual symbolism that distinguishes these objects and the metallurgical techniques employed to make them reflect distinct regional characteristics.

In most areas, people adhered to local metallurgical traditions and a specific range of metals, depending on their availability and the proficiency of local craftsmen. Correct identification of the birds and animals represented is essential to understanding an artifact. To a certain extent, zoomorphic images are area specific and the ability to recognize an artifact's regional features helps to determine its origin and authenticity. Nevertheless, trade, migration, marriage alliances, and warfare frequently involved not only the movement of people but the dissemination of objects. Artifacts can thus document the long-distance contacts that were not recorded in ancient texts. For example, a third- to second-century B.C. belt plaque made in North China was recovered from a grave in the Ural Mountains at Petrovka, thousands of miles west of where it was made.[4]

The northern frontier zone of the Eurasian steppes can be divided geographically into three cultural spheres. Northeast China—known as the Dongbei, encompassing Jilin, Liaoning, and Heilongjiang Provinces, and southeastern Inner Mongolia—was inhabited by agro-pastoral peoples whose economies depended on livestock, hunting, and agriculture. The land was fertile, watered by many rivers, so there was little seasonal migration. The groups living in northern Hebei Province were primarily hunters and trappers, who supplied furs and other animal products to their Chinese neighbors to the south. Long-distance mobility for these peoples was not a concern. By contrast, west of the Taihang Mountains—in a large area that includes northern Shanxi and Shaanxi Provinces, southwestern Inner Mongolia Autonomous Region, Ningxia (Hui Autonomous Region), southeastern Gansu, and parts of Xinjiang Uyghur Autonomous Region—the regional economies were grounded in large-scale herding and livestock trading, necessitating the adoption of transhumance, seasonal migration in search of pasture and fresh water.

Ancient Chinese texts refer to numerous non-Chinese peoples who inhabited the northern frontier zone during the first millennium B.C., but whether these names are the same as those used by the people to refer to themselves, Chinese transcriptions of foreign names, or merely generic terms is difficult to say. Long lists of named groups and their general geographic locations can be gleaned from ancient Chinese texts, but little or no information is available concerning their individual customs and artistic traditions.[5] Such information remains elusive until the late third century B.C., and by the first century B.C., when Sima Qian wrote the *Shiji,* their separate identities are already lost.

Problems of identity also surround the many Eurasian peoples discussed by Herodotus.[6] Only the "Scythians" of the Black Sea area, whose Central Asian counterparts were known by the Iranian name of Saka, can be described with any confidence. The importance of early literary citations is the repeated reference to those people considered "others," alien peoples with whom the Greeks, Iranians, and Chinese must have had complex and mutually beneficial relationships. Cultural encounters between these civilizations and their nomadic neighbors are seldom mentioned in ancient literature but can often be detected in the art of both groups.

THE DONGBEI (9TH – 3RD CENTURY B.C.)

The most distinctive artifacts produced in the Dongbei are knives, short swords, helmets, horse and chariot gear, and small personal ornaments, including belt decorations, and implements appropriate for settled agro-pastoral and hunting cultures. The chariot ornaments are frequently equipped with jingles, typical steppe paraphernalia intended to make a bell-like sound (cat. no. 26). The jingles themselves derive from northern metalworking traditions in which, long before they were produced by casting, they were formed by smithy work (cat. nos. 26, 28, 29).[7] The small bronze weapons also exhibit characteristic features—blades that are integrally cast with the hilts, not separately, as they were in China (cat. nos. 44, 45, 49–52).

Chariot ornaments decorated with hunting scenes were a regional specialty of the Dongbei. A fragmentary bone plaque excavated from tomb 102 at Nanshan'gen, Ningcheng county, southeastern Inner Mongolia, shows a hunter with drawn bow aiming at two stags while two hunting dogs stand beside horse-drawn vehicles (fig. 17). The two-wheeled vehicles are similar in design to those represented on two plaques in the present exhibition (cat. no. 23). A bronze ornament (cat. no. 26) shows two mounted hunters accompanied by dogs pursuing their prey, a counterpart to the bronze ornament

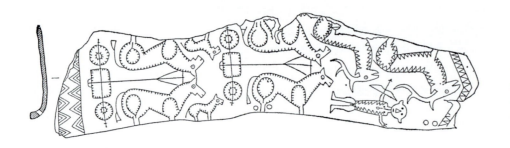

Figure 17. Drawing of a bone plaque with hunter and horse-drawn carts, tomb 102, Nanshan'gen. 8th century B.C. (after *Kaogu* 1981, p. 307, fig. 6)

Figure 18. Bronze fitting with mounted rabbit hunters, tomb 3, Nanshan'gen. 8th century B.C. (after *Kaogu xuebao* 1975, p. 137, fig. 18.4)

Figure 19. Deerstone, Hentii aimag, eastern Mongolia, June 1996. Photo: Emma C. Bunker

excavated in the Nanshan'gen vicinity, which depicts two hunters pursuing a wild hare (fig. 18).[8] This type of pictorial decoration appears to have no counterpart in the art of Northwest China. Instead, Dongbei pictorial traditions may be traced back to narrative scenes represented on deerstones (fig. 19) and petroglyphs (fig. 20) that are still visible throughout Mongolia and southern Siberia, where unexplored Bronze Age tombs still dot the landscape (fig. 21).[9]

Closer connections existed between the Dongbei, northern Mongolia, and eastern Siberia than between the Dongbei and Northwest China. The geographic location of the Dongbei gave access to Inner Asia by routes that led north through the Amur Valley and westward along the so-called Fur Route, a complex trading network crossing Eurasia north of the fiftieth parallel. The Fur Route completely bypassed Northwest China and was roughly the same as that traveled by the Trans-Siberian Railroad today.[10]

The zoomorphic motifs that embellish Dongbei ornaments and weapons feature horses, wild animals, amphibians, and birds native to the area. Such representations, often realistically rendered (cat. nos. 44, 155), are quite distinct from the stylized zoomorphic symbols on many artifacts produced west of the Taihang Mountain range (cat. nos. 90, 140, 141), a region culturally different altogether.

One motif that deserves special attention is the reindeer with folded legs and flowing, backswept antlers, represented

Figure 20. Petroglyphs, Mongolia. Photo courtesy of Nora Novgorodova

Figure 21. Bronze Age slab grave, Mongomor't, Tov aimag, eastern Mongolia, June 1996. Photo: Emma C. Bunker

on garment plaques and amulets found throughout the Dongbei and in northern Hebei Province (cat. no. 158). Its legs are drawn inward in such a way that they overlap, with the hooves pointing both forward and backward.

The cervid represented is a reindeer—identifiable by its brow tines—an image that must have evolved somewhere in the heartland of the Eurasian steppes. From there, it spread east to the Dongbei and west to the Black Sea region, where it became one of the hallmarks of Scythian art.[11] An early rendition of this image occurs on a seventh-century B.C. gold fragment from the Ziwiye Treasure found in northern Iran (cat. no. 168).

Fertility and procreation were also popular Dongbei themes.[12] Animal copulation and prominent male organs appear on many artifacts (fig. 22), reflecting a concern with the propagation of wild game and livestock, on which the livelihoods of the inhabitants depended (cat. no. 155). Early hunting societies must have been far more environmentally aware than has been acknowledged. By contrast, fertility symbols and sexual motifs do not occur in the art of the herding peoples in Northwest China. Rather, it was animal combat—a subject not depicted on artifacts from the Dongbei[13]—that was the popular subject matter west of the Taihang Mountains, where the attack on livestock by wild animals was a fear and concern. The psychology of the northeastern hunter was different from that of the northwestern herder, and this difference is reflected in the artistic

motifs that gave visual form to the symbolic systems regulating their lives.

There is no evidence that foundries in China produced artifacts designed specifically for Dongbei consumption. The ritual vessels and other items included among the grave offerings are orthodox Chinese objects with Chinese decor that reflected the wealth of the owner but were not designed

Figure 22. Rubbing of a bronze plaque discovered near Chifeng, southeastern Inner Mongolia (after Bunker et al. 1997, p. 166, fig. 71.1)

to appeal to his taste. Rather, they are exotica obtained through trade and demonstrate the lively commercial relations that must have existed between the two diverse cultures. Mining and foundry debris discovered in the Dongbei indicates that other artifacts were cast in local foundries.[14] Most objects were piece-mold cast, but a few, such as helmets (cat. nos. 46, 47) and chariot jingles (cat. nos. 26, 28, 29), were cast by lost wax, as this process was more suited to the complexities of the designs.[15]

NORTHERN HEBEI PROVINCE (9TH – 3RD CENTURY B.C.)

The material culture of the hunting peoples who inhabited the rugged Jundushan and Yinshan ranges of northern Hebei Province is different from that found in the Dongbei. The many funeral canopy decorations, bridle fittings, short swords, knives, personal ornaments, tools, and other practical items discovered in graves are decorated with zoomorphic images—representations of the local fauna, such as leopards, deer, ibex, gazelles, snakes, frogs, and birds.

The burials, situated in large cemeteries rather than in isolated graves, have been tentatively associated with a non-Chinese group referred to in ancient texts as the Shanrong, a hunting people known to have supplied the Chinese with fur and leather goods.[16] In northern Hebei, fur trading and leather tanning are still major occupations today, especially in Zhangjiakou, a city that throughout history has served as a point of departure for northern Eurasian destinations, such as Ulaanbaatar in Mongolia and Lake Baikal in eastern Siberia.

The most distinctive artifacts are pectorals (cat. nos. 155–157), which appear to have been more prestigious than the many small ornaments attached to necklaces and belts (cat. no. 139). The repetition of a limited number of zoomorphic motifs suggests that pectoral designs were a sign of kinship ties and beliefs and the hierarchy of metals used an indication of status and rank. Those of higher rank wore gold pectorals (cat. no. 156), some of which had turquoise inlays (now often missing). Pectoral designs also appear to have been gender specific. Men's pectorals were primarily leopard shaped (cat. no. 157), while pectorals depicting frogs encircled by snakes were favored by women and may have symbolized fertility (fig. 23).[17]

Figure 23. Pectoral ornament in the shape of a frog encircled by snakes, northern Hebei Province. 6th–5th century B.C. (after Bunker et al. 1997, p. 188, no. 110)

The most unusual artifacts found in northern Hebei are bronze finials surmounted by standing animals that were cast by the lost-wax process (cat. nos. 24, 25). Similar lost-wax-cast bronze finials surmounted by standing wild sheep (fig. 24) were discovered at Arzhan, a site dated from the seventh to the sixth century B.C. in Tuva, in southern Siberia.[18] Apparently, these were used to decorate the corner poles of canopies that had been placed over biers during funeral rituals, a function also suggested here for the Hebei examples. This is a custom that can be traced back to the third-millennium B.C. burials at Maikop, in southern Russia, as noted below (note 1 on p. 56).

Small weapons, especially short swords, are prominent among the grave goods in Hebei burials, where they are found at the waist of the deceased attached to belts, essential items in a hunter's toolkit (fig. 25). Some small weapons from northern Hebei are quite unlike those of the Dongbei. One sword (cat. no. 54), for example, has a much shorter blade marked by a raised median ridge, a feature not found in the Dongbei (cat. no. 45). The median ridge, a device for strengthening the blade, is seen in the early Bronze Age, where it occurs on a short sword excavated at Zhukaigou, in the Ordos Desert region (fig. 26).[19] The scabbard of the Hebei sword has a bronze cover cast with an openwork interlace design punctuated by turquoise inlays. This design derives from the interlace dragon patterns seen on sixth-century B.C. bronze ritual vessels cast in North China,

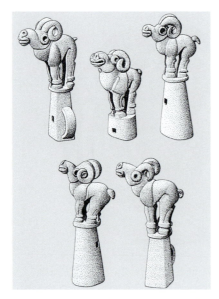

Figure 24. Drawing of bronze canopy finials, Arzhan, Republic of Tuva, southern Siberia. 7th–6th century B.C. (after Griaznov 1984, p. 52, fig. 25)

Figure 25. Small weapon at the waist of the deceased, grave 174, Yuhuangmiao, Yanqing county, Beijing district. 6th century B.C. Photo courtesy of Jin Fengyi

suggesting that such weapons and scabbards may have been made by Chinese metalworkers for northern consumption.[20]

A more abstract type of interlace pattern embellishes the guard and the pommel of another short sword in the exhibition (cat. no. 56). The distinctive openwork hilt featuring animal heads in the round is a type of hilt decoration found on short swords excavated in the Ural Mountains in the west, evidence of long-distance cultural continuity that appears to have existed between pastoral communities in the east and those in the west, a subject that has yet to be fully explored.[21]

Certain types of horse bits in some of the early-sixth-century B.C. graves at Yanqing, north of Beijing, were designed specifically for riding (fig. 27).[22] The presence of these bits, along with animal-shaped cheekpieces (cat. no. 3), indicates that riding astride was practiced in the north and perhaps even in a few of the northern feudal states, during the Spring and Autumn period (770–481 B.C.), long before the introduction of mounted warfare into China by Wuling, king of the state of Zhao, in 307 B.C.[23]

The hunting peoples in northern Hebei appear to have used a combination of metallurgical processes similar to those of the Dongbei. For simple objects, such as small personal ornaments (cat. no. 139), piece-mold casting was used, whereas for more complex items, such as finials surmounted by hollow ungulates (cat. nos. 24, 25), lost wax was the preferred casting method.

NORTHWEST CHINA (9TH – 4TH CENTURY B.C.)

Northwest China was culturally subdivided into three separate areas defined by distinctly different material remains. One pastoral group occupied the region just west of the

Figure 26. Bronze knife and short sword, tomb 1040, Zhukaigou, southwestern Inner Mongolia. 15th–13th century B.C. Photo courtesy of Guo Suxin

Figure 27. Bronze snaffle bits and cheek-pieces from a horse bridle, Yuhuangmiao, Yanqing county, Beijing district. 6th century B.C. Photo: Emma C. Bunker, 1990

Taihang Mountains in south-central Inner Mongolia, including parts of northern Shanxi; another group was centered farther west in the Ordos Desert and included northern Shaanxi; and the third group occupied an area encompassing southern Ningxia and southeastern Gansu, centered in the vicinity of Guyuan and the Qingyang plateau.

The archaeological remains of the pastoral groups living west of the Taihang differ noticeably from those found at sites east of the mountain range, as did their lifestyles. The inhabitants in the west were chiefly mobile herders in search of pasture, while those in the east were settled stockbreeders and hunters. The most prominent artifacts are belt plaques, small weapons, and funerary cart and canopy ornaments, all decorated with zoomorphic motifs, occasionally in predatory scenes. In the northwest, the use of tinned bronze was an emblem of status, while in the northeast status was signified by gold, evidence of significantly different metalworking traditions on either side of the Taihang.

SOUTH CENTRAL INNER MONGOLIA

The most characteristic artifacts found at burial sites in south-central Inner Mongolia, especially in Horinger and Liangcheng counties, are short swords, belt plaques, and hook buckles. Eight plaques similar to cat. no. 37 and dated from the sixth to the fifth century B.C. were recovered from a disturbed grave at Fanjiayaozi, Horinger county. Each plaque is cast in the shape of a crouching carnivore consuming a herbivore, of which only the head remains. The introduction

of scenes of animal predation on northern frontier zone belt plaques roughly coincides with their appearance on late Spring and Autumn bronzes cast at Houma, the Jin foundry in southern Shanxi Province (fig. 28).[24] The carnivore in another animal predation scene that occurs on belt plaques excavated at the nearby site of Guoxianyaozi, Liangcheng county,[25] is shown in an awkward half-crouching pose with flexed legs, a position also seen in the artistic vocabulary at Houma (fig. 29), providing visual evidence for the close relationship that existed between the state of Jin and its northern neighbors.[26]

Several other plaques at Guoxianyaozi are shaped like raptors' heads similar to catalogue no. 140. These appear to be stylized abstractions of eagles' heads, such as those that decorate a saddle excavated at Bashadar (fig. 30), the sixth-century B.C. site in the Altai Mountains,[27] indicating indirect long-distance contact with pastoral groups far to the north.

The importance of belt ornaments as status symbols among the pastoral peoples west of the Taihang is confirmed by their distribution in graves at Maoqinggou, a major cemetery site in Liangcheng county dated typologically to the seventh through the third centuries B.C.[28] The choice between such metals as plain and tinned bronze, and, in later tombs, iron was another indication of prestige and status. Of the seventy-nine graves at Maoqinggou, twenty-eight contained belt ornaments and seven of the twenty-eight, large feline-shaped plaques. The men were buried with short swords suspended from belts adorned with plaques. One female burial, M5, dating from the late sixth to the fifth century B.C.,

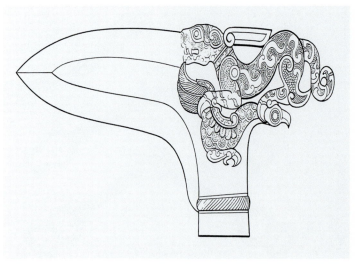

Figure 28. Drawing of a belt boss mold, Houma, southern Shanxi Province (after Li, Liang, and Bagley 1996, p. 326, fig. 699)

Figure 29. Drawing of a *ge* blade with zoomorphic decorations, Houma, southern Shanxi Province (after Li, Liang, and Bagley 1996, p. 333, fig. 721)

yielded a complete belt with two large tinned bronze plaques, each representing a stylized standing tiger with prominent claws, whose anatomical details are marked by indented lines (fig. 31), suggesting that the owner must have had some special status. Unlike the occupants of the male graves, the female in M5 was not provided with weapons.

The smaller belt plaques on the belt from M5, like catalogue no. 89, are quite different in style and design from those at the two earlier sites, Fanjiayaozi and Guoxianyaozi. The small plaques have S-shaped designs represented by sunken lines that derive from abstract zoomorphic forms similar to those represented on late Spring and Autumn

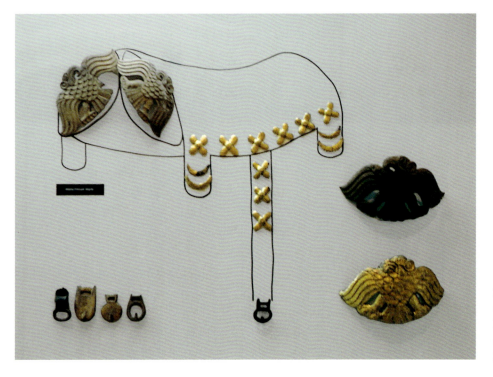

Figure 30. Saddle ornaments, tomb 2, Bashadar, Altai Mountains, southern Siberia. 6th century B.C. The State Hermitage, St. Petersburg

22

Figure 31. Belt with tinned bronze plaques, tomb 5, Maoqinggou, Liangcheng county, Inner Mongolia. 6th–5th century B.C. Photo: Emma C. Bunker

bronze and jade items found at Shangcunling, Henan Province.[29] Some of the grave goods also include Chinese-style belt hooks. By contrast, the obvious source for the standing tiger on the belt plaques from M5 are the felines carved on a sixth-century B.C. wooden coffin at Bashadar, in southern Siberia (fig. 32). The combination of styles at Maoqinggou suggests some connection with both China and the pastoral peoples far to the north, presumably through marriage alliances and trade.

THE ORDOS DESERT REGION

The most characteristic artifacts from the Ordos Desert region are animal figures cast in the round to embellish vehicles used in burial rituals (cat. nos. 31, 35, 37–39). The

finials surmounted by ungulates (cat. nos. 36, 38) are typologically similar to finials from northern Hebei Province (cat. nos. 24, 25), but they are cast by a different method. The Ordos examples are piece-mold cast, while those from Hebei are cast by the lost-wax process, suggesting that the two are not directly related but, instead, derive from a shared heritage. While piece-mold casting was more typical of Chinese foundry practices during this period, it may be that Chinese craftsmen in sedentary communities were involved in producing artifacts for the nomadic herders as they moved from one place to another on the northwestern frontier. In this case, the artifacts were probably made by craftsmen in the predynastic state of Qin. Some Ordos finials are tinned (cat. no. 38), indicating that the person interred must have been someone of influence and prestige. Tinning,

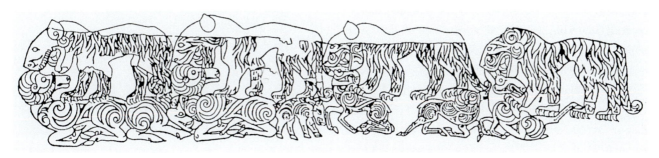

Figure 32. Drawing of animal-combat scenes on a wooden coffin, tomb 2, Bashadar, Altai Mountains, southern Siberia. 6th century B.C. (after Bunker et al. 1997, p. 215, fig. 156.1)

a surface enrichment also practiced by the Qin, was used to indicate status in the Ordos region until it was superseded by gold and silver in the late fourth century B.C.

Numerous animal figures from the Ordos have been identified as yoke covers by their association with a wheeled vehicle excavated at Yulongtai, Jungar banner.[30] Each animal is cast with a hollow, open body that fits over the yoke of a cart (cat. nos. 31, 35, 37), as do similarly designed animal figures excavated from a Qin tomb at Bianjiazhuang, Long county, southwestern Shaanxi Province.[31] Yoke covers were made in sets (cat. no. 32), many of which have been broken up over the years, such as catalogue no. 37.

Some animals on yoke covers are shown recumbent (cat. nos. 31, 35). This pose is quite different from that of the ungulate images found on artifacts in the Dongbei, which seems to suggest speed (cat. no. 2). In the Ordos, the animal is the red deer shown in a recumbent pose (cat. no. 35). The legs overlap, and the undersides of the hooves on the forelegs face up, while those on the hind legs face down. The pose derives from Qin artistic conventions, as seen on a lacquer animal from the sixth-century B.C. tomb of a Qin duke,[32] and can be traced back to the Shang dynasty (ca. 1523–ca. 1027 B.C.).[33] This particular articulation of the hooves also occurs, surprisingly, in a fifth-century B.C. context in the Black Sea region. There is as yet no explanation for its sudden appearance in the west.[34]

Many small garment plaques made of bronze appear to have been mass-produced by piece-mold casting.[35] Most of these, similar to catalogue nos. 148, 149, are chance finds without cultural context, so it is difficult to determine their precise dates and provenance.

SOUTHERN NINGXIA AND SOUTHEASTERN GANSU

The artifacts associated with the pastoral peoples of southern Ningxia and southeastern Gansu display a highly complex cultural admixture compared with those of the Ordos region. Grave goods include yoke covers, harness ornaments, and large, impressive belt buckles of diverse styles, casting techniques, and zoomorphic motifs. Animal-shaped yoke covers are commonly found in graves. Typologically they are the same as yoke covers from the Ordos, but with one minor difference: they are cast with open-ended muzzles, a distinguishing local feature (cat. nos. 32–34).

By contrast, the harness ornaments and belt plaques from southern Ningxia and southeastern Gansu are distinctly different from grave goods in the Ordos. The harness fittings are mainly small bridle ornaments (cat. nos. 8, 11, 12) and larger decorative plaques, such as the superb coiled wolf, catalogue no. 7, which relates stylistically to late-sixth-century B.C. images found far to the west—for example, a bridle ornament from Simferopol, a major Scythian site in the Crimea (fig. 33). The motif of an animal curled into a ring has an East Asian priority and occurs on numerous Western Zhou (ca. 11th century–771 B.C.) bridle ornaments and on Mongolian deerstones.[36] Coiled feline images have also been discovered on artifacts in the Dongbei and northern Hebei, and a large coiled feline plaque was excavated at Arzhan, a seventh-to-sixth-century B.C. site in the Sayan Mountains (fig. 34).[37] The motif was transmitted to Central Asia, where it appeared in Saka art (cat. no. 138), and farther west, where it appeared in Scythian art, such as the Simferopol example, although the connecting links remain obscure.[38]

Perhaps the most distinctive artifacts from the Ningxia–Gansu region are large belt plaques that depict some form of animal predation in which a standing carnivore is shown savaging a mangled herbivore (cat. nos. 63, 94). The buckles are

Figure 33. Bronze horse bridle ornament, Simferopol, Crimea. Late 6th century B.C. (after Artamonov 1969, pl. 78)

Figure 34. Bronze harness ornament in the shape of a coiled feline, Arzhan, Tuva Republic, southern Siberia. 7th–6th century B.C. (after Basilov 1989, p. 20)

cast in the shape of a pair of mirror-image plaques that are frequently tinned to achieve a pleasing silvery surface. This type of buckle had an earlier priority in the Tagar culture of Minusinsk, Siberia,[39] and among pastoral groups in the Altai Mountains,[40] suggesting long-distance commercial ventures between Minusinsk, the Altai, and the Guyuan–Qingyang region, as such buckles do not appear during this period in the Ordos vicinity.[41]

The animal-combat motif, which derives from earlier traditions in West Asia, probably served as an emblem of power for herders, who had to protect their stock and grazing lands. As the motif was transmitted eastward, the West Asian lion and the panther were replaced by the tiger, leopard, and wolf, local East Asian predators.

History provides much evidence of contact between the peoples of the steppes and West Asia in the first millennium B.C. The Assyrians and the Iranians are known to have reinforced their cavalries with mercenaries and riding horses imported from the mounted pastoral peoples of the eastern frontiers of Central Asia.[42] Cyrus the Great, the Achaemenid ruler of Iran, met his death in 530 B.C. while fighting the Massagetae, a horse-riding people that Herodotus placed east of the Caspian Sea. In 519 B.C., Darius I led a campaign against the Saka in Central Asia in the vicinity of the Oxus River (Amu Dar'ya), precipitating the displacement of certain Saka groups farther east across the Eurasian steppes, perhaps to the western borders of China.[43]

By contrast, some buckles have shapes common to the steppes but display purely Qin-style decoration, consisting of raised curls, striations, pseudogranulation, and superimposed zoomorphs (cat. nos. 62, 95), suggesting that such items were made by Qin craftsmen expressly for pastoral consumption.[44] Other, smaller belt ornaments display designs that derive from Chinese zoomorphic images found earlier on Western Zhou vessels which appealed to pastoral taste, such as raptors with hooked beaks and curvy wings (cat. no. 63). The enthusiasm for raptor images (cat. nos. 173, 176) may refer to falconry, a sport popular among the pastoral peoples; it is still practiced today in Northwest China, Central Asia, and Mongolia (fig. 35).

Images of camels occur for the first time in southern Ningxia, in the decoration of harness and belt ornaments (cat. nos. 14, 15, 92). The camel, with its big padded feet, made travel in sandy desert terrain possible, as it did in trans-Asian travel along the Silk Road. Riders of camels were portrayed as foreigners with big noses, such as the rider on catalogue no. 92, which documents the perception of an exotic people on the outskirts of China during the latter half of the first millennium B.C. The earliest evidence for the motif in Chinese art appears to be a bronze lamp in the shape of a camel and rider, excavated from a fourth-century B.C. Chu tomb at Wangshan, Jiangling county, Hubei Province.[45]

Other artifacts display stylistic traits that derive from the carving traditions of southern Siberia. Bone artifacts testify to the existence of these traditions in southern Ningxia (cat. no. 175). With the exception of a few minor fragments, gold and silver were not major status markers among the pastoral peoples in the area at this time and have not been found among grave goods. Instead, tinning continued to be the major metallurgical indicator of status, and it enhances the surface of numerous artifacts from the southern Ningxia–southeastern Gansu region (cat. nos. 62, 63, 94, 172).[46]

Toward the end of the fourth century B.C., images of carnivores display raptors' heads at the tips of their crests and tails (cat. nos. 63, 94), indicating the appropriation of images associated with nomadic groups living farther north

Figure 35. Kazakh falconer with eagle, Bayanolgi, western Mongolia, 1997. Note metal plaques on belt. Photo: John Stevenson

and farther west.[47] Raptor-headed appendages belong to a little-known symbolic system that suddenly blossomed in the Ordos Desert region during the fourth and third centuries B.C. and later appeared as exotica and *xiangrui* (auspicious signs) in the art of Han China (cat. nos. 161, 180).

NORTHWEST CHINA (4TH – 3RD CENTURY B.C.)

The arrival to the Ordos region of peoples from the north and west who practiced mounted warfare instigated dramatic changes in the character of grave goods and visual symbolism. These changes roughly coincide with the Asian campaigns of Alexander the Great in Central Asia (ca. 334–323 B.C.) and the introduction of mounted warfare to the state of Zhao in 307 B.C. by groups referred to in ancient Chinese literature as the Hu and the Linhu.[48] By the beginning of the third century B.C., yoke covers had gone

out of fashion and were no longer included among grave goods, and the chariot, which had played a major role in earlier funerary rites of the pastoral elite, became less important, as primacy was given to the horse rather than to the horse-drawn vehicle.

The iconography of some artifacts found in the Ordos region is related to that represented on artifacts found in eastern Central Asia, and the iconography on others indicates long-distance associations with pastoral groups in the Altai Mountains. A spectacular mythological gold ungulate with exaggerated antlers discovered in northern Shaanxi Province at Nalin'gaotu, just south of the Ordos Desert (fig. 36), exemplifies the intrusive iconography that appeared late in the fourth century B.C. along with an entirely new group of artifacts. And a hierarchy of metals based on gold and silver replaced tinned bronze as emblems of high-ranking individuals.

The extraordinary creatures with raptor-headed appendages, similar to the creatures tattooed on a man buried in Pazyryk tomb 2 in the Altai Mountains (fig. 37), belong to a poorly understood symbolic system employed by certain Eurasian nomads living between Bulgaria in the west and the Great Wall of China from the seventh to the sixth century B.C. to the first century A.D.[49] To date, the earliest known example of this iconography is a gold goat-shaped plaque with horns in the shape of round-eyed birds' heads. The plaque was found in a seventh-to-sixth-century B.C. Saka burial at Chilikta, eastern Kazakhstan.[50] By contrast, the image depicted by the Scythians in the Black Sea region is a cervid with antler tines terminating in raptors' heads that, by the fourth century B.C., had acquired ears and almond-shaped eyes, like the Greek and Iranian griffin. This classicizing of a nomadic motif was the result of increasing Greek involvement in the manufacture of Scythian art. Carnivores were also provided with raptor-headed appendages, especially on artifacts from Northwest China dating to the late fourth and third centuries B.C. (fig. 40 and cat. no. 94).

The fact that raptor-headed appendages occur on animals earlier in southeastern Gansu and southern Ningxia than they do in the Ordos suggests that the pastoral bands that introduced them into the area were mounted warrior herdsmen who came through the Gansu corridor, China's main route to the west, and then moved north along the Yellow River to reach the Ordos. These groups must have come in several waves from regions in both Central Asia and southern

Figure 36. Gold headdress ornament, Nalin'gaotu, Shenmu county, Shaanxi Province. Late 4th century B.C. (after Bunker 1989, p. 54, fig. 3)

Siberia, as suggested by the new types of artifacts and iconography in the Ordos region.

The Hu, who appeared on the northwestern frontier and impressed the king of Zhao with "archery from horseback," may have come from farther west and joined the Rouzhi.

According to Sima Qian, the Rouzhi (sometimes given as Yuezhi) controlled a large confederation of mixed linguistic and ethnic backgrounds located in Gansu.[51] The Chinese texts describe the Hu as mounted archers and make a clear distinction between the Hu and the Xiongnu, who had united all the peoples of eastern Eurasia into a vast steppe empire by the end of the third century B.C.[52]

The artifacts excavated in the Ordos include flamboyant headdresses, necklaces, ear ornaments, belt plaques (figs. 38, 39), and bridle ornaments, often of precious metals encrusted with colored stones (fig. 40). The use of silver as a mark of status, and as a means of achieving a shiny white surface, appears to have replaced tinning (fig. 41). Many of these artifacts display metallurgical techniques new to the area that had been transmitted across the Eurasian steppes from metalworking centers farther west.[53] The appearance of these techniques, such as granulation, on China's northwestern frontier had a major impact on Chinese metallurgy.

Two of the most important artifacts in the Ordos region to show such a technique are a pair of gold plaques that depict an animal combat between a tiger and a wild boar and display Chinese characters on the back (figs. 42, 43); these refer to the weight of the plaque and the subject matter.[54] The subject matter is not Chinese, but the presence of the characters and the realistic rendition of the animals indicate that the plaques were cast in China rather than by metalworkers in the Ordos.

The backs of the two plaques display a coarse woven pattern which reproduces the piece of textile that originally supported the wax model when it was removed from the

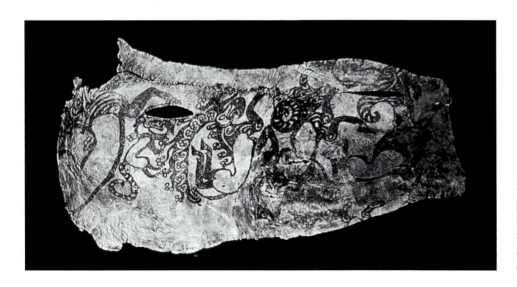

Figure 37. Tattoos of zoomorphic symbols on a male buried in kurgan 2, Pazyryk, Altai Mountains, southern Siberia. 4th century B.C. Photo courtesy of Yevgeny Lubo-Lesnichenko

Figure 38. Gold headdress and torque, Aluchaideng, Hanggin banner, southwestern Inner Mongolia. 3rd century B.C. (after Bunker et al. 1997, p. 49, fig. A53)

Figure 39. Pair of gold and turquoise earrings, Xigoupan, Jungar banner, southwestern Inner Mongolia. 3rd century B.C. (after Yang Boda 1987, vol. 10, pl. 13)

mother-mold in the lost-wax and lost-textile casting process. This is a variation of the indirect lost-wax technique that was developed during the fourth and third centuries B.C. for casting artifacts made of precious metals and later for bronze examples that were to be gilded, tinned, or silver-plated.[55]

Several gold artifacts adorned with distinctly northern subject matter were unearthed from tomb 30 at Xin-zhuangtou near Yixian, Hebei Province.[56] Many display both the textile pattern and characters denoting the weight. During the late Warring States period, Yixian was the location of Yanxiadu, the southern capital of the state of Yan from 311 until 222 B.C., when the city was destroyed by the armies of the Qin. It would appear that metalworkers in Yanxiadu produced luxury items for northern pastoral

Figure 40. Pair of gold belt plaques, Aluchaideng, Hanggin banner, southern Inner Mongolia. 3rd century B.C. Photo courtesy of Guo Suxin

Figure 41. Silver belt plaque, Shihuigou, Eijin Horo banner, southwestern Inner Mongolia. 3rd century B.C. (after Beijing 1993, no. 104)

peoples that were designed to appeal to northern taste; on rare occasions, they would depict an individual identifiable as a nomad who had acquired one of these items (fig. 44).

The major preferences of the pastoral peoples in the Ordos region during the late fourth and third centuries B.C. included the extensive use of precious metals, the representation of fantastic mythological animals, a range of artifacts not seen earlier in the region, new metalworking techniques, and major Chinese involvement in manufacture. Curiously, these features did not spread eastward into south-central Inner Mongolia and the Dongbei and were of only minimal importance in the Ningxia and Gansu areas at this time.

NORTH CHINA (3RD – 1ST CENTURY B.C.)

By the end of the third century B.C., the Xiongnu had unified all the pastoral groups of East Asia into a vast steppe empire that rivaled the Han state which had recently come to power in China. The complex organization of the Xiongnu empire— stretching from Liaoning Province in the east to Xinjiang in the west and northward through Mongolia to Lake Baikal and the Yenisei River valley in eastern Siberia—was repeated by many of the great seminomadic states that were to follow.

The creation of the empire was accompanied by substantial changes in the metallurgy and iconography of belt plaques (the most important indicators of clan and status) and by an increase of Chinese luxury goods, such as lacquers and silk, in burials. The lost-wax and lost-textile technique continued to be used to cast plaques of precious metal, such as the superb silver horse in the collection of the Metropolitan Museum (cat. no. 101) and bronze plaques that were to be gilded, such as catalogue nos. 67, 68, 73, 76, and 77. The majority of these items were produced in China proper or locally by Chinese metalworkers in the employ of the Xiongnu (there is no evidence that the Xiongnu themselves practiced mercury gilding, a chemical gold-plating technique invented in China in the fourth century B.C. by Daoist alchemists searching for man-made gold). One buckle, catalogue no. 75, represents the same scene as catalogue no. 68 but is not gilded and has no textile pattern on the back. This would suggest that it was cast at a different workshop, as its style as well as its casting method is completely different.

Casting models (cat. no. 112) used to create a mother-mold, in which a wax model of a plaque to be cast is formed, not only facilitated the production of identical plaque designs

Figure 42. Gold belt plaque, one of a mirror-image pair, tomb 2, Xigoupan, Jungar banner, southwestern Inner Mongolia. 3rd century B.C. Photo courtesy of Guo Suxin

Figure 43. Reverse of gold belt plaque in figure 42, with textile pattern and Chinese inscription. Photo: Emma C. Bunker

at more than one metalworking center but promoted mass production. The iconography of the Xiongnu displays a shift during the second and first centuries B.C. from that of the pre-Xiongnu pastoral peoples in the northwestern Chinese border areas away from the representation of composite fantastic creatures with raptor-headed attributes to a renewed interest in real animals and people, frequently shown in an abbreviated landscape setting (cat. nos. 79–81, 108, 116). Many belt plaques depict ungulates antithetically posed on either side of a tree or vegetal form, a scene associated with fertility in the Near East, where it originated. Whether the scene carried the same meaning among the Xiongnu is not known, but fertility would surely have been a focus of interest in a herding economy, in which the increase of livestock was of major importance.

Belt buckles and plaques dating to the Xiongnu period have been recovered in quantity from burials in both Northeast and Northwest China.[57] The plaques are decorated with a limited number of zoomorphic scenes, which may indicate clan affiliation, and the alloys of some of them contain arsenic. The artifacts with arsenic are similar to Xiongnu material excavated in Buryatia, where the Xiongnu summer camps were situated, and in Mongolia, the seat of power, both areas where arsenic can be detected in the copper alloys.[58]

The Xiongnu are first mentioned in ancient Chinese texts as owing allegiance to the Ruizhi before they conquered the

tribes in East Asia, including the Ruizhi, to form their empire,[59] although the lengthy prehistory frequently attributed to the Xiongnu cannot be substantiated either archaeologically or in the texts.[60] The Xiongnu have frequently been associated with the Ordos sites that yielded artifacts showing the mythological creatures with raptor-headed appendages. But, in fact, it could not have been the Xiongnu who brought this iconography to China's northwestern borders. First, there is no indication that they were in this region during the fourth century B.C., when these motifs first appeared. The few plaques adorned with such creatures (cat. nos. 67, 68, 72, 76, 99, 103) must instead have belonged to the conquered Ruizhi, who were absorbed by the Xiongnu confederation. Second, with the rise of the Xiongnu and the subsequent expulsion of the Ruizhi between 176 and 160 B.C., the depiction of raptors' heads decreases significantly and eventually disappears from the visual vocabulary of the area.[61]

The mythical animal most favored by the Xiongnu was a sinuous, lupine-headed dragon that must have been an amalgamation of steppe and Chinese features (cat. nos. 17, 102, 105). The earliest representation of this image occurs on a gold belt buckle excavated at Szidorovka, a site near Omsk in western Siberia dated to the late first millennium B.C. (fig. 45). The dragon is shown being attacked by two tigers, a combat scene identical to that represented on a pair of bronze openwork plaques discovered in a female Xiongnu

Figure 44. Gold ornament depicting the
head of a nomad, tomb 30, Yinzhuangtou,
Yi county, Hebei Province. 3rd century B.C.
Photo: Emma C. Bunker

burial at Ivolga, Buryatia, dated to the second century B.C.
(cat. no. 105). Plaques cast with openwork designs were
probably backed with colored fabric or leather to imitate the
color achieved by the earlier inlay tradition.[62] An openwork
jade plaque in a private collection in London (cat. no. 106)
depicts the same scene and may also have been backed with
colored material. The jade is a dark green nephrite visually
similar to nephrite found in northern Mongolia and eastern
Siberia, suggesting that it was carved in the north rather than
in China itself.[63]

The discovery at Szidorovka of the gold buckle with the
lupine-headed dragon suggests that the Xiongnu may originally
have come from much farther west than has heretofore been
realized. A gold plaque in the famous Peter the Great collection of Siberian art in the State Hermitage, St. Petersburg,
that also depicts a lupine-headed dragon on either side of a
vegetal motif (fig. 46), is similar in design to a later bronze
version from a Xiongnu burial at Daodunzi, Tongxin county,
Ningxia (fig. 47), which has a dragon not unlike the one on
catalogue no. 102. Interestingly, both the Szidorovka and
the Peter the Great plaques are inlaid with semiprecious
stones and glass paste, and both have a textile pattern on the
reverse, indicating the lost-wax and lost-textile casting technique.[64] The relationship of the Szidorovka buckle to the
Peter the Great plaque, said to have been found somewhere
in western Siberia, adds credence to the idea of the Xiongnu's
more western origin. Further connections with western
Eurasia are demonstrated by the similarities between the
tear-shaped borders that frame the plaques from Szidorovka,
from the Peter the Great collection, and from Daodunzi
and the tear-shaped border on a gold-inlaid plaque in the
exhibition associated with the Sarmatians (cat. no. 115).
A recent article pointing out other similarities between
zoomorphic scenes on Xiongnu plaques and earlier animal
representations in West Asia would also seem to support a
western origin and argues for further scholarly attention.[65]

Many artifacts from the Xiongnu culture found in North
China provide a means for comparative dating of objects in
collections formed before the twentieth century, such as that
of Peter the Great. Several large gold belt buckles in that
collection are stylistically and iconographically related to belt

Figure 45. Gold inlaid
belt plaque, one of a pair,
Szidorovka, western Sibe-
ria. 3rd century B.C. Photo
courtesy of Jacov Sher

Figure 46. Gold inlaid belt plaque, 3rd century B.C. Peter the Great collection, The State Hermitage, St. Petersburg (after Jettmar 1967, p. 193, pl. 39)

Figure 47. Bronze openwork belt plaque with pair of dragons, tomb 1, Daodunzi, Tongxin county, Ningxia. 2nd–1st century B.C. Photo courtesy of Wu En

plaques dated to the last quarter of the first millennium B.C. that have been found at sites in North China.[66] The sixth- to fourth-century B.C. dates given to many of these objects may be too early, in view of their similarities to bronze plaques depicting the same scenes found in North China dating to the much later Xiongnu period. For example, catalogue no. 72 is a simplified version of a gold Peter the Great plaque, said to have been found at Verkhneudinsk (present-day Ulan-Ude), near Lake Baikal (fig. 48), a similarity that calls into question the fifth- to fourth-century B.C. date traditionally given to the Peter the Great plaque.[67] Another gold plaque in St. Petersburg, depicting a tiger attacking a camel under a leafy tree (fig. 49), is dated to the sixth century B.C.,[68] yet the composition of the animal-combat scene and the style of the tree relate to examples portrayed on bronze plaques that do not date any earlier than the late third to second century B.C., as evidenced by the date of catalogue no. 78. These few observations indicate that a complete reevaluation of many gold treasures in the Peter the Great collection should be undertaken in light of recent archaeological discoveries in China.

Vessels associated with the northern frontier zone peoples were piece-mold cast and primarily utilitarian, with almost no decoration. The complex ceremonies associated with vessels in China were ill-suited to a herding and hunting lifestyle. The most common steppe vessel was a stem-footed cauldron, called a *fu* by the Chinese (cat. no. 186). Although the eighth-century B.C. cauldron with Zhou-style decor in the exhibition was obviously cast in late Western

Zhou China, the shape has no Chinese antecedents and must copy a non-Chinese example (cat. no. 185). The origins of the nomadic cauldron must instead be sought in the west, where numerous early examples of pottery, wood, and hammered metal have been discovered, such as a hammered vessel from the Trialeti cemetery in Transcaucasia, Georgia.[69] It may be that Chinese metalworkers were the first to cast a cauldron in this shape, but they must have done so under nomadic influence, as the vessel shape has a far earlier priority in the Eurasian steppes than it does in China.

XIANBEI ART FROM NORTH CHINA (1ST–3RD CENTURY A.D.)

By the end of the first century B.C., the Xiongnu had been replaced by the Xianbei, who succeeded them as masters of the eastern steppes. The Xianbei enhanced their belt ornaments with motifs of animals, both mythological and real — deer, rams, gazelles, and horses, with and without wings (cat. nos. 117, 152–154)—that reflected their own beliefs. A winged horse that guided an early Xianbei leader and his people on their migration southward figures prominently in ancient Xianbei mythology and is depicted on numerous belt ornaments and plaques (cat. nos. 22, 85).

Xianbei artifacts are made of gold (cat. no. 152), silver (cat. no. 22), and bronze (cat. no. 153) that was either hammered or cast. Some bronze plaques are gold-plated either by mercury gilding (cat. no. 85) or by overlaying the surface with thin sheet gold (cat. no. 154).

Figure 48. Gold inlaid belt plaque found at Verkhneudinsk (present-day Ulan-Ude), Lake Baikal. 3rd–2nd century B.C. (Aruz 2000, pp. 288–89, no. 210)

Figure 49. Gold belt plaque, 3rd–2nd century B.C. Peter the Great collection, The State Hermitage, St. Petersburg (Aruz 2000, p. 290, no. 211)

CONCLUSION

The artifacts associated with the hunting and herding peoples of the Eurasian steppes appear to have served two main purposes. On the one hand, their images were totemic and proclaimed their owners' individual heritage. On the other, they gave visual form to the supernatural world that guided their lives. The mythologies of the nomads were closely related to shamanism, a nature-oriented religion rooted in the distant past, which stimulated the creation of symbols that represented the complex relationships between man and the forces of nature and the supernatural. Small, portable drums, traditionally made of wood and leather, have always been associated with shamanism. The bronze drum body in the exhibition (cat. no. 166) reflects an earlier pottery or wood construction and perhaps indicates the presence of shamanism in ancient Dongbei beliefs, but we would be on dangerous ground if we were to accept this theory as fact.

There are no authorities to consult to tell us exactly what each symbol means, and we must be careful not to impose our own unsupported interpretations on the past. The art of the steppe peoples was created to transmit information to those who saw and wore it, both the living and the dead, but if we try to attribute specific meanings to the various motifs and symbols, we run the risk of being profoundly wrong. Their meanings were not meant for us and can probably never be retrieved. Instead, the information transmitted to us through these artifacts is the visual record of countless incidents of cultural exchange that occurred between the Eurasian steppe peoples and their settled neighbors. The peoples of the steppes served as cultural intermediaries between regions east and west, north and south throughout the first millennium B.C. The discovery of Han Chinese mirrors in nomadic tombs far to the west beyond the Oxus River, for example, attests to the long-distance trade that existed throughout Eurasia.[70]

Since antiquity, a traditional Sinocentric perspective has so dominated the historical accounts that the role of the northern pastoral peoples in the development of Chinese culture has often been misrepresented or overlooked. The interactions between the herding and the planting worlds created a hybrid vigor that, in turn, produced the extraordinary dynamism which characterizes some of the art created during the Western Han. Important metalworking techniques—for example, strip-twisted wire, granulation, and loop-in-loop chains—were introduced into China by way of the steppes during the late Warring States period. Four superb gold buckles in the exhibition (cat. nos. 82–84, 86) are excellent illustrations of Sino–steppe contacts. The omega shape of the buckles derives from the steppes (cat. no. 71), but the workmanship is Chinese, using western metalworking techniques transmitted by way of the steppe peoples into China.

The appearance of northern motifs in the artistic vocabulary of China during the first millennium B.C. is a phenomenon demonstrated by several Chinese artifacts in the exhibition. A perfect example of steppe exotica in Chinese art is the beak-

Figure 50. Underside of a gilded bronze censer (detail) from a Western Han tomb, Maoling, Xingping county, Shaanxi Province. Dated by inscription to 137–136 B.C. Photo courtesy of Masahiro Hashiguchi

headed creatures that embellish the lowest register on the superb Western Han gilded bronze censer from Maoling, Yingping county, Shaanxi (fig. 50). Another example is the mythical ungulate with inverted hindquarters on a gold horse frontal from a Han tomb at Luozhuang, in Zhangyu, Shandong Province.[71] The prototypical Han lupine-headed dragon, with its partial northern lineage (cat. nos. 7, 102, 105), represents the ultimate symbol of Sino–steppe contact. Wheeled transport, horseback riding, riding gear, mirrors, ornamental belt fittings, the scabbard slide (cat. no. 170), and lost-wax casting were also introduced into China through contact with northern peoples beyond its frontiers.

Recent publications have presented tantalizing evidence for the Chinese appropriation of certain steppe architectural elements, tomb designs, and other features, including tents and canopies like those excavated at Zhongshan, Hebei.[72] The similarity between steppe kurgan burials and a tomb filled with horses at Linzi, Shandong, is not so far-fetched when one considers that nomadic kurgans have been discovered near Almaty in Kazakhstan, just west of Xinjiang (fig. 51). As more scholars turn their interests to Sino–steppe relations, a word of caution is in order. Before any conclusion is reached as to the Chinese appropriation of some aspect of steppe culture, it must first be demonstrated that the cultural

Figure 51. Saka kurgan near Almaty, Kazakhstan. Photo: Emma C. Bunker

Figure 52. Bronze incense burner in the shape of a mountain landscape. 2nd – 1st century B.C. Hebei Provincial Museum (after Beijing 1998, pl. 128)

spectacular headdress worn by the man buried at Issyk-Kul in Kazakhstan (fig. 54).

Trade and tribute were the primary means of cultural intercourse, fueled by the insatiable desire of the Chinese for horses, fur, leather, and other animal products. By the Western Han, the list of desirable imports recorded in the *Yan tie lun* (On Salt and Iron) included mules, donkeys, camels, and horses of many colors and types, plus furs, rugs, carpets, and all manner of semiprecious stones.[75]

The artifacts in the present exhibition are the physical embodiments of the ever-changing relationships between the nomads of Central Asia and the settled communities with which they came in contact. They are the only unbiased testament to the long associations that either went unrecorded or were misrepresented in the literature. Visual footnotes to the history of the Eurasian steppes, they not only celebrate the pastoral peoples who produced them but allude to the far-reaching impact of the nomads on Eurasian history. Were it not for the survival of these small but remarkable creations, a significant link in the cultural history of the ancient world might have been lost forever.

1. Yablonsky 2000, pp. 3–4.
2. For an in-depth discussion of the social organization among mobile pastoral peoples, see Barfield 1993 and Linduff 1997, pp. 33–34.
3. Hall 1997.
4. Yablonsky 1994, fig. 83.13.
5. For a discussion of the northern frontier zone peoples, see Prušek 1966; Prušek 1971; Tian 1983; Bunker et al. 1997, pp. 14–16; and Di Cosmo 1999, 2002.

element in question—the motif or the metalworking technique, and so forth—occurred in the steppes before, not concurrent with or after, it made its appearance in China.

The most surprising implication of Sino–steppe contact is the possibility of northern influence on the development of early plucked instruments in China, such as the *se* and the *qin*. A *qin* tuner surmounted by a bear (cat. no. 178), a *se* string anchor decorated with a coiled beaked ungulate (cat. no. 180), and a *se* string anchor surmounted by a mountain inhabited by wild animals (cat. no. 179) all display images that derive from the pastoral world beyond the Great Wall.[73] That a three-dimensional mountain image depicted on a Western Han *se* string anchor (cat. no. 179) may also have a steppe ancestry suggests that contact with the nomadic world may have been a major catalyst to the development of integrated Chinese landscape representations during this period.[74] Incense burners in the shape of mountain landscapes (fig. 52) abound with scenes that are comparable to those with tiny animals and galloping hunters represented on nomadic artifacts (fig. 53) such as on the

Figure 53. Gold belt plaque. 3rd–2nd century B.C. Peter the Great collection, The State Hermitage, St. Petersburg. Photo courtesy of Yevgeny Lubo-Lesnichenko

Figure 54. Reconstruction of clothing found at a male burial at Issyk-Kul, Kazakhstan. 4th century B.C. (after Arbore-Popescu, Grigore, Silvi Antonini, and Baipakov 1998, p. 175, no. 27)

6. Herodotus bk. 4.

7. Lawergren 1988; So and Bunker 1995, pp. 34–35; Bunker et al. 1997, p. 117.

8. So and Bunker 1995, pp. 29, 47.

9. Novgorodova 1980, chaps. 2, 3.

10. So and Bunker 1995, p. 65.

11. Chlenova 1963; Bunker et al. 1997, p. 171.

12. So and Bunker 1995, p. 65; Bunker et al.1997, pp. 166–67.

13. Bunker (in So and Bunker 1995, p. 64) suggests that the few minor images of animal predation may refer to local hunting practices in which felines were used as hunting partners.

14. Linduff 1997, p. 72.

15. Bunker 1994b, p. 41; So and Bunker 1995, pp. 59–61.

16. So and Bunker 1995, p. 63; Bunker et al. 1997, pp. 175–76.

17. So and Bunker 1995, pp. 64–65; Bunker et al. 1997, p. 188.

18. Griaznov 1984, pl. 25; Bunker et al. 1997, p. 177. The change in date is based on unpublished carbon 14 dating and dendrochronology supplied by Sergei Miniaev, Institute of the History of Material Culture, Russian Academy of Sciences, St. Petersburg.

19. So and Bunker 1995, p. 97, fig. 37; Linduff 1997, p. 21, fig. A1.

20. So 1995b, pp. 190–91.

21. Aruz 2000, pp. 80–81.

22. Linduff 1997, p. 37, fig. A23.

23. So and Bunker 1995, p. 29.

24. So in Fong 1980, no. 69; Li, Liang, and Bagley 1996, p. 326, no. 699. According to references in ancient Chinese literature, the Jin were related to northern peoples, referred to as the Di and the Rong, through trade and marriage alliances. Thus it is not surprising to find evidence for the relationships reflected in the manufacture and decoration of certain northern artifacts.

25. *Kaogu xuebao* 1989, no. 1, p. 66, fig. 11:10.

26. Li, Liang, and Bagley 1996, pp. 331 no. 713, 333 no. 721.

27. Bunker et al. 1997, fig. B5; Barkova 1987.

28. For details of this site see Höllmann 1992; Höllmann and Kossack 1992; and Linduff 2000a.

29. Tian and Guo 1986, p. 117, fig. 82.

30. *Kaogu* 1977, no. 2, pp. 111–14.

31. *Wenwu* 1988, no. 11, p. 16, fig. 3:39–42, p. 17, fig. 4.

32. Beijing 1992, p. 71.

33. Beijing 1980c, colorpl. 30.4.

34. Chlenova 1963.

35. Bunker et al. 1997, nos. 168, 169, 173, 174, 176–78. This type of ornament was not cast in gold.

36. W. Watson 1971, pp. 107–8.

37. Griaznov 1984, pl. 4.

38. Chlenova 1967, pl. 31.

39. Zavitukhina 1983, p. 158.

40. Polosmak 1991, p. 8, fig. 10:5–6.

41. It is possible that the bronze belt plaque in the shape of a walking carnivore found in Maoqinggou, M55, which has a hole in its shoulder, was not made locally but is an exotic import from farther north; see Linduff 1997, p. 57, fig. A74.

42. Dalley 1985.

43. Dandamayev 1994, p. 44.

44. So 1995a.

45. Li Xueqin 1985b, no. 137.

46. Bunker 1994b, pp. 48–49.

47. Jacobson 1984; Bunker 1989; Bunker 1992b.

48. Bunker 1992b, pp. 111–12; So and Bunker 1995, p. 29.

49. Jacobson 1984; Bunker 1989; Bunker 1992b.

50. Bunker 1989; Aruz 2000, p. 248.

51. Sima Qian locates the Rouzhi "in the area between the Ch'i-lien or Heavenly Mountains and Tun-huang" in present-day Gansu; B. Watson 1961, vol. 2, p. 168. The name Rouzhi is the modern equivalent of the old textual reading of Ruzhi, which has in the past been read as Yuezhi as the result of confounding the 130th radical with the 74th radical; see Bunker 1992b, esp. p. 115 n. 56.

52. Prušek 1971, pp. 204, 224; Bunker 1992b, p. 112.

53. For a description and history of these techniques, see Bunker 1994b, pp. 44–47.

54. Li Xueqin 1985a, pp. 333–36; Bunker 1992b, fig. 19; Bunker 1993, fig. 25.

55. Bunker 1994b, pp. 41–42; So and Bunker 1995, pp. 59–61.

56. Bunker 1992b, fig. 20; Bunker 1993, fig. 24; So and Bunker 1995, pp. 59–61, fig. 24.

57. For a complete list of sites associated with the Xiongnu, see Bunker et al. 1997, p. 343.

58. Ibid., p. 270.

59. B. Watson 1961, vol. 2, pp. 160–62; Pulleyblank 1983, pp. 457–58.

60. Haskins 1988.

61. Ibid., pp. 1–2; Yü 1967, pp. 123, 127.

62. A plaque in the Arthur M. Sackler collections still retains a wooden backing that would have held a piece of fabric in place, see Bunker et al. 1997, pp. 266–67, no. 233.

63. *Mongol Messenger*, June 12, 1996, p. 6; personal communications from Janet Douglas, FGA/AMSG, 1995. This type of jade occurs in Siberia as well.

64. Bunker 1992a, pp. 213–15; personal communication from M. P. Zavitukhina, 1996.

65. Miniaev 1995b.

66. Bunker 1992a; Bunker 1992b, pp. 109–11.

67. Aruz 2000, pp. 287–89, no. 210.

68. Ibid., p. 290, no. 211. This gold plaque in the Peter the Great collection is actually one of a mirror-image pair of plaques, a fact that is never mentioned in the catalogue entry. For the other matching plaque, see Rudenko 1962, pl. v:3.

69. So and Bunker 1995, p. 108, no. 22; for a discussion of early cast cauldrons, see Bunker et al. 1997, pp. 178–79, no. 93.

70. Musée Cernuschi 2001, p. 231.

71. I would like to thank Zhixin Sun, associate curator, Department of Asian Art at The Metropolitan Museum of Art, for bringing this reference to my attention.

72. Rawson 1999, pp. 21–25.

73. So and Bunker 1995, pp. 148–51.

74. Akishev 1978, p. 47; Rawson and Bunker 1990, p. 302, fig. 7.

75. Gale 1931, pp. 14–15.

Catalogue

1. HORSE HARNESS FITTINGS

Harness fittings were used as adornments for horses, which were so important in the lives of the hunting and herding peoples of northern Eurasia. While many bridle ornaments are typologically the same, they are differentiated by regional artistic styles and motifs.[1] Although we cannot hope to understand the precise meaning of the visual symbols that distinguish these artifacts, the obvious intention was to give horses, whether ridden or driven, supernatural traits that would enable them to serve their owners both in life and in death. One has only to look at the horse decorations discovered in the frozen nomadic kurgans at Pazyryk, in the Altai Mountains of southern Siberia, to imagine how spectacular a fully caparisoned horse could have looked (fig. 12).

1. For the various kinds of strap-crossings found throughout northern Eurasia, see Janse 1932.

1.
Harness fitting in the shape of an ibex

> Western Asia, late 7th–6th century B.C.
> Bronze
> Height 1⅝ in. (4.1 cm); width 2⅛ in. (5.4 cm)
> Ex coll.: Ariadne Galleries, Inc. New York

This small harness fitting is cast in the form of a recumbent ibex with the head turned back 180 degrees. The ibex is naturalistically depicted, with ridged horns and a short beard. The underside displays a projecting square with holes in each side, indicating that the fitting probably served to hold and distribute the strap-crossings of a bridle. The piece was solid cast by the lost-wax process.

No harness fittings identical to the Thaw example have been found in archaeological context, but a plaque nearly identical in shape and function is in the Mildenberg collection.[1] The Mildenberg plaque has been attributed to western Asia and dated to the late seventh to the early sixth century B.C. by comparison with an unfinished object decorated with a similar animal motif excavated at Sardis, Turkey.[2]

1. Kozloff, Mitten, and Sguaitamatti 1986, pp.14–15.
2. Ibid., p. 15.

2.

Two harness ornaments in the shape of gazelles

Northeast China, 6th–5th century B.C.
Bronze
Each: Height 1⅞ in. (4.6 cm); width 2¼ in. (5.7 cm)
Ex coll.: J. J. Lally & Co., New York; Calon da Collection
Published: So and Bunker 1995, pp. 119–20, no. 35.

Two sensitively portrayed gazelles in mirror image face one another on these harness ornaments. Each gazelle is shown, with folded legs, in profile. The almond-shaped eyes are indicated by intaglio lines, and the S-shaped horns are marked by a row of raised dots between two parallel lines. The placement of four loops on the reverse of each plaque, vertical ones at both top and bottom and horizontal ones at either end, suggests that they are harness ornaments, most likely for a bridle. Each plaque was cast integrally with its loops in a multipiece mold. The ornaments may originally have belonged to a much larger set. Another pair of nearly identical fittings is in the Tokyo National Museum.[1]

A plaque from northwestern Jilin Province[2] and a garment hook excavated at Wudaohezi, Lingyuan county, Liaoning Province,[3] are also cast in the shape of a gazelle with S-shaped curved horns and folded legs very similar to the present examples. The pose is characteristic of ungulate images on artifacts belonging to the hunting tribes of Northeast China and is distantly related to early representations found in southern Siberia and western Eurasia.[4] This particular articulation of the legs and hooves is not found on artifacts associated with Northwest China, because there the ungulates' hooves point upward and downward, with the soles parallel to a hypothetical ground line. (See also cat. no. 35.)

1. Takahama and Hatakeyama 1997, no. 139.
2. Nelson 1995, p. 210, fig. 7:2.
3. *Wenwu* 1989, no. 2, p. 56, fig. 8:12.
4. Chlenova 1963, pp. 66–67, tables 1, 2.

3.
Cheekpiece for a bridle in the shape of leopard

> Northeast China, 6th–4th century B.C.
> Bronze
> Length 5½ in. (14 cm)
> Ex coll.: J. J. Lally & Co., New York; Calon da Collection

An attenuated racing leopard forms this cheekpiece for a riding-horse bridle. The divided ends of a headstall cheek strap would pass through the holes that pierce the leopard's shoulder and haunch, and the ring end of a snaffle bit would be fitted loosely around the leopard's midsection. A longitudinal mold mark visible under the neck and jaw confirms piece-mold casting.

A complete pair of cheekpieces with the same shape as the present example was published in 1990 by the Hong Kong Ceramic Society.[1] The particular riding-horse bridle system to which this cheekpiece belongs was originally developed by the Scythians in Northwest Asia and then spread eastward across the Eurasian steppes to the borders of China.[2] The first such cheekpieces had three holes but were superseded by cheekpieces with two holes during the sixth to the fifth century B.C., providing a terminus ad quem for the present example. Bronze cheekpieces that have vertical attachment holes with the same bulging sides occur also at sixth-to-fourth-century B.C. sites in Kazakhstan[3] and among the grave goods in the fourth-to-third century B.C. barrows at Pazyryk, in the Altai Mountains.[4]

1. Rawson and Bunker 1990, no. 211.
2. So and Bunker 1995, p. 29.
3. Arbore-Popescu, Silvi Antonini, and Baipakov 1999, pl. 239–42.
4. Rudenko 1970, pls. 88, 118A.

4.
Harness ornament in the shape of a carnivore

> Northwest China and southwestern Inner Mongolia,
> 6th–4th century B.C.
> Bronze
> Height 2¾ in. (7 cm); length 5½ in. (14 cm)
> Ex coll.: J. J. Lally & Co., New York

This harness ornament, cast in the shape of a carnivore clutching a ram in its paws, exhibits an odd combination of feline and canine features that makes specific identification difficult. The animal displays all four legs, with five prominent claws on each paw: four semicircular front claws and one semicircular dewclaw curved in the opposite direction. The jaws are wide open, revealing fangs and teeth represented by half circles. The ears were precast and then cast on by inserting them into the casting mold. The tail has been broken off.

This powerful carnivore figure derives from earlier southern Siberian artistic traditions, exemplified by the fifth-century B.C. carved wooden tigers on harness ornaments from Tuekta, in the Altai Mountains.[1] The manner in which the teeth are represented, as semispheres, reflects a wood-carving tradition. The back is concave, and the head is hollow. Two vertical loops are provided for attachment, one behind the haunches and the other close to the edge at the back of the head.

The location of the loops and the orientation of the ornament suggest that it may originally have decorated the breast strap of a horse's harness. Breast-strap ornaments from southern Siberian sites, such as Pazyryk, also have a similar shape.[2]

Two tiger-shaped ornaments of gold that may have been harness decorations were recovered from a disturbed grave at Nalin'gaotu, Shenmu county, northern Shaanxi Province,[3] and are quite similar in shape to the Thaw ornament. The ram's forelegs are shown pointing forward rather than folded under the body on both the present example and on the rim of a gold torque excavated at Aluchaideng, Hanggin banner, in the Ordos Desert region, southwestern Inner Mongolia.[4] The stylistic similarities between the Thaw ornament and artifacts found in the Ordos suggest an attribution to Northwest China and southwestern Inner Mongolia. Two pieces in the Shelby White and Leon Levy collection are nearly identical to this one.[5]

1. Rudenko 1970, pl. 80.
2. Ibid., pl. 89.
3. Dai and Sun 1983, p. 24, fig. 2:4,5.
4. Bunker et al. 1997, p. 49, figs. A53, A54.
5. So and Bunker 1995, pp. 115–16, no. 30; Takahama and Hatakeyama 1997, no. 184.

5.
Strap-crossing in the shape of a coiled wolf

> Eastern Eurasia, 5th century B.C.
> Bronze
> Diameter 2 ¼ in. (5.7 cm)
> Ex coll.: Anthony Plowright, Paris

This harness fitting, in the shape of a delightful small wolf curled into a circle, is a device used to distribute the crossed straps of a bridle. The artisan has ingeniously represented all four legs rather than just two, as most Eurasian steppe coiled carnivore images are shown, such as catalogue no. 7. The wolf's jaws are slightly open, revealing two sharp fangs and four molars. The ear is indicated by a comma shape that begins with a spiral at the inner base. The texture of the pelt is suggested by striated intaglio enclosures with pebbled areas, surface patterns that may have first developed in wood and bone carving or in stamped leather. The reverse displays thick folded-over edges and four loops to accommodate the straps. The ornament was cast by the lost-wax process, indicated by marks on the back that were left in the bronze by wax joins.

Strap-crossings were introduced into China along with the chariot during the Shang dynasty but have an earlier priority in West Asia.[1] To date, no harness ornament cast in the same style as the Thaw strap-crossing has been found in archaeological context, but the coiled carnivore was a popular image throughout the Eurasian steppes. The particular carnivore represented in each geographic region reflected the local fauna. Panthers were represented in western Eurasia, whereas wolves and tigers appear in the artistic vocabulary of eastern Eurasia. The comma-shaped ear with a spiral at the base appears to be a specifically eastern Eurasian stylistic trait and occurs on several artifacts in the Thaw collection (cat. nos. 7, 94).

1. Janse 1932.

6.
Strap-crossing in the shape of three bears

> Eastern Eurasia, 5th century B.C.
> Bronze
> Diameter 2 ⅜ in. (6 cm)
> Ex coll.: Anthony Plowright, Paris

This strap-crossing takes the form of three crouching bears—identified by their very short, stumpy tails—in a circle, each biting the tail of the bear in front. Each is shown in profile with only two legs represented. The mouths are open, revealing fangs and teeth, and the ears are indicated by an oval with a depression in the center. The back of the plaque displays a hollow square frame on four posts that accommodate the crossed straps of a bridle. The heavy folded edges seen on the reverse suggest that the ornament was cast by the lost-wax process.

Archaeological research has not revealed any other harness ornament similar in style to this one. The prominence given to the bears' sharp claws is related to the claws of the tigers depicted on a sixth-century B.C. coffin from Bashadar, in southern Siberia (fig. 32). The ornament appears to be cast in an as yet unrecognized style of the eastern Eurasian steppes.

tradition, or a carving tradition such as that seen on catalogue no. 159, a bone cylinder from Northwest China.[4] The representation of the wolf's teeth by semicircles can be seen on earlier carved wooden artifacts from burials in the Altai.[5]

1. Bunker et al. 1997, pp. 194–95, nos. 123–25.
2. Artamonov 1969, pl. 78.
3. Yan and Li 1992, p. 574, fig. 1.11.
4. For artifacts in stamped leather and carved wood from burials in the Altai Mountain region showing these techniques, see Rudenko 1970, pls. 131L, 130B, and Debaine-Francfort and Idriss 2001, p. 167, no. 52.
5. Aruz 2000, pp. 252–53, no. 174.

7.
Harness ornament in the shape of a coiled wolf

> Northwest China, 5th–4th century B.C.
> Bronze
> Height 2⅞ in. (7.4 cm); width 2⅝ in. (6.7 cm)
> Ex coll.: J. J. Lally & Co., New York; Calon da Collection; Alvin Lo, New York
> Published: So and Bunker 1995, pp. 129–30, no. 47.

This harness ornament represents a wolf coiled into a circle and shown in profile. The hind- and forelegs form a smaller circle within the perimeter of the body. Four claws are shown on each paw, and the ear is described by an elongated spiral that begins at the inner edge. The wolf's body is slightly fluted and marked with finely patterned striations, and a large volute marks the shoulder and haunch. On the reverse are three squared attachment loops. The way in which the loops are formed confirms that the ornament was cast by the lost-wax process. Each loop was made by placing a thin, unevenly shaped strip of wax on two projecting round wax posts.

The coiled wolf appears to derive from coiled-wolf images found far to the west that date to the late sixth century B.C. rather than from the coiled felines found at earlier sites east of the Taihang Mountains.[1] A bridle ornament in the shape of a coiled wolf from a late-sixth-century barrow near Simferopol, in the Crimea, is startlingly close in concept to the present example.[2]

The Thaw wolf relates stylistically to a similar small coiled wolf represented on a fitting found at Xinyangxiang, Guyuan county, southern Ningxia.[3] The artisan who designed the Thaw plaque has caught the essential lupine characteristics, including the soft paws and slightly swollen forehead. The designs on the pelt may derive from a stamped-leather

8.

Harness ornament with zoomorphic motifs

> Northwest China, 5th–4th century B.C.
> Bronze
> Height 2 in. (5.1 cm); width 1 1/4 in. (3.2 cm)
> Ex coll.: J. J. Lally & Co., New York; Calon da Collection

This harness ornament is decorated in relief with an unusual combination of zoomorphic motifs. The upper part displays a coiled carnivore shown *en face* with one front and one hind paw visible, as if seen from above. A curved element that terminates in an eared bird's head at one end and a bird's head with a long curved beak at the other hangs below. The hollow reverse of the plaque has two squared vertical loops, formed the same way as those on catalogue no. 7, an ornament in the shape of a coiled wolf, indicating that the ornament is lost-wax cast.

Harness ornaments with zoomorphic designs similar to this one have been found throughout Northwest China.[1] Although no plaques identical to the present example have been excavated archaeologically, the similarity of its casting method to that of the coiled wolf suggests that it can be attributed to the same geographic region. A bronze harness ornament recently unearthed in the Honggou Mountain valley, Xinjiang, displays a bird's head that is very similar to this one.[2]

1. Bunker et al. 1997, p. 252, no. 213.
2. *Xinjiang wenwu* 1998, no. 4, p. 61.

9.

Harness ornament with bird's head

> Bulgaria, Thracian period, late 5th–4th century B.C.
> Bronze
> Height 1 1/2 in (3.8 cm); width 1 1/4 in. (3.2 cm)
> Ex coll.: Madelon Hedden, Santa Fe

This small plaque, used to decorate a horse's harness, takes the form of a fantastic bird's head. The eye is indicated by a sunken circular line, the ruff is textured by striations, and the beak is described by raised curved lines. The reverse reveals the remains of two attachment loops, and the presence of mold lines suggests that the ornament was piece-mold cast.

Small metal appliqués were made by the Thracians not only as personal ornamentation but also to adorn their horses.[1] Several small plaques intended as harness decoration and similar to the Thaw example have been recovered from Bulgaria.[2]

1. Ariadne Galleries 1998, nos. 8–10.
2. Berti and La Porta 1997, p. 155, fig. 221.

10.

Harness ornaments with raptors and carnivores

Bulgaria, Thracian period, late 5th—4th century B.C.
Silver with gilded details
a. Height 3 in. (7.6 cm); width 5¼ in. (13.3 cm)
b. Diamater 3⅞ in. (9.8 cm)
c. Height 1⅝ in. (4.1 cm); width 2⅜ in. (6 cm)
Ex coll.: Ariadne Galleries, Inc., New York

These handsome gilded-silver bridle ornaments represent mythological raptors and carnivores. A diagonal line across the largest plaque shows wear from rubbing, perhaps by a leather harness strap. The two largest ornaments were formed by hammering; the smallest one is lost-wax cast. The surface details on all three are chased, the outside borders highlighted by diffusion gilding, a process used in Europe before the introduction of mercury gilding.

Although sold as a set, the ornaments display minor differences in production method and attachment devices. The largest plaque displays a horizontal tube for attachment. The middle-sized piece has an attachment loop on the back that was soldered on, while the squared loop on the smallest plaque was cast.

The Thracians paid particular attention to the decoration of their horse harnesses, and many rich equestrian fittings have been found in burials throughout Bulgaria.[1] Plaques decorated with whorls composed of three animal heads very similar to the example in the middle have been excavated from burial mounds at Mezek.[2] Raptors' heads and carnivores were major symbols of the Thracians and must have played an important role in their rich mythology. Obvious stylistic and iconographic relationships exist between Thracian and Scythian art in the frequent use of zoomorphic symbols as an expression of cultural beliefs.

1. Marazov 1998, p. 99, nos. 7, 8, and p. 128.
2. National Museum of India 1981, no. 202.

a.

b.

c.

I I.
Harness ornament with bird's-head terminals

> Northwest China, 4th century B.C.
> Tinned bronze
> Height 2 in. (5.1 cm); width 1⅝ in. (4.1 cm)
> Ex coll.: Michael Dunn, New York

This harness ornament is cast in the shape of a round boss from which depends a curved element with bird's head terminals. One bird, with a somewhat menacing demeanor, has a short curved beak, round eye, and prominent ear, while the other has a longer hooked beak and a smaller ear. The ornament is tinned on the front to give it a silvery appearance, and the curved element, which serves as a neck for both birds, is textured by a central pebbled band. A vertical loop is placed behind the hollow boss, and mold marks indicate that the piece was piece-mold cast integrally with the loop.

Harness ornaments similar to this one have been excavated in the Guyuan region of southern Ningxia.[1] The type derives from earlier examples found at Tuekta, kurgan 1, in the Altai Mountains,[2] which also depict eared birds' heads. The surface pebbling indicated by pseudogranulation relates the Thaw ornament to workmanship by the Qin of the late fifth century B.C., suggesting that it may have been made specifically for trade with their pastoral neighbors.[3]

1. Tian and Guo 1986, p. 155, fig. 110.1; Luo and Han 1990, p. 415, fig. 14.10; Yan and Li 1992, p. 574, fig. 1:7; Bunker et al. 1997, pp. 252–53, no. 213.
2. Piotrovskii 1987, pl. 91.
3. So and Bunker 1995, p. 162, no. 85.

I 2.
Harness ornament with owl's head and bird

> Northwest China, 4th century B.C.
> Tinned bronze
> Height 3¼ in. (8.3 cm); width 1¾ in. (4.4 cm)
> Ex coll.: Michael Dunn, New York

The shape of this harness ornament is that of a stylized owl's head with a coiled bird in its beak. The owl's bulging eyes are formed by a convex boss within a raised circular rim, and the ruff is described by two openwork loops below the pointed ear tufts. The pendant bird is so abstracted that it is recognizable only by comparison with slightly earlier versions, such as catalogue no. 11. The remains of tinning mark the surface around the eyes, and the reverse shows a crude-looking vertical loop inside the hollow owl's head. Flashing in the openings indicates that the ornament was piece-mold cast.

Typologically related to the other harness ornaments with pendant bird forms in the Thaw collection (cat. nos. 8, 11), this one can be associated with the pastoral peoples on the frontiers of Northwest China. The owl intended may be the long-eared owl that is widespread throughout Eurasia.[1]

1. Zhao 1990, p. 87.

1 3.
Bridle ornaments with raptors and carnivores

Ukraine or Bulgaria, Scythian or Thracian period,
4th century B.C.
Gold
a. Height 1 ⅜ in. (3.5 cm); width 1 ⅞ in. (4.8 cm)
b. Height 1 ⅞ in. (4.8 cm); width 3 ⅜ in. (8.6 cm)
c. Height 1 ½ in. (3.8 cm); width 1 ⅞ in. (4.8 cm)
Ex coll.: Ariadne Galleries, Inc., New York

These three flat bridle ornaments, made from cast gold blanks that were hammered and chased, represent the heads of mythological raptors and carnivores. Texture and definition are heightened by hatching, and hammer marks are still visible on the backs. The reverse of each plaque has attachment straps that have been soldered in place. A fluid resinous red material remaining from unknown burial rituals highlights certain areas on each plaque.

Numerous similarly decorated harness ornaments have been recovered from both Scythian burials in Ukraine[1] and Thracian burials in Bulgaria.[2] The majority display raptors' and carnivores' heads comparable to those seen here, and like them much of the surface detail is produced by hatching and indented lines.[3]

1. Reeder 1999, pp. 317–19, nos. 166, 167.
2. Marazov 1998, nos. 7, 8.
3. Berti and La Porta 1997, no. 228.

tinning the bronze with molten tin. The reverse has a turned-over edge and displays a vertical loop between and below the ear and eye. The plaque was cast by the lost-wax process.

The camel does not appear in the art of China or that of the neighboring pastoral peoples until the fourth century B.C., although the animal had been well known in Central Asia from the third millennium B.C.[1] The camelid species first introduced into eastern Eurasia was the two-humped Bactrian camel represented here.

1. Knauer 1998, pp. 11, 36, 38.

14.
Harness ornament in the shape of a camel's head

> Northwest China, 4th – 3rd century B.C.
> Tinned bronze
> Height 2 in. (5.1 cm); width 2⅝ in. (6.7 cm)
> Ex coll.: J. J. Lally & Co., New York; Calon da Collection

This harness ornament is cast in the shape of a stylized camel's head shown in profile. The eye is represented by a round boss with a circular rim, and the ear by an elongated oval with a central depression. An upper and a lower tooth are visible within the slightly open jaws. The artist has caught the essential characteristics of a camel, suggesting even its rather disagreeable disposition. The silvery sheen of the surface is the result of

15.
Strap-crossings in the shape of camels' heads

> Northwest China 4th – 3rd century B.C.
> Tinned bronze
> a. Height 2⅛ in. (5.4 cm); width 2⅞ in. (7.3 cm)
> b. Height 2⅛ in. (5.4 cm); width 2 in. (5.1 cm)
> Provenance: Susan Chen & Company, Hong Kong

This pair of strap-crossings, each one cast in the shape of a camel's head, is stylistically similar to catalogue no. 14, with the eyes represented by a round boss surrounded by a raised circular rim. The back of each ornament has a square frame on each of four posts to accommodate the crossed straps of a bridle. The frames have been piece-mold cast separately, while the two camels' heads appear to have been lost-wax cast, with the strap-crossing frames soldered in place.

16.
Set of ten harness fittings with zoomorphic motifs

North China, 3rd century B.C.
Gilded bronze
Max. height 1 ¾ in. (4.4 cm); max. width 1 ½ in. (3.8 cm)
Ex coll.: Joseph G. Gerena Fine Art, New York

The ten gilded-bronze ornaments that make up this group of harness fittings are distinguished by zoomorphic motifs. Three of the ornaments have scalloped oval shapes and depict rhinoceros heads seen from above, each flanked by a medley of antelope heads and hooves. Three other ornaments are circular and decorated with beaked ungulates curled around a central boss. The three tear-shaped ornaments portray frontal animal heads, again flanked by antelope features. And the remaining single fitting shows the same frontal animal head. The ornaments all have hollow backs with some attachment loops or broken stubs. They were cast by the lost-wax process and then mercury-amalgam gilded. A substantial amount of rust is visible on the stubs that project from each back, suggesting that some element in the fastening mechanism was made of iron.

The presence of a beaked ungulate among the zoomorphic motifs and the likely use of iron in the fastening mechanism suggest that these bridle ornaments were made in China specifically for the pastoral peoples on the northern frontier. Excavations at Xinzhuangtou, Yi county, Hebei Province, site of the southern capital of the state of Yan during the late fourth and third centuries B.C., have yielded similar ornaments decorated with distinctly northern subject matter that were locally made but intended for a northern market.[1]

1. So and Bunker 1995, pp. 58–61.

17.
Bridle fitting with mythological landscape

North China, 3rd–2nd century B.C.
Gilded bronze
Diameter 5⅜ in. (13.7 cm)
Ex coll.: Eskenazi Ltd., London
Published: Eskenazi 1996, no. 13.

This gilded bronze disk, a bridle fitting, is embellished with a complex mythological landscape scene in relief. Two horned and winged dragons stride through a cloudy mountain landscape as they bite each other's bifurcated tail. Half hidden in the mountains below are various wild animals: two pairs of deer, a bear, a wild boar, and two tigers. The fitting, which is lost-wax cast, is distinguished by a wide circular aperture with a reinforced inner rim. A red residue is visible around the edge of the aperture.

A comparable Western Han gilded-bronze disk, described as a chariot harness fitting, was excavated from a princely tomb in Qi state south of Wetuo village, Dawu township, about fourteen miles southwest of the Qi capital in Zibo

City, Linzi district, Shandong Province,[1] and another example was recovered from the tomb of Tou Wan, the concubine of Prince Liu Sheng of Zhongshan, at Mancheng, southern Hebei Province.[2] The function of the disk has been clarified by the reconstruction of a driving bridle from the tomb complex of Qin Shihuang Di outside Xi'an, Shaanxi Province, showing that such a disk served as a cheekpiece for the bridle worn by the outside chariot horse.[3]

The two dragons have fierce-looking lupine heads that relate them to the dragons represented on several belt plaques associated with the Xiongnu, such as catalogue nos. 102 and 105, and the landscape scene populated with wild animals recalls that on catalogue no. 116. Many artifacts produced during the late Qin and Western Han are embellished with similar mountain landscapes. Populated with dragons and wild animals, they reflect the Daoist belief that such images represent a sacred realm between heaven and earth, and were therefore appropriate decorations for tomb offerings.[4] The animals in these fantastic landscapes were frequently interpreted as *xiangrui* (auspicious omens), supernatural reflections of a ruler's authority and benevolence.[5]

1. Jia 1985, p. 250, fig. 24:8.
2. Beijing 1980a, vol. 1, p. 325, fig. 219:6, vol. 2, pl. 228:2.
3. Beijing 1983, pl. 7, and p. 32, fig. 4.
4. Munakata 1991, p. 82.
5. For a discussion of the *xiangrui* phenomenon, see Miho Museum 1997, p. 212.

18.
Strap-crossing with crouching bear

> North China, 3rd – 2nd century B.C.
> Silver
> Diameter 1¼ in. (3.2 cm)

A superbly cast crouching bear adorns the domed cap of this silver strap-crossing. The bear's ruff continues as outward spirals at both ends to form the ears, a stylistic feature of bear representations during the Western Han period. The fitting has four loops that project from the back of the fitting to form a strap-crossing device. It is lost-wax cast, and the loops are soldered in place.

The bear, an animal most commonly found in the northern forests, was frequently represented on artifacts during the late

Warring States and Western Han periods. Bears may have signified immortality or rebirth, as they reemerge each spring after a long period of hibernation.

A bear stylistically similar to this one is seen on a *se* (zither) string anchor in the Harris collection,[1] as well as on many other Han artifacts, such as catalogue nos. 19 and 20. Also related is a bear head depicted on a belt buckle made for northern consumption (see cat. no. 68).

1. So and Bunker 1995, pp. 150–51, no. 72.

19.
Two bridle fittings with crouching bears

> North China, 3rd – 2nd century B.C.
> Gilded bronze
> Each: Diameter 1 in. (2.5 cm)
> Ex coll.: Michael Dunn, New York

Each of these two gilded-bronze bridle fittings represents a crouching bear. The back of each fitting is concave and displays a cagelike device, or strap-crossing, formed by an open square supported by four posts at the corners. The cages were probably precast and then cast on when the bear plaques were cast. (See also cat. nos. 5, 15, 18.)

A foreshortened crouching bear with rounded ears, long muzzle, and four paws is shown on the front of each of these four gilded-bronze harness fittings. Curvilinear indented lines mark the shoulders to suggest fur. The back of each ornament is concave and displays two sturdy vertical attachment loops.

20.
Four harness ornaments with crouching bears

> North China, 2nd–1st century B.C.
> Gilded bronze
> Each: Diameter 1 in. (2.5 cm)
> Ex coll.: Roger Keverne Ltd., London

21.
Two harness ornaments with gazelle and stag

> North China, 1st century B.C. – 1st century A.D.
> Gold-plated iron
> Each: Height 5¼ in. (13.3 cm); width 2⅝ in. (6.7 cm)
> Ex coll.: Jonathan Tucker Asian Art, London

Each of these two cast-iron harness ornaments is plated with gold foil to simulate the appearance of gold. One plaque is decorated with the raised design of a winged gazelle with long ribbed horns that turn up at the tips, and the other displays a standing stag.

No ornaments identical to the present examples have been archaeologically excavated, but silver plaques of similar shape have been unearthed from regions as far apart as Korea[1] and

Mongolia.[2] Those found in Korea originally belonged to an elaborate set of harness decorations. Two bronze plaques with similar raised designs of winged gazelles were excavated from a late Western Han tomb at Xucungang, Zhulin township, Qi county, Henan Province, and may represent exotica from beyond the Great Wall.[3] And two belt plaques made of cast iron covered with thin gold foil were excavated from tomb 4 at Xigoupan, Jungar banner, southwestern Inner Mongolia, a northern site with a late Western Han date.[4]

Such plaques have traditionally been associated with China's northern neighbors, but whether the present examples were made by Han craftsmen for local consumption or as items to trade with the pastoral nomads is unclear. The subject matter relates to the design of catalogue no. 17, a bridle ornament dating from the third to the second century B.C. that was definitely made for the Chinese market.

1. Umehara 1956, fig. 17.
2. Haussig 1992, pl. 64.
3. *Kaogu* 2000, no. 1, p. 42, fig. 10.
4. Kessler 1993, fig. 36.

22.
Harness ornament with winged stallion

> Northeast China, 1st century B.C. – 1st century A.D.
> Silver
> Height 2¾ in. (7 cm); width 5 in. (12.7 cm)
> Ex coll.: J. J. Lally & Co., New York
> Published: Lally 1998, no. 21.

A dramatic winged stallion shown in flight over a mountain landscape with tiny peaks and curved cloud formations adorns this silver pear-shaped plaque. The same landscape elements are also present on two other plaques in the Thaw collection, catalogue no. 21. The ornament was formed by hammering, and the design worked in repoussé from the back with details enhanced by chasing on the front. Folded over, and showing considerable wear, the edges are pierced by fourteen small attachment holes punched through the silver from inside.

The winged stallion, which figures prominently in ancient Xianbei mythology, is believed to have guided an early Xianbei leader and his people on their migration southward. Plaques that depict winged horses are found at numerous sites associated with the Xianbei people to the north of China.[1]

A pair of gilded-bronze pear-shaped ornaments excavated in Hulun Buir league, eastern Inner Mongolia, and dating from the first to the third century A.D., are decorated with a similar winged horse.[2] And another gilded-bronze plaque, depicting a goat rather than a horse, was discovered in a tomb in Putuo, Xilin county, Guangxi, and may reflect an elite taste for the exotic during the Han dynasty.[3]

1. Kessler 1993, fig. 46.
2. Fu Tianqiu 1985, p. 141, no. 140, and p. 52.
3. Pirazzoli-t'Serstevens 1994, fig. 12.

2. WHEELED TRANSPORTATION

Artifacts associated with wheeled transportation include yoke covers, finials, and jingles or bells, which would have made a tinkling sound as the vehicle moved. Although referred to as chariots, which were used in warfare, many of these vehicles were not exclusively intended for military purposes but were also used for hunting and transporting goods during migrations. The discovery of finials and decorated vehicles in burials indicates that they were also used in funerary rituals. Finials surmounted by animals (cat. nos. 24, 25) probably decorated the corners of funerary canopies placed over the dead during burial rituals, a custom that can be traced back to southern Russia, as exemplified by a burial at Maikop dating to the third millennium B.C.[1]

1. Phillips 1961, p. 320.

23.

Two chariot-shaped plaques

Northeast China, 8th–7th century B.C.
Bronze
Each: Height 4 in. (10.2 cm); width 3¾ in. (9.5 cm)
Ex coll.: Joseph G. Gerena Fine Art, New York

Each of these two plaques represents a two-horse chariot. The horses are depicted in profile with only two legs in view, while the chariot is shown as if seen from above. No harness equipment is depicted on the horses, but the way the center pole of the chariot branches into three prongs suggests that they may have had yoke saddles.[1] The chariot has a square box with a rounded front and a centrally placed axle with two wheels, each of which has sixteen spokes. A low diagonal attachment loop is placed on the reverse side of each plaque behind the horse's head, and another loop projects sideways from the chariot box. The presence of flashing within the perforated centers of each wheel indicates that each plaque was cast in a two-piece mold.

The chariot and two horses are similar to the two horse-drawn chariots with a deer hunter depicted on a carved bone fragment from tomb 102 at Nanshan'gen (fig. 17), Ningcheng county, southeastern Inner Mongolia, a site dated from the eighth to the seventh century B.C.[2] Both the Nanshan'gen and the Thaw chariot images are similar in design to those found in petroglyphs in Mongolia and Central Asia but have a different harness arrangement from that represented in Shang pictographs, which also do not include horses, indicating that the northern harness fittings are different from those found in China.[3]

1. A yoke saddle is an inverted Y-shaped element for adapting a yoke to the conformation of a horse; see Littauer and Crouwel 1979, p. 7.
2. *Kaogu* 1981, no. 4, p. 307, fig. 6; So and Bunker 1995, p. 49, fig. 16.
3. Lin Yun 1998, p. 298.

24.
Four finials with wild rams

North China, Hebei Province, 7th–6th century B.C.
Bronze
Each: Max. height 6⅜ in. (16.2 cm)
Ex coll.: R. H. Ellsworth, Ltd., New York

A standing wild ram with large curved horns surmounts each of these four finials that once adorned the corners of a canopy used during burial rituals. The rams' eyes are indicated by rimmed perforations that pierce through to the opposite side, and the horns are marked by anterior ridges. The two taller finials, at the right, each have a loop on opposite sides of the socket, while the two shorter ones, at the left, have a loop at the back of the socket and two holes in either side. Some sockets still retain the remains of the object to which they were attached. The finials seem to be fashioned of a very dense alloy, and no mold marks can be detected, indicating that they were cast by the lost-wax process.

Several finials cast in the same style as these four were discovered in non-Chinese graves in northwestern Hebei Province.[1] Others, related technically and stylistically to the present examples, are included in several Western collections.[2]

The custom of adorning canopies and funerary carts used in elite burial rituals was confirmed by discoveries dating from the seventh to the sixth century B.C. at Arzhan, near Uyuk in Tuva, in the Sayan Mountains of southern Siberia.[3] There, the canopy covering the bier was distinguished by five finials, each surmounted by a standing wild ram, one at each corner and one at the apex. Two of the Arzhan finials have side loops identical to those seen here.

It is not surprising that finials associated with northwestern Hebei Province reflect contact with southern Siberia. Long-distance trade between the two regions has existed since ancient times along routes that led through Zhangjiakou and Ulaanbaatar, the same route followed today by the train that connects with the Trans-Siberian railroad at Irkutsk.

1. Zheng Shaozong 1991, p. 22, nos. 110–12; Bunker et al. 1997, p. 177, figs. 92.1, 92.3; Takahama and Hatakeyama 1997, nos. 131–34.
2. Bunker 1981, no. 771; Bunker et al. 1997, p. 177, no. 92.
3. Griaznov 1984, pl. 25. For dating, see note 18 on page 36.

25.
Finial with standing ibex

North China, Hebei Province, 7th–6th century B.C.
Bronze
Height 6⅛ in. (15.5 cm); width 3⅝ in. (9.2 cm)
Ex coll.: J. J. Lally & Co., New York

Surmounting this finial is a standing ibex with prominent horns and gathered feet. The tips of the ears are broken off, and the remains of a beard are visible under the chin. The horns sweep back over the neck and are supported by a strut that extends to the shoulders. The figure is hollow cast in the round, and the oval socket is pierced front and back for attachment. The absence of mold seams indicates that the finial was cast by the lost-wax process.

Like catalogue no. 24a–d, this example must once have belonged to a set of finials used by the hunting peoples who inhabited northern Hebei Province during the seventh and sixth centuries B.C. Finials from this region are lost-wax cast, while similar finials from the Ordos Desert region of Northwest China are piece-mold cast (see cat. no. 38). Comparison with the preceding set and the set excavated at Arzhan in southern Siberia confirms their date and function as funerary canopy ornaments (fig. 24).

bronze ringlike fitting excavated from tomb 3 at Nanshan'gen, Ningcheng county, southeastern Inner Mongolia, which has been dated to about the eighth century B.C. (fig. 18).

1. So and Bunker 1995, pp. 34–35.
2. Eliade 1964, pp. 91, 178.
3. *Wenwu ziliao congkan* 1985, no. 9, p. 56, fig. 59.

26.
Harness jingle with mounted hunters

Northeast China, 7th–6th century B.C.
Bronze
Height 5⅛ in. (13 cm); width 3¼ in. (8.1 cm)
Ex coll.: J. J. Lally & Co., New York

Two mounted hunters with a dog driving a doe toward them are shown in the round moving along the edge of a bronze harness ornament with a pendant openwork jingle. On the opposite side, another hunting dog confronts a raptor's head. The jingle still appears to have a tiny pebble within it. The ornament was cast by the indirect lost-wax method, in which the wax model is formed in a two-piece mold.

Jingles cast with tiny pebbles inside, which would have made a tinkling sound as the horse moved, were especially popular among the herding and hunting peoples north of China during the second and first millennia B.C. They are found atop weapon and tool handles, harness fittings, and vessels and other utensils. Such ornaments are conspicuously absent among Chinese finds, suggesting that they belonged exclusively to the northern cultures, where they had specific ritualistic meanings and functions.[1] Noisemakers and rattles have always figured prominently in cultures in which some form of shamanism is practiced, and pebbles, such as those used in rattles and jingles, are considered to be imbued with animistic spirits.[2]

A jingle of this type, with horse and chariot fittings, was recovered from a burial at Xiaoheishigou, Ningcheng county, southeastern Inner Mongolia.[3] The figures seen here are very similar to the mounted hunters chasing a wild hare on a

27.
Harness ornament with tiger and bird's head

Northeast China, 7th–6th century B.C.
Bronze
Max. height 2¼ in. (5.7 cm); width 4⅛ in. (10.6 cm)
Ex coll.: J. J. Lally & Co., New York

This hook-shaped harness ornament represents a tiger with a long tail ending in a simplified bird's head. A doe and two more felines are depicted on the tail, which serves as a ground line and forms the hook. Ribbed lines indicating stripes mark the tigers' pelts, while the doe's body is left undecorated. A strut connecting the large tiger's jaw to its feet serves as a suspension loop. The ornament is lost-wax cast using a wax model formed in a two-piece mold. The raised spiral line that encircles the tail may have been formed by the use of a cord wrapped around the wax model.[1]

Typologically and iconographically related to catalogue nos. 26 and 28, this harness ornament is also comparable, in the perforations in the shoulders and haunches, to an ornament found in the Irkutsk region of eastern Siberia that displays the same stylistic features and is dated from the seventh to the sixth century B.C.[2]

1. This casting method is known as the lost-cord process. For a technical description, see Bulbeck and Barnard 1996–97, vol. 1, pp. 34–36.
2. Berdnikova, Vetrov, Lykhin 1991, p. 199, fig. 6.

28.
Harness ornament with crouching tiger

> Northeast China, 7th – 6th century B.C.
> Bronze
> Height 2¼ in. (5.7 cm); width 4 in. (10.2 cm)
> Ex coll.: J. J. Lally & Co., New York; Lord Cunliffe
> Collection; Calon da Collection
> Published: Cheng 1963, pl. 37a; So and Bunker 1995,
> p. 119, no. 34; Takahama and Hatakeyama 1997, pl. 91.

This harness ornament is hollow cast in the shape of a crouching tiger with bared, jagged teeth and a long, gracefully curved tail from which a jingle with a tiny pebble inside is suspended. The shoulders and haunch are indented with concentric circles, and two rows of pseudobeading mark the tail longitudinally. Evidence of wear is visible within the circular suspension loop that projects from the tiger's front paws. A mold mark running the length of the tail suggests that the piece was cast by the indirect lost-wax process, in which the wax model was formed in a two-piece mold.

29.
Harness jingle with stag

> Northeast China, 7th – 6th century B.C.
> Bronze
> Height 5¼ in. (13.3 cm); width 5½ in. (14 cm)
> Ex coll.: J. J. Lally & Co., New York

This hollow-cast harness jingle takes the form of a stag with its legs extending into two long S-curved loops, each with a knobbed spherical jingle suspended below and another jingle suspended beneath the grooved terminal arc. Each jingle contains a tiny pebble. The stag's antlers are conceived as twin parallel rows of four tangent circles that extend over the neck and are connected by a strut in between and secured by two other struts attached to the stag's withers. Attachment must have been accomplished by the two large vertical holes through the back that show wear around the edges. The absence of mold marks suggests that the piece was cast by the lost-wax process. The surface displays a dark green patina mottled in reddish brown.

Like the other harness jingles in the Thaw collection, this one can be associated with the hunting and pastoral peoples of Northeast China. The representation of stags' antlers as a series of circles tangent to each is an artistic convention introduced into North China east of the Taihang Mountains sometime before the sixth century B.C.[1] Images of stags found at northern sites west of the Taihang do not display this characteristic.

1. Bunker et al. 1997, p. 166, no. 71.

30.
Animal's head harness jingle

> Northeast China, 7th–6th century B.C.
> Bronze
> Height 2⅞ in. (7.3 cm); width 1¼ in. (4.4 cm)
> Ex coll.: Michael Dunn, New York

This jingle takes the shape of a hollow animal's head in the round. It is attached to the underside of a flat openwork plaque depicting a mirror-image design of two animal protomes joined at the shoulder. The eyes of both the animal's head and the animal protomes are indicated by round perforations

enclosed within raised rims, and the shoulder of each protome is marked by a perforation centered within a raised tear-shaped rim. The three-dimensionality of the jingle and the absence of mold marks indicate that the fitting was cast by the lost-wax process.

The body markings are similar to those found on several plaques and other artifacts dated from the seventh to the sixth century B.C. and excavated at Xiaoheishigou, Ningcheng county, southeastern Inner Mongolia.[1] The jingle itself also relates the ornament to other harness fittings from Northeast China that are in the Thaw collection (cat. nos. 26, 28, 29).

1. Takahama and Hatakeyama 1997, pls. 67–69, see cat. no. 45 for revised Xiaoheishigou date.

31.
Two chariot yoke ornaments in the shape of recumbent rams

> Northwest China and southwestern Inner Mongolia,
> 5th–4th century B.C.
> Bronze
> Each: Height 2½ in. (6.4 cm); max. width 5 in. (12.7 cm)
> Ex coll.: Christie's, New York, March 25, 1998

These two recumbent rams with folded legs are hollow cast, allowing them to fit over the rounded yoke on either side of the pole of a two-wheeled vehicle (see also cat. no. 32). The legs overlap, with the hind hooves facing downward and the front hooves facing upward. Each ram is shown with its tongue protruding from its mouth. A longitudinal mold line between the horns bisects the body of each ram, indicating piece-mold casting. Mold lines along the edges of the horns indicate that they were cast separately and then soldered on.

Hollow-cast recumbent deer with neatly folded legs are common among the grave goods of the pastoral peoples who inhabited the grasslands on the northwestern frontier of China during the fifth and fourth centuries B.C., but their exact function had long perplexed scholars. The discovery of a set of late Spring and Autumn period animal-shaped ornaments that fit over the yoke of a conveyance excavated in a pre-dynastic Qin state tomb at Bianjiazhuang, Long county, southwestern Shaanxi Province, solved the puzzle.[1] The specific placement of the hooves is a local feature of southwestern Inner Mongolia

and Northwest China. It derives from a Chinese convention illustrated by a lacquer animal from the tomb of Duke Jing of Qin, near Xi'an, Shaanxi, who died in 537 B.C.[2] This type of yoke ornament appears to have been discontinued during the third century B.C., when, with the increased practice of mounted warfare, status came to be associated more with vehicles than with horses.

Originally, these rams must have belonged to a larger set of four or more identical figures. The two recumbent rams in the Shelby White and Leon Levy collection are identical to the pair shown here and most likely belonged to the same set.[3]

Yoke ornaments such as these are peculiar to burials of the herding peoples of the northwest and, to date, have not been found in burials east of the Taihang Mountains, where different burial rituals must have prevailed. Animal figures with a protruding tongue, a feature which indicates that the animal is in rut, are invariably male. Such an image provided an appropriate symbol for the nomadic peoples, whose livelihoods depended on a proliferating and thriving herd and whose wealth was measured by its size (see also cat. no. 39).[4]

1. *Wenwu* 1988, no. 11, pp. 16, 17, figs. 3:39–42, 4.
2. Beijing 1992, p. 71.
3. So and Bunker 1995, pp. 95–96, no. 9.
4. For other animal figures with protruding tongues, see Bunker 1981, nos. 775, 779.

32.
Set of six yoke ornaments in the shape of recumbent does

Northwest China, Ningxia and Gansu, 5th–4th century B.C.
Bronze
Each: Height 2½ in. (6.3 cm); width 3¼ in. (8.2 cm)
Ex coll.: R. H. Ellsworth, Ltd. New York
Published: Rawson and Bunker 1990, p. 322, no. 205.

These six alert recumbent does are represented with heads held erect and legs folded beneath them. The bodies are hollow to fit over the rounded poles of the two-wheeled vehicles used in burial rituals. The position of the legs is the same as that of catalogue nos. 31 and 35, but the muzzles, with open ends, are differently cast.[1] The figures are distinguished by their complex mold marks. One mark bisects the body longi-

tudinally, while others can be seen on the back of the ear extending from the base to the tip, indicating that each doe was cast integrally with its ears in a multipiece mold.

Like the ungulates with scooped-out bodies associated with the Ordos region, these six does also served as yoke ornaments, but they were made by nomads inhabiting the grazing lands of southern Ningxia and southeastern Gansu. The cir-

cular aperture in the hollow head of each doe is a characteristic of deer figures found in this region.[2]

1. For a discussion of this feature, see Rawson and Bunker 1990, p. 322.
2. For deer figures in southern Ningxia, see *Kaogu xuebao* 1993, no. 1, p. 42, fig. 24:1–10; and *Kaogu xuebao* 1995, no. 1, p. 94, fig. 15:6–7. For deer figures in southeastern Gansu, see Liu and Xu 1988, p. 414, fig. 2:9.

33.
*Pair of yoke ornaments in the shape of
recumbent deer*

Northwest China, Ningxia and Gansu, 5th–4th century B.C.
Tinned bronze
Left: Height 4 in. (10.2 cm); length 4⅞ in. (12.4 cm)
Right: Height 3¾ in. (9.5 cm); length 5 in. (12.7 cm)
Ex coll.: Joseph G. Gerena Fine Art, New York

These two yoke ornaments are cast in the shape of a doe and a stag. The stag's antlers are now missing from the sockets between the ears. The eyes of both deer are represented by small, almond-shaped bosses and the mouths by open slits. The ornaments are hollow cast, with open-ended muzzles and inside cores. Although the surface is quite worn, the remains of tinning are still visible under the corrosion. A longitudinal mold mark bisects the body, and a V-shaped mold mark

below the ears indicates that each deer was cast integrally with the ears.

The ornaments originally belonged to a larger set similar to catalogue no. 32 and functioned the same way. Apparently, such ornaments often represented both male and female deer, exemplified by the stag and doe figures excavated at Sujigou, Jungar banner, southwestern Inner Mongolia.[1]

1. Gai 1965, pl. 6.

34.
Doe-shaped yoke ornament

Northwest China, Ningxia or Gansu, 5th–4th century B.C.
Tinned bronze
Height 2¼ in. (5.7 cm); length 2⅝ in. (6.7 cm)
Ex coll.: Joseph G. Gerena Fine Art, New York; Taylor Dale, Santa Fe; Calon da Collection

Like all yoke ornaments, this recumbent doe is hollow cast. A sunken, almond-shaped mark indicates each eye, and each ear is represented by a triangle begun by a spiral at the inside base. A socket protrudes vertically from the back and probably once held some sort of banner or tassel. The piece has been wiped with molten tin to give it a flashy, silvery appearance. A longitudinal mold mark bisects the entire figure including the socket.

Like catalogue nos. 32 and 33, the muzzle of this small recumbent doe is open at the end, a common characteristic of deer figures discovered in the vicinity of southern Ningxia and southeastern Gansu. Tinning is also a surface enrichment frequently found on artifacts excavated in this region, and was used to signify status before the development of mercury gilding and the accompanying increase in the use of precious metals.[1]

1. Bunker et al. 1997, p. 241.

35.
Chariot yoke ornament in the shape of a recumbent doe

Northwest China and southwestern Inner Mongolia,
5th–4th century B.C.
Bronze
Height 4¼ in. (10.8 cm); length 5¼ in. (13.3 cm)
Ex coll.: Nathanial Hammer, New York; Bluett's, London
Published: Eskenazi 1977, pp. 60–61.

At Yulongtai, Jungar banner, southwestern Inner Mongolia, recumbent deer similar to this one were excavated with the remains of a wheeled vehicle.[1] This would suggest that the present ornament was once part of a matched set that adorned a conveyance, perhaps one used in funerary rituals.[2] (See also cat. no. 32.)

1. *Kaogu* 1977, no. 2, pls. 2:1, 3:3.
2. For a set of such ornaments, see Rawson and Bunker 1990, no. 205.

36.
Finial surmounted by a gazelle

> Northwest China and southwestern Inner Mongolia,
> 5th–4th century B.C.
> Bronze
> Height 2⅝ in. (6.7 cm); length 2⅜ in. (6 cm)
> Ex coll.: J. J. Lally & Co., New York; Calon da Collection

A sensitively modeled gazelle with its feet drawn in stands on the remains of a damaged socket. The gazelle has almond-shaped eyes, formed by indented lines, and a slightly open mouth. A longitudinal mold line, especially visible under the chin, indicates piece-mold casting.

   Like catalogue nos. 37 and 38, this ornament must once have belonged to a large set of finials designed to decorate a funerary canopy or vehicle and had a socket that fit over some upright element. Piece-mold casting relates the finial to other finials associated with Northwest China, where gazelles were prevalent among the local fauna.[1]

1. Bunker et al. 1997, p. 230, no. 181.

37.
Doe-shaped chariot yoke ornament

> Northwest China and southwestern Inner Mongolia,
> ca. 4th century B.C.
> Bronze
> Height 3¾ in. (9.6 cm); length 4⅝ in. (11.6 cm)
> Ex coll.: J. J. Lally & Co., New York; James Marshall
> Plummer; Calon da Collection
> Published: So and Bunker 1995, pp. 117–18, no. 32.

This standing doe originally belonged to a set of chariot decorations.[1] It has almond-shaped eyes, indicated by indented lines, and an open mouth. The feet are connected laterally by a horizontal strip that functions as a baseline and reinforces the slender legs. The figure is hollow cast and retains some of the casting core. Remnants of red cinnabar are visible on the face.

   Standing deer with similar baselines were excavated at Sujigou, Jungar banner, a fourth-century B.C. site in the Ordos region of southwestern Inner Mongolia.[2] Several other similar yoke ornaments were also found in conjunction with the remains of a wheeled vehicle at the site of Yulongtai, Jungar banner.[3] It has been suggested that such ornaments were used by the Xiongnu people,[4] but according to the archaeological remains this type was popular before the appearance of the Xiongnu on the northern frontiers of China and quickly went out of fashion after the Xiongnu came to power.[5]

1. See Bunker and So 1995, p. 117, no. 32.
2. Gai 1965, pl. 6:2.
3. *Kaogu* 1977, no. 2, pp. 111–14.
4. Hearn 1987, nos. 81, 82.
5. See p. 26 in the present publication.

38.
Pair of finials in the shape of kulans

> Northwest China and southwestern Inner Mongolia,
> 4th century B.C.
> Tinned bronze
> a. Height 2 in. (5.1 cm); max. width 2½ in. (6.2 cm);
> length 2⅞ in. (7.3 cm)
> b. Height 2⅛ in. (5.4 cm); max. width 2 in. (5.1 cm);
> length 2½ in. (6.4 cm)
> Ex coll.: Michael Dunn, New York

Two delightful kulans (wild asses) here surmount a pair of finials that may once have decorated a funerary cart. The oversized ears identify the animals as kulans, which were common to the grasslands of China's northern frontier. Each is represented in the round, but with the front and back legs merged into one. The eyes are naturalistically indicated by intaglio areas, and the mouth of each is shown slightly open. The sockets are rectangular in shape and have two holes cut into each through which an attachment pin would have been inserted. The shiny surface of the bronze indicates that the finials were intentionally tinned, and a longitudinal seam confirms that each finial was piece-mold cast.

Two finials very similar to these examples were excavated at Yulongtai, Jungar banner, in the Ordos Desert region, from a burial site that has been dated to the fourth century B.C. and associated with the pastoral peoples who once grazed their herds in the area.[1] Like the Thaw finials, the Yulongtai ornaments are also tinned and piece-mold cast.

Finials surmounted by animals were popular not only among the nomads of southern Siberia as decoration for funerary canopies but also among the Scythians in northwestern Eurasia, as decoration on two-wheeled vehicles used in funerary rituals.[2] Yulongtai also yielded the remains of a two-wheeled vehicle, suggesting that the Thaw finials once belonged to a larger set that adorned the four corners of a funerary cart.[3]

1. Duan 1995, p. 161, pl. 227.
2. Cherednichenko and Fialko 1988, p. 163, fig. 8.
3. *Kaogu* 1977, no. 2, pp. 111–14.

39.
Chariot pole ornament with ram's head

Northwest China and southwestern Inner Mongolia,
4th century B.C.
Bronze
Height 2¼ in. (5.7 cm); width 7⅜ in. (18.7 cm)
Ex coll.: J. J. Lally & Co., New York

This sensitively modeled ram's head was used to embellish the end of a pole used on a wheeled vehicle. The ram is shown with its tongue protruding and its characteristically ribbed horns curled around the ears. A small loop projects from beneath the ram's chin. The figure is hollow cast and terminates in an open socket into which the pole end could be inserted, and the bottom has two open rectangular slots, presumably for attachment purposes. A longitudinal mold mark, especially visible under the tongue, indicates piece-mold casting of the head and body; the horns were cast separately and then inserted into sockets in the head and soldered into place.

Similar pole ends associated with wheeled vehicles have been found in burials of the pastoral peoples inhabiting the Ordos Desert region of southwestern Inner Mongolia.[1] The protruding tongue relates this pole ornament to catalogue no. 31, where the same gesture indicates that the animal is represented in rut.

1. *Kaogu* 1977, no. 2, pl. 3:2; Gai 1965, p. 46, fig. 4.

3. WEAPONS, HELMETS, AND TOOLS

In spite of their fearsome descriptions in historical literature, the ancient peoples of the Eurasian steppes do not appear to have possessed vast stores of life-threatening weapons compared with the arsenals of the settled civilizations with which they came in contact. All of the examples in this section can be associated with the pastoral peoples to the north of China, but their shapes, decoration, and methods of production relate them to weaponry traditions found throughout the steppes rather than to traditions in China's Central Plains, as has been suggested in the past. The short sword (*duan jian* in Chinese archaeological literature and a dagger in the West) is one of the most characteristic steppe artifacts. The blade was traditionally cast integrally with its hilt (cat. no. 40), whereas in China they were cast separately and then assembled (cat. no. 48).[1] The short sword was primarily a small personal weapon for thrusting and stabbing rather than a slashing, battle-ready weapon.[2] Axe heads used by pastoral groups (cat. no. 42)

all have tubular sockets, a hafting device first conceived in the west and then introduced into the periphery of the Chinese world via the steppes during the second millennium B.C.[3] Such axes belonged to a broad Eurasian steppe tradition and would have been more a prestige item than a weapon worthy of great strength to wield.

1. In some scholarly literature, such weapons are described as *acinaces,* a Greek term used by Herodotus (4.70). An *acinaces* was employed by the Saka people to stir blood in a bowl. The blood was then imbibed as an oath was sworn to blood brotherhood. As we do not know what an *acinaces* looked like, however, the term is best avoided.
2. Although there are certain similarities between Scythian short swords used in the West and those of the eastern Eurasian pastoral peoples, the two types do not appear to be directly related. Rather, they may both derive from a common Central Asian weapon tradition that has not yet been identified. I am very grateful to P. R. S. Moorey for his helpful comments concerning this subject.
3. Chernykh 1992, p. 220. See Bunker et al. 1997, p. 125, esp. n. 4.

40.
Short sword

> Northwest China, 13th–12th century B.C.
> Bronze
> Length 10⅞ in. (27.7 cm)
> Lent by Shelby White and Leon Levy

The flattened ovoid hilt, animal's head pommel, and tapering leaf-shaped blade that characterize this short sword were all cast in one piece. The hilt and blade are separated by a notched guard which has two straight blunt wings that project sideways. The hilt is slightly curved at the end and decorated longitudinally with alternating plain and pebbled bands, and the blade is distinguished by a median ridge that extends from one of the plain bands. The use of a median ridge to strengthen the blade can be traced back to mid-second-millennium B.C. traditions at Zhukaigou, in the Ordos region of Northwest China.[1] The pommel takes the form of a horned mythological animal with open jaws that reveal sharp teeth.

This short sword is typical of the personal weapons and tools used by the northern hunting and herding peoples in the eastern Eurasian steppes during the last centuries of the second millennium B.C.[2] Short swords with similar shapes have

been found at numerous sites on China's northwestern frontier as well as at Anyang, the last capital of the Shang dynasty, where they represent exotica from beyond the northern fringes and indicate cultural contact between the Chinese and their pastoral neighbors.[3]

Short swords with oval, slightly curved hilts are earlier than those with flat, straight hilts. The mythological animal's head that forms the pommel is highly unusual, with no known parallel.

1. Bunker et al. 1997, p. 21, fig. A1.
2. Wu En 1985, pp. 136–37; Yan Jinzhu 1985; So and Bunker 1995, pp. 100–101, no. 14.
3. Linduff 1997a, pp. 29, 32.

41.
Knife with ram's head

> North China, 12th–11th century B.C.
> Bronze inlaid with turquoise
> Length 10⅝ in. (27 cm)
> The Metropolitan Museum of Art, Gift of Mrs. John Marriott, Mrs. John Barry Ryan, Gilbert W. Kahn, and Roger Wolfe Kahn (children of Addie W. Kahn), 1949 (49.136.9)
> Published: Asia Society 1970, no. 20; So and Bunker 1995, p. 102, no. 16.

This handsome knife has a curved hilt terminating in a ram's head distinguished by prominent curled horns. The junction between the hilt and the blade is marked by a ridge and a projecting tang on the cutting side. The eyes and nostrils are punctuated by turquoise inlays, and a series of nine indented lines marks the hilt two-thirds of the way down. A small loop under the ram's chin serves as a suspension ring, and longitudinal mold marks along the edge of the hilt indicate that the knife was piece-mold cast integrally with the blade and pommel.

A knife with an ibex-head pommel and a shape similar to that of this knife is in the Arthur M. Sackler collections.[1] Knives with zoomorphic pommels have been excavated together with non-Chinese material throughout North China at sites in Shaanxi, Shanxi, and Hebei provinces.[2] A knife with a ram's-head pommel that is stylistically related to the present knife was also reported from Tazigou, Lindong county, Chifeng city, southeastern Inner Mongolia.[3]

A knife of this type was discovered in the late-thirteenth-century B.C. tomb of Fu Hao, consort of the Shang king Wu Ding, at Anyang, Henan Province.[4] The presence of such an artifact in a royal Shang tomb is firm evidence of contact between China and the northern pastoral peoples from whom the Shang acquired wheeled transport and horse-drawn chariots.[5] It is possible that Fu Hao was not herself Shang but from one of the peripheral non-Chinese (fang) groups with whom the Shang interacted, a fact that would explain some of the steppe-related artifacts in her tomb.[6]

1. Bunker et al. 1997, p. 121.
2. Wu En 1985, pp. 138–39.
3. Wang Weixiang 1994, p. 31.
4. Beijing 1980c, pl. 66:1.
5. So and Bunker 1995, pp. 26–27.
6. Ibid., p. 27; Linduff 1997b.

42.
Axe head with oval-shaped blade

> Northeast China, 10th–8th century B.C.
> Bronze
> Width 3¼ in. (8.1 cm); length 5 in. (12.7 cm)
> Ex coll.: James Freeman, Kyoto

This axe head is distinguished by an oval-shaped blade and a tubular socket. Two arrowheads and a five-pronged whorl star mark each side. A rounded butt plate projects from the back

of the socket, and a small vertical loop is placed near its lower rim. A mold mark visible between the blade and the socket indicates that the axe head was cast in a two-piece mold.

A nearly identical axe head is in the Reitberg Museum, Zürich,[1] and a similar example is in the Museum of Far Eastern Antiquities, Stockholm, said to have been acquired in Tianjin, northeastern Hebei Province.[2] This type of axe has not been found in archaeological context, but the presence of a crudely cast tiger in the round surmounting the socket of another version[3] relates the present example stylistically to early-first-millennium B.C. Bronze Age finds in Northeast China, where tiger figures with similar markings frequently occur.[4] Axe heads of this kind have traditionally been dated to the late second millennium B.C., but stylistic associations suggest a later date, which is more compatible with the date of around the tenth century B.C. suggested by Loehr.[5]

Axe heads with tubular sockets first developed in West Asia and were then introduced into the periphery of China during the late second millennium B.C. Axe heads with oval blades have not been found in Siberia, but five-pointed whorls, traditionally interpreted as solar symbols, occur on other artifacts discovered to the north of China, such as the gold ornaments found at a fifth-to-fourth-century site in Tuva.[6]

1. Brinker 1975, p. 116, no. 63.
2. Andersson 1932, pl. X.
3. Loehr 1956, p. 6, fig. 5; Rawson and Bunker 1990, p. 158, no. 58.
4. Bunker et al. 1997, p. 69, fig. A103, and p. 139, no. 31.
5. Loehr 1956, p. 7.
6. Kilunovskaya and Semenov 1995, pl. 60.

43.
Knife-spoon

> Northeast China, 1st half of 1st millennium B.C.
> Bronze
> Length 10⅜ in. (26.5 cm)
> Katherine and George Fan

This utensil would have been a very appropriate item for the toolkit of a member of a hunting people living beyond the frontiers of Northeast China, as it would have served two purposes. One end is a spoon with an oblong bowl, and the other is a knife with a long, slender blade. The blade is an extension of the hilt, with no guard or transverse element. Rounded S-shaped spirals decorate one side of the handle, and squared

spirals the other side. The handle was cast integrally in a piece mold with the blade and bowl. A mold mark is visible along the edge of the handle.

To date, the present knife-spoon appears to have no excavated or collected counterpart. The Arthur M. Sackler collections include three knife-spoons that have been attributed to southern Siberia or Mongolia based on the presence of arsenic in the alloys from which they were cast and that are stylistically related to knives cast between the twelfth and the tenth century.[1] The long slender blade, without a guard, is related to knives associated with Northeast China dating from the eighth to fifth century B.C.,[2] and the oblong spoon bowl occurs in tiny spoons also associated with Northeast China.[3] The S-shaped spiral embellishment is identical to the linear decoration of a Dongbei scabbard in the present exhibition that has been dated from the seventh to the sixth century B.C. (cat. no. 45), so that it would seem plausible to give this knife-spoon the same date.

1. Bunker et al. 1997, p. 144, no. 33.
2. Ibid., pp. 158–59.
3. Ibid., pp. 173–74.

44.
Knife with bird's head

Northeast China, 8th–6th century B.C.
Bronze
Length 6⅞ in. (17.4 cm)
Ex coll.: J. J. Lally & Co., New York; Calon da Collection

An openwork bird's head in profile serves as the pommel for this knife. Two recumbent does represented with sunken lines decorate one side of the hilt, and three standing boars with down-turned heads and bristling manes adorn the other side. Mold marks and metal flashing in the bird's head confirm that the piece was cast in a two-piece mold.

Although no identical knife has been found in archaeological context, the drawing of the animals is consistent with Loehr's knife typology, which would date such a piece from the eighth to the sixth century B.C.[1] Numerous knives with similar animal representations associated with the ancient hunting cultures of Northeast China are included in the Arthur M. Sackler collections.[2] The zoomorphic images on artifacts found at sites in Northeast China are far more sensitively drawn than those on artifacts found at sites west of the Taihang Mountains in North China.

1. Loehr 1951, p. 86, pl. v:28–29.
2. Bunker et al. 1997, pp. 155, 157, 159.

45.
Short sword and sheath with animal motifs

Northeast China, 7th–6th century B.C.
Bronze
Short sword: Length 11⅞ in. (30.2 cm)
Sheath: Length 8½ in. (21.6 cm)
Ex coll.: Anthony Plowright, Paris

Animal figures embellish this short sword and sheath. The sheath carries an intaglio design of six does and six S-shaped spirals on each side. Seven standing horses in profile, with only two legs shown, adorn one side of the hilt. Raised spirals mark the horses' shoulders and rumps, as they do the deer on the sheath. The other side of the hilt is decorated with four back-to-back stags' heads with their antlers arranged vertically. The short sword has a notched straight blade with a raised longitudinal ridge, a straight guard, and a perforation below the bar at the top for attachment purposes. Both the sheath and the sword are piece-mold cast, as indicated by mold marks on the side edges of the sheath and on the hilt of the short sword. The blade and hilt were integrally cast.

Short swords were not major battle weapons. Rather, they were small personal weapons used for stabbing and cutting that would have been useful in a pastoral society. The sheath was suspended from the belt and tied to the thigh by two straps attached to the two pairs of loops on the sides, a practical way to carry such a weapon, whether one is on foot or on horseback.

A short sword of the same shape with similar intaglio decoration on the hilt was excavated at Xiaoheishigou, Ningcheng county, southeastern Inner Mongolia, a site that has traditionally been dated from the eighth to the seventh century B.C.[1] A similar short sword in the Chaoyang City Museum is given a Warring States date,[2] as is one in the collection of the Tokyo National Museum, dated from the ninth to the seventh century B.C.[3]

The motif of a stag with vertically extended antlers occurs in the Koban culture of the Caucasus in the eighth to the seventh century,[4] on Tagar artifacts dated from the sixth to the fifth century,[5] and again on Sauromatian objects of the fifth century.[6] This conventionalized way of representing a stag's antlers appears to have had priority in the west and was then transmitted eastward. Such trans-Asian comparisons suggest a date no earlier than the seventh century for the Thaw and similar examples. A date of the eighth to the seventh century for Xiaoheishigou is thus too early. A later date is also indicated by the trans-Asian comparisons presented for catalogue no. 46, a helmet.

1. Shanghai 2000, p. 96.
2. Yang Tienan 1997, p. 89.
3. Takahama and Hatakeyama 1997, no. 74.
4. Aruz 2000, no. 137.
5. Ibid., no. 206.
6. Ibid., no. 128.

46.
Helmet surmounted by a horse

Northeast China, ca. 7th century B.C.
Bronze
Height 9½ in. (24.1 cm); width. 6¾ in. (17.1 cm);
depth 8 in. (20.3 cm)
Ex coll.: Ariadne Galleries, Inc., New York

A figure of a horse in the round surmounts the top of this helmet. Flashing in the opening between the legs and a mold mark bisecting the body longitudinally indicate that the horse was cast in a two-piece mold and then soldered in place. The helmet's face opening has a small point projecting downward over the forehead, and the border around the edge of the helmet is embellished with a running design of triangles that appears to have been chiseled into the surface. Two small attachment loops are soldered onto each side near the bottom rim. Unlike the horse, the helmet displays no mold marks, having been cast by the lost-wax method.

A very similar helmet, also surmounted by a horse figure and decorated with a triangle-patterned border, was excavated at the Bronze Age site of Xiaoheishigou, Ningcheng county, southeastern Inner Mongolia, but whether the opening in front has a point over the forehead is not clear from the published drawing.[1] A helmet of this type, surmounted by a horse, in the David-Weill collection does not have a point,[2] but there is one on another helmet, also surmounted by a horse, in the National Palace Museum, Taibei.[3] It would appear that the frontal point is a feature that originated in Russia, where it is first found on seventh-century B.C. helmets

excavated at Kelermes.[4] For this reason, helmets with this feature from Northeast China cannot be dated before the seventh century B.C.

Earlier helmets found within China are piece-mold cast, as indicated by mold marks along the vertical central line on Shang-dynasty helmets from Anyang, Henan Province.[5] The first archaeological evidence for lost-wax casting in China was discovered at the sixth-century B.C. Chu state cemetery in Xiasi, Xichuan county, Henan Province.[6] The possibility that lost-wax casting was practiced earlier on the northeastern periphery of China and that the northern hunting and herding peoples played some role in its transmission from the west warrants further consideration.

1. Xiang 1984, p. 121, fig. 5:2.
2. Egami and Mizuno 1935, p. 63, fig. 33:2.
3. Chen Fangmei 2000, fig. 29.
4. I am most grateful to Karen Rubinson for sharing with me her extensive research on bronze helmets made during the second and first millennia B.C. (article forthcoming). For archaeological references to Russian helmets, see Smirnov 1961. For a redating of the Kelermes helmets, see Galanina 1994, p. 105
5. Yang Hong 1992, p. 59.
6. Li Xueqin 1991; So and Bunker 1995, p. 59.

47.
Helmet surmounted by a horse

Northeast China, 7th century B.C.
Bronze
Height 9½ in. (24.1 cm); width 7⅞ in. (20 cm);
depth 8⅜ in. (21.3 cm)
Ex coll.: James Freeman, Kyoto

This helmet is nearly identical to catalogue no. 46, with the exception of a horned animal head in relief on the front. The animal's-head design was most likely produced by hammering the cast metal over a matrix. To date, this is the only known helmet of its type that carries a repoussé decoration formed by hammering. The raised decoration on helmets found in China was produced by piece-mold casting.[1] Helmets such as this one and catalogue no. 46 belong not to casting traditions in China but to those found far to the west.

The alloy from which the helmet is formed is a leaded bronze. The remains of a coarse fabric are visible on the right side of the helmet, indicating that it may have been wrapped in fabric at the time of burial. It is possible that the helmet was also lined with cloth of some type when worn.

The animal mask on the front of the helmet must have provided magical protection for the wearer and was possibly a clan marker. The presence of the mask suggests that the wearer enjoyed a higher rank than a person whose helmet did not display such decoration. Helmets are the earliest known form of body armor and remain today an essential means of protection not only in war but also in sports. They frequently display images that transform or identify the wearer, as suggested here.

1. Yang Hong 1992, p. 59.

48.
Short sword

> North China, ca. 7th century B.C.
> Blade, bronze; hilt, gold with turquoise inlay
> Length 24.7 cm (9¾ in.)
> Private Collection

The hilt of this short sword is cast in brilliant gold. Its double-edged blade with prominent median ridge, which tapers gradually to a pointed tip, retains some sharpness in spite of corrosion. The guard is formed by a stylized animal's head with short horns and broad jaws, and two raised parallel lines spiral upward toward the pommel around the shaft. The evenly spaced spikes between the lines are accented with brightly colored turquoise inlays.

Bronze short swords are commonly found among the steppe cultures, but those with luxurious embellishment are rare. A comparable but less lavishly decorated example, cast in one piece in bronze, is in the Tokyo National Museum, its hilt decorated with similar spiraling lines and spikes.[1] Among archaeological finds, a bronze short sword found at Fengxiang, Shaanxi Province, comes closest to the present example. Apparently, it has the same design and the same decoration, but the hilt is cast in bronze.[2]   ZS

1. Takahama and Hatakeyama 1997, pl. 77.
2. Zhao Congcang 1991, p. 6, fig. 5:5.

49.
Knife surmounted by a tiger

Northeast China, 7th–6th century B.C.
Bronze
Length 11 ¾ in. (29.8 cm)
Ex coll.: Michael Dunn, New York

A small standing tiger in the round, its long tail touching its hind paws, serves as the pommel for this sturdy knife. The tiger's striped pelt is indicated by worn intaglio chevrons, and an indented tear-shaped mark emphasizes its powerful haunches. The eyes and nostrils are represented by round indentations, and the hilt is decorated with bird images. One side displays six birds of prey with outspread wings and the other side six birds in profile, with one shown upside down. Mold marks in the opening between the tiger's legs and along the spine of the blade indicate that the entire knife was cast in a two-piece mold.

Knives with similar tiger-shaped pommels and bird-decorated hilts have been excavated at Bronze Age sites in Northeast China, such as Xiaoheishigou, Ningcheng county, in southeastern Inner Mongolia, a site with an eighth-to-seventh-century B.C. dating, here revised to the seventh-to-sixth century B.C.[1] The bird images that adorn the hilt follow earlier pictorial traditions found in petroglyphs throughout Inner Mongolia, Mongolia, and southern Siberia.[2]

Knives were very common among the non-Chinese people who inhabited the northern frontier zone east of the Taihang Mountains, where such implements were designed as tools to be used in hunting and skinning rather than as weapons in warfare.

1. Xiang 1984, p. 121, fig. 3:2; Shanghai 2000, p. 104. In the text, the dates suggested are contemporary with the late Western Zhou–early Eastern Zhou period, which translates to about the eighth century B.C. In cat. no. 45, they have been revised to the seventh to sixth century B.C.
2. For petroglyphs in Inner Mongolia, see Gai 1989.

50.
Knife surmounted by a tiger

Northeast China, 7th–6th century B.C.
Bronze
Length 12⅛ in. (30.8 cm)
Ex coll.: Susan Chen & Company, Hong Kong

A standing tiger with five-clawed paws serves as the pommel of this knife. Its pelt is marked with indented chevrons and its haunches accentuated by tear-shaped ovals. Each side of the hilt is decorated with two vertical, striated sunken panels separated by a plain panel and framed by the hilt's unadorned borders. Mold marks within the opening between the tiger's legs indicate that the knife and pommel were cast integrally in a two-piece mold.

This knife, with its tiger-shaped pommel, belongs to the same category as catalogue no. 49, and it too should be associated with Northeast China of the seventh to the sixth century B.C. The only difference between the two knives is the slightly straighter blade that curves up almost imperceptibly at the tip on the present knife. Such a tip would have prevented a hunter from piercing the pelt when skinning an animal.

51.
Knife with standing bear

Northeast China, 7th–6th century B.C.
Bronze
Length 10½ in. (26.7 cm)
Ex coll.: Susan Chen & Company, Hong Kong

The pommel of this knife is formed by a standing five-clawed bear with a slightly open mouth and punched round eyes. Like the tigers on catalogue nos. 49 and 50, the pelt is marked by chevrons, and indented ovals emphasize the haunches. A vertical panel with a striated design between two sunken plain panels adorns the hilt, and a mold mark along the back of the hilt indicates that the knife was cast in a two-piece mold.

There is no question that this sturdy knife and catalogue nos. 49 and 50 date from the same period and were produced by the same culture in Northeast China. The hilts of all three knives comfortably fit the hand, as those of a tool should. The close similarity between the three knives further suggests that they were all cast in the same region, perhaps even at the same foundry. Several other published knives appear to belong to the same group.[1] The possibility that there were regional foundries established specifically to supply the hunting and herding peoples beyond the frontiers of China should be considered.

1. Ariadne Galleries 1998, nos. 74, 78; Takahama and Hatakeyama 1997, no. 82; Shanghai 2000, p. 104.

52.
Knife surmounted by a hedgehog

Northeast China, 7th–5th century B.C.
Bronze
Length 5 ¼ in. (13.3 cm)
Ex coll.: James Freeman, Kyoto

A small hedgehog adorns the stud that projects outward from the hilt of this knife. Shown in profile with its head down, the hedgehog has tiny raised marks on its body to indicate the spines. One side of the hilt has a vertical intaglio design in sequence: three thin horizontal lines, two single birds with outspread wings, three horizontal lines, three single birds, and three more horizontal lines. The other side is decorated by two standing animals. The hedgehog was probably precast and then cast onto the knife, which displays mold marks along the edges, the result of piece-mold casting. The knife tip has broken off.

Hedgehogs, friendly nocturnal creatures, are represented on numerous artifacts associated with the nomadic peoples beyond the northern frontier of China.[1] A finial in the Museum of Far Eastern Antiquities, Stockholm, depicts a hedgehog that is very similar to this one.[2] The Thaw knife must have served as a minor tool, as it is too small to grasp firmly with the whole hand. Knives with a decorated stud at the end of the hilt are found chiefly among grave goods in Northeast China dating from the eighth to the fifth century B.C.[3]

Two subspecies of hedgehog are known in China: *Erinaceus echinus deablatus* has long ears and is found in Shandong, Hebei, Hubei, and Jiangsu provinces; *E.e. miodon* has short ears and inhabits the northern Shaanxi desert area. They were among the sacred animals of Siberian shamanism and also figure prominently in European folktales. In ancient Egypt, hedgehogs were believed to signify renewal and rebirth because they would emerge in spring after a long winter in hibernation.[4] Hedgehogs may also have been associated with similar beliefs in East Asia. Today, hedgehog skins are nailed over doorways in Mongolia for protection and good luck.

1. So and Bunker 1995, p. 94, no. 7; Bunker et al. 1997, p. 237, no. 192.
2. Andersson 1933, pl. 8:1.
3. So and Bunker 1995, p. 122, no. 39; Shanghai 2000, p. 102.
4. Arnold 1995, pp. 22–23.

53.
Knife scabbard with birds in a row

Northeast China, 7th – 5th century B.C.
Bronze
Length 9½ in. (24.1 cm)
Ex coll.: James Freeman, Kyoto

Nine birds in a row perch on the top edge of this curved knife scabbard. The heads of three of the birds have broken off, but the remaining figures are depicted in profile, with the eye marked by a circular depression. The scabbard itself is cast in openwork, with slanting rectangular openings that form a chevron pattern banded by raised hemispheres on the front and seven slanting rectangles on the back. Two squared attachment loops project from the edge, and flashing and mold marks indicate piece-mold casting. A raised vertical line on the reverse of each bird must have facilitated the attachment of the figures during the casting process.

A very similar scabbard in the David-Weill collection was published by Salmony,[1] but no identical scabbard of this type has been found in archaeological context. A curved scabbard of a similar type was excavated at Xiaoheishigou, Ningcheng county, southeastern Inner Mongolia, which suggests that the Thaw scabbard can be attributed to Northeast China.[2] Two other artifacts from this site are also decorated with birds in profile not unlike those seen here.[3] By contrast, nothing similar has been found at pastoral sites in Northwest China.

1. Salmony 1933, pl. 40:2; David-Weill sale 1972, no. 74.
2. Xiang and Li 1995, p. 17, fig. 22:5. The find contains Chinese ritual vessels of the Western and Eastern Zhou periods.
3. Ibid., p. 18, figs. 24:1, 25:1.

54.
Short sword and sheath with crouching feline

North China, Hebei Province, ca. 6th century B.C.
a. Short sword: Bronze, length 9 in. (22.9 cm)
b. Sheath: Bronze with turquoise inlay, length 5¾ in.
(14.6 cm); width 2½ in. (6.4 cm)
Ex coll.: Susan Chen & Company, Hong Kong

A feline in the round crouches atop the pommel of this handsome short sword. Flat, with rounded edges, the hilt is perforated in the middle for suspension, and the guard is embellished with an interlace design. The thin tapering blade displays a rounded midrib that springs from the base of the guard. Jagged zigzag lines indicate the feline's toothy jaws, and circular depressions mark the shoulders and haunches. The blade and hilt of the sword are integrally cast, with visible mold join seams running down the edges.

The piece-mold cast sheath has an openwork interlace design accented by circular turquoise inlays that may once have been backed with colored leather or fabric. The casting process has been described by Pieter Meyers, conservator at the Los Angeles County Museum of Art: "Make decorated model; take mold impressions and make molds; add circular decoration in molds; cut down model so that it can be used as core; assemble and cast. Alloy compositions are very similar for both short sword and sheath: leaded tin-copper alloy (leaded bronze)."

No identical short sword and sheath have been found in archaeological context, but in shape and style they are related to artifacts associated with northern Hebei Province and Northeast China, where zigzag lines indicating a feline's mouth and indented marks on the shoulders and haunches are characteristic artistic motifs. The interlace designs on the guard and scabbard derive from the dragon-inspired interlace patterns seen on early-sixth-century B.C. Chinese bronze ritual vessels.[1] A close examination of the scabbard reveals vestigial indented circular eyes that remain from the earlier dragon design. Such a stylistic relationship with Chinese bronze decoration suggests a sixth-century date for both the short sword and the scabbard.

The rounded median ridge, which serves to strengthen the blade, is an imported feature that became extremely common on short swords produced in North China during the Spring and Autumn period.[2] Because the ridge occurs earlier, on a

short sword from the second-millennium B.C. site of Zhukaigou, in the Ordos region, its presence on late Spring and Autumn blades testifies to extensive contact between the Chinese and their northern neighbors.[3] As a type, the scabbard also appears to have originated in the north.[4] The unusual combination of Chinese and non-Chinese northern features on both the short sword and the scabbard suggests that they may have been manufactured by Chinese artisans for northern, non-Chinese consumption.

1. So 1995b, pp. 190–91, 300–301.
2. Chen Fangmei 1995, pp. 100–101.
3. Bunker et al. 1997, p. 180, fig. A1.
4. Loehr 1949, pp. 54–55.

55.
Knife with zoomorphic decoration

East-Central Asia, 6th century B.C.
Bronze
Length 8½ in. (21.6 cm)
Ex coll.: Susan Chen & Company, Hong Kong

Three felines—perhaps panthers—in the round, their paws transformed into stylized raptors' heads, adorn the hilt of this elegant knife. The paws appear to terminate in such a way that the ring formed by the claws serves as the circular eye of each raptor. The felines' eyes are described by a round depression. A mold seam along the edges of the hilt suggests that the knife was cast in a two-piece mold.

No other knife with a similar zoomorphic hilt has been identified in the archaeological literature, but the representation of the claws as raptors' heads is a well-known instance of zoomorphic juncture that occurs in Scythian art of the Black Sea region, as in the case of a seventh-century B.C. gold panther from Kelermes, whose claws are transformed into tiny coiled panthers.[1] A similar example of feline claws metamorphosed into raptors' heads occurs on several artifacts from the Tuva region in southern Siberia.[2] Knives are not typical Scythian tools and are more common among the nomadic peoples of the eastern Eurasian steppe world.

1. Jettmar 1967, p. 34, pl. 5.
2. Kenk 1986, p. 126, fig. 22:42, 45.

56.
Short sword with four kulans

North China and south-central Inner Mongolia,
6th–5th century B.C.
Bronze
Length 9⅝ in. (24.5 cm)
Ex coll.: J. J. Lally & Co., New York

This handsome short sword has an openwork hilt featuring the heads of four kulans depicted in the round. The hilt is surmounted by a flat, oval pommel decorated with an angular blind strap-work design that also marks the rounded V-shaped guard. The double-edged blade tapers to a point and displays a pronounced median ridge. The nicks along the side of the blade are the result of wear, and the transverse perforation through the pommel allows the piece to be suspended. Longitudinal mold lines along the edge of the hilt indicate that the short sword was piece-mold cast.

No short swords of this type have been excavated archaeologically, but there are short swords with similar openwork hilts in several collections.[1] An identical example is in the Hellstrom collection in Göteborg.[2] Typologically, the present short sword relates to catalogue no. 54.

It is interesting to note that the hilt of a short sword excavated from kurgan 1, Filippovka, in the southern Urals, has a similar openwork hilt featuring raptors' heads dating from the fifth to the fourth century B.C.[3] This similarity between a short sword traditionally associated with North China and a weapon from the southern Urals suggests that the two may have a common heritage in the earlier Iron Age of Central Asia that has yet to be identified.

1. Takahama and Hatakeyama 1997, no. 121; Ariadne Galleries 1998, no. 66.
2. Andersson 1929, fig. 1.
3. Aruz 2000, pp. 80–81, no. 6.

57.
Short sword with birds' heads

North China and south-central Inner Mongolia,
6th–5th century B.C.
Bronze
Length 9¾ in. (24.8 cm)
Ex coll.: J. J. Lally & Co., New York

The pommel and guard of this short sword are formed by two stylized outward-facing birds' heads represented in intaglio. The hilt is flat and enhanced by three sunken claws resembling those of an eagle, the most powerful raptor in the Eurasian steppes. The tapering double-edged blade is strengthened by a strong median ridge, and the concave channels along either side would have helped to increase the flow of blood when the weapon pierced the flesh. A circular perforation for attachment is located on the hilt below the pommel, and mold marks within the perforation indicate that the sword was cast in a two-piece mold.

No exact counterpart to this example has been archaeologically excavated, but similar weapons with a variety of bird's-head pommels and guards are associated with the pastoral peoples west of the Taihang Mountains, in North China and south-central Inner Mongolia, around the middle of the first millennium B.C.[1] Such short swords, with bird's-head decoration and dating from the sixth to the fifth century B.C., have been found at Maoqinggou, Liangcheng county, on the southern slopes of the Manhan Mountains.[2]

1. Rawson and Bunker 1990, no. 196; Bunker et al. 1997, nos. 139, 140.
2. Bunker et al. 1997, p. 56, fig. A71.

58.
Knife with recumbent horse

Northeast China and southeastern Inner Mongolia,
5th century B.C.
Bronze
Length 8 in. (20.3 cm)
Ex coll.: J. J. Lally & Co., New York

A recumbent horse at the hilt of this elegant knife is shown
in profile, with a perforated eye and folded legs. The blade is
curved, with a tip that turns up slightly, a single edge, and two
angular bends along the crest. Decorated longitudinally, the
hilt has two parallel lines of raised bosses between two ridged
edges. A seam visible under the horse's belly and under the
neck indicates that the knife was cast integrally with the hilt in
a two-piece mold.

Nothing similar has been found archaeologically, but there
is a nearly identical example in the Katherine and George Fan
collection that is said to come from the Ningcheng region of
southeastern Inner Mongolia and Northeast China. Horse
figures appear to have been quite popular among the frontier
peoples in Northeast China, and they adorn numerous artifacts associated with that region. The present knife was probably not a weapon but a tool of some sort useful to hunters and
horse people.

4. BELT ORNAMENTS

Belt ornaments are the most distinctive artifacts associated with the Eurasian steppe peoples. Belts were not just a practical means of holding up and fastening items of clothing. To the pastoral peoples of northern Eurasia, belt ornaments were necessary regalia, which they adorned with visual symbols that identified the owner's clan, rank, and prestige. By contrast, the belt hooks worn by the Chinese indicated power and wealth, but never clan and rank. The source for detached metal belt plaques strung on some sort of perishable material is somewhat obscure, but belts embellished by metal date back to the third millennium B.C. in the ancient Near East. Belts ornamented with a series of metal plaques first occurred in the Caucasus early in the first millennium B.C.[1] The earliest excavated evidence for this type of belt ornament in East Asia occurs around the seventh century B.C. in a nomadic burial at Zhoujiadi,

Aohan banner, southeastern Inner Mongolia[2] and slightly later in the Guo state cemetery at Shangcunling, Henan Province.[3] A belt decorated with metal plaques became an important prestige item among successive nomadic groups, such as the Avars, Turks, Kitan, and Mongols, throughout the first and second millennia A.D. The decorated belt was also introduced into Europe during the Migration (ca. A.D. 400–800) and medieval periods, when it came to represent military prowess, honor, and all the heroic virtues associated with chivalry.

1. Moorey 1967, pp. 83–85. Belts adorned with metal sheets can be traced back to the third-millennium B.C. burials at Ur, in the ancient Near East, where they are found in burials with small personal weapons suspended from them.
2. *Kaogu* 1984, no. 5, pl. 6.
3. Beijing 1959, pls. 2.1, 23.9.

BELT ORNAMENTS: BUCKLES

59.
Hook buckle in the shape of three raptors' heads

North China and south-central Inner Mongolia,
6th–5th century B.C.
Tinned bronze
Height 1⅞ in. (4.8 cm); width 2⅞ in. (7.3 cm)
Ex coll.: Joseph G. Gerena Fine Art, New York

This hook buckle is cast in the shape of three raptors' heads. The two smaller heads have long curved beaks and are represented on the larger section (the wearer's right), from which projects an attachment hook. The beaks are each marked by a row of five pseudogranulated dots within a sunken area. A larger bird's head with a curled beak, nearly identical in design to catalogue no. 140, forms a side extension that carries a vertical attachment loop on the reverse. The buckle was cast integrally with the loop in a multipiece mold, and the silvery appearance of the surface indicates that it was intentionally tinned on both sides.[1]

No hook buckle identical to this one has been excavated archaeologically, but a nearly identical example was recovered with scrap metal by workers in a Beijing factory,[2] and

another example is in the collection of the Museum of Far Eastern Antiquities, Stockholm.[3]

1. For a discussion of the tinning technique, see Bunker 1994b, pp. 48–49.
2. Cheng and Zhang 1982, p. 31, fig. 23.
3. Unpublished.

60.
Wolf-shaped belt buckle

> Bulgaria, Thracian period, 6th–4th century B.C.
> Bronze
> Height 1 1/8 in. (2.9 cm); width 3 3/4 in. (9.4 cm)
> Ex coll.: Four Corporation, New York; Mathias Komor

This Thracian belt buckle is cast in the shape of a crouching wolf. The back is flat and displays a horizontal hook behind the head pointing toward the tail, where a tiny loop remains; the rest of the fastening device is missing. The buckle is lost-wax cast.

A nearly identical buckle in the shape of a wolf was excavated in Apollonia, Bulgaria.[1] In antiquity, a neophyte Thracian warrior was often awarded a belt as a sign of his having reached maturity and completed the initiation into manhood.[2]

1. Marazov 1998, p. 62, fig. 17.
2. For a similar wolf-shaped buckle misidentified as a Scythian fibula, see Ariadne Galleries 1998, p. 28, no. 16.

61.
Hook buckle with heads of a bird and a deer

> North China, 6th–4th century B.C.
> Bronze
> Length 2 in. (5 cm)
> Katherine and George Fan

This small buckle has a circular center section with a hook in the shape of a bird's head on one side and an attachment loop at the other end in the shape of a deer's head seen frontally; the loop is formed by a strut connecting the two ears. Ribbing marks the sides of the buckle, which display mold marks indicating that it was cast in a multipiece mold.

This type of simple buckle is found among pastoral peoples throughout the Eurasian steppes during the early part of the first millennium B.C. as well as in ancient Iran.[1] They also occur in China with horse gear and chariot fittings in the sixth to the fifth century B.C.[2] and as belt accessories in the northern

pastoral world during the same period.[3] A similar belt buckle in bone and with a fixed tongue was found at Zhoujiadi, an eighth-to-seventh-century B.C. site in Aohan banner, southeastern Inner Mongolia, suggesting that the type occurs earlier in the Dongbei than in Central China.[4]

1. Grach 1983, pp. 32–33, nos. 41–43; Moorey 1971, pp. 134–36, pl. 27:146.
2. Wang Renxiang 1986, pp. 65–75, fig. 1:1; Bunker et al. 1997, pp. 210–11, no. 149.
3. For various theories on the origins of this type of buckle, see Bunker et al. 1997, pp. 210–11.
4. So and Bunker 1995, p. 78; So 1997.

62.
Belt buckle with writhing bodies

Northwest China, 5th–4th century B.C.
Tinned bronze
Height 1⅝ in. (3.9 cm); width 2⅞ in. (7.3 cm)
Ex coll.: J. J. Lally & Co., New York; Calon da Collection
Published: So and Bunker 1995, p. 135, no. 53; Takahama and Hatakeyama 1997, no. 192.

This pentagonal buckle is embellished with writhing bodies enclosed within a narrow border of scalelike motifs. A large dragon mask with typically Chinese heart-shaped ears and rolled-up muzzle fills the blunt end. Behind the mask the body splits in two, each part bordered by two pebbled strips, with one fore- and one hind leg emerging from spiral haunches. Between the haunches and facing the buckle opening is a smaller, bovine mask. Two diminutive animals, also rendered with pebbled bodies, fill the space on either side. On the border of the squarish opening is a fixed projection for fastening;

a stemmed stud on the underside, near the blunt end, is also part of the fastening device. There is considerable wear around the button and the opening. The buckle was cast by the lost-wax process, and the silvery sheen on the surface is the result of tinning. The marks left by fingers pushing the wax into the mold to make the casting model are visibly impressed in the metal on the reverse.

In form and decoration, this buckle exemplifies a blend of Chinese and northern steppe traditions. The buckle with a stationary hook is a northern feature, and the serpentine zoomorphic motif prevails on Chinese ritual vessels of the fifth century B.C.[1] Buckles similar in shape and decoration are included in many collections[2] and have been discovered in non-Chinese graves in Zhongwei county, Ningxia,[3] and in the Qingyang region of southeastern Gansu Province.[4] They were probably made expressly for trade with the neighboring pastoral peoples in a Qin metalworking center somewhere in Shaanxi Province.

1. Extensively discussed by Jenny So in So and Bunker 1995, p. 135, no. 35.
2. Bunker et al. 1997, pp. 242–43, no. 198.
3. Zhou 1989, p. 976, fig. 6:1.
4. Liu and Xu 1988, pp. 414 fig. 2:11, 415 fig. 4:2.

63.
Sixteen belt ornaments

Northwest China, 4th century B.C.
Tinned bronze
a. Height 2 in. (5.1 cm); width 3⅛ in. (7.9 cm)
b–p. Height 1⅛ in. (2.9 cm); width 2 in. (5.1 cm)
Ex coll.: Michael Dunn, New York

This partial set of sixteen belt ornaments consists of one buckle plaque and fifteen smaller plaques. The large plaque, in the shape of a fantastic standing wolf mauling a fallen deer, is the wearer's right-hand half of a mirror-image pair of plaques that together would have formed a complete belt buckle. The ear is a heart shape, and the tail and crest each terminate in an eared raptor's head. Beneath the wolf are three scalloped elements, the vestigial remains of a representation of a pup, such as the one shown beneath the carnivore in catalogue no. 94. The deer is shown lying with a twisted body, its muzzle in the wolf's open jaws. The reverse displays a vertical loop behind the wolf's haunches and the remains of

another loop behind the head. The plaque was cast by the lost-wax process and then intentionally tinned on one side to give it a pleasing, lustrous surface.

Each of the fifteen small belt plaques takes the form of two tangent coiled raptors joined by a boss. The raptors are shown in profile, with a curvy wing and tail distinguished by longitudinal ridges. Each plaque once had a vertical loop, now mostly missing, on the reverse behind the boss. Like the buckle plaque, their surfaces have been tinned, a bronze enrichment that may have indicated that the owner had a higher status than someone who wore only plain bronze belt ornaments.

The large buckle plaque displays an animal-combat scene very similar to that of plaque catalogue no. 94. The raptors on the smaller plaques have been reduced to conventionalized designs that can ultimately be traced back to bird images found on Western Zhou ritual vessels.[1] Even those with ears, as shown here, can be found in the Western Zhou bronze vocabulary.[2] Such raptors have been inaccurately described as griffins. These raptors have round eyes, while those on the mythological griffin are almond shaped.[3]

This belt set exhibits both northern and Chinese features. Similar belt ornaments have been recovered from the Qingyang region of southeastern Gansu Province and the adjacent Guyuan region of southern Ningxia, where they must have been worn by the herding peoples who inhabited the area during the late fourth century B.C.[4] In all probability, they were made by Qin craftsmen specifically for these peoples. How many plaques originally constituted a complete belt set is unknown, since to date no complete sets that are similar have been found intact.

1. Rawson 1990, nos. 53, 54.
2. Ibid., no. 91.
3. For a discussion of the difference between bird and griffin images, see Loehr 1956, pp. 189–92; for griffins see Mayor 1994.
4. Liu and Xu 1988, pp. 414 fig. 2:12, 420 fig. 17:3, 4. See So and Bunker 1995, pp. 165–66, no. 90, for a similar buckle plaque with excavated, but unpublished, counterparts from Guyuan.

64.
Belt buckle with walking tigers

Southern Siberia, 3rd century B.C.
Bronze
Each: Height 2½ in. (6.4 cm); width 4⅝ in. (11.7 cm)
Ex coll.: Eskenazi Ltd., London

The two openwork mirror-image plaques that together form this complete belt buckle are each cast in the shape of a walking tiger. The fastening hook protrudes from the front right-hand edge of the wearer's left-hand plaque. The face of each tiger is shown frontally and its body in profile. The paws have three prominent sharp claws, and the pelt is distinguished by raised striated lines. A leafy bush beneath each head lends the scene a wooded ambience. The alloy is an arsenical copper with traces of iron and antimony but no tin or lead, suggesting that the plaques were cast in southern Siberia.

The striated treatment of the tigers' pelts is stylistically related to the tigers on the wooden coffin from tomb 2 at Bashadar, in the Altai Mountains of southern Siberia, dating from the sixth to the fifth century B.C. (fig. 32). The plaques also foreshadow slightly later tiger plaques, such as catalogue no. 97 and those found at sites in Guyuan county, Ningxia.[1] The leafy bush is related to the vegetation represented on catalogue nos. 78 and 80, which were also cast somewhere north of the Chinese frontier regions.

1. Tian and Guo 1986, p. 94, fig. 62.1.

65.
Belt buckle with bovines

North China, 3rd – 2nd century B.C.
Gilded bronze
Height 2⅛ in. (5.4 cm); width 3½ in. (8.9 cm)
Ex coll.: J. J. Lally & Co., New York

This complete belt buckle comprises two bovine-shaped, mirror-image plaques. Each bovine is shown with its head turned downward and slightly back toward the rump. The facial features are represented naturalistically, and the body of each is marked by ridges and curved surface designs similar to those seen on the carved bone cylinder, catalogue no. 159. The reverse of each plaque displays two squared vertical loops that were probably soldered on. The plaques were cast by lost wax and then mercury gilded. There is evidence of post-cast tooling to sharpen the details before gilding.

Similar plaques have been found all over North China and are in several collections.[1] One pair was collected in Shouzhou, Anhui Province, the capital of the state of Chu from 241 until 223 B.C., when it was conquered by the Qin.[2] Apparently, it was a city of some sophistication, with important bronze foundries. Another pair was excavated in Suide county, northern Shaanxi Province, from a Western Han tomb.[3] All these plaques exhibit minor differences, as they were probably products of different workshops. If they were commissioned by northern pastoral peoples, the designs would have

remained basically consistent, with only technical details varying from foundry to foundry.

1. Bunker 1990, pp. 69–70, no. 49; So and Bunker 1995, pp. 140–42, no. 59.
2. Karlbeck 1955, pl. 32:1, 2.
3. Fu 1985, pl. 139.

66.
Belt buckle with standing oxen

North China, 3rd–2nd century B.C.
Gilded bronze
a. Height 1 ⅝ in. (4.1 cm); width 2 ⅛ in. (5.4 cm)
b. Height 1 ⅝ in. (4.1 cm); width 2 ¼ in. (5.7 cm)
Provenance: J. J. Lally & Co., New York

This belt buckle is cast in the form of two openwork mirror-image plaques, each of which depicts a standing ox with its body in profile within a rope-patterned frame. Each ox is shown with all four legs, its head in three-quarter view, and its tail curving between its legs. The wearer's left-hand plaque has a projecting semicircular ring that is part of the fastening device and a rounded vertical loop on the reverse. The plaque on the left has two rounded, vertical loops. Both plaques were cast by the lost-wax process and mercury gilded.

Plaques like these are found in both North China and Inner Mongolia,[1] and there are other examples in many collections.[2] One was excavated at Daodunzi, Tongxin county, Ningxia,[3] and another from a tomb in Chengdu, Sichuan. The Chengdu buckle was buried with coins that date the tomb to the late

third or second century B.C.,[4] a date that can also be applied to the Thaw buckle.

1. Tian and Guo 1986, pl. 58:6, 7.
2. Andersson 1932, pl. 24:5; Bunker 1981, pl. 157, no. 838; Rawson and Bunker 1990, pp. 340–41, no. 220; Bunker et al. 1997, p. 257, no. 218.
3. Duan 1995, pl. 113.
4. Hu 1983, p. 27, figs. 2:6, 3:1.

67.
Belt buckle with zoomorphic design

North China, 3rd–2nd century B.C.
Gilded bronze
Each: Height 1 ¾ in. (4.4 cm); width 3 ½ in. (9 cm)
Ex coll.: J. J. Lally & Co., New York

The surface of these two gilded bronze belt plaques is decorated with a complex design of zoomorphic forms in mirror image. The central animal is a recumbent wolf shown in profile, with pointed ear, almond-shaped eye, turned-up snout, open jaws revealing fangs and teeth, and two paws, each with five claws. Two wild sheep, coiled and with their hindquarters slung over their heads, are superimposed on the wolf's body. Above the wolf is a row of horned gazelles' heads, above which is a series of eared raptors' heads. The front of each plaque has been mercury gilded, and the back displays two vertical rounded attachment loops that have been soldered on. A woven pattern on the reverse indicates that the plaque was cast by the lost-wax and lost-textile process.[1]

A nearly identical plaque was found among the grave goods from Xichagou, Xifeng county, northeastern Liaoning Province,[2] and a buckle similar to the Thaw buckle but cast in solid gold was found in an elite Western Han burial in Jiangsu Province, evidence for contact between the Chinese and the northern nomads.[3] The animal-combat scene, so dramatically portrayed on earlier nomadic plaques, such as catalogue no. 94, has been reduced here to a pleasing design that is almost impossible to decipher at first glance. The eared raptors' heads refer to antlers with raptors'-head tines found on earlier plaques, but only someone initiated in this iconography would recognize them; the symbolic content has been overwhelmed by a stylized design of curves and countercurves. The presence of mercury gilding and the emphasis on pattern are typical of Western Han workmanship and confirm manufacture by the Chinese specifically for their northern neighbors.

1. For a discussion of this unusual casting technique, see Bunker 1994b, pp. 41–42.
2. Bunker et al. 1997, p. 78, fig. A110 (with photograph in reverse).
3. Wei, Li, and Zou 1998, p. 18, fig. 23:3.

68.

Belt buckle with animal-combat scene

North China, 3rd – 2nd century B.C.
Gilded bronze
Each: Height 2¼ in. (5.7 cm); width 4⅝ in. (11.7 cm)
Ex coll.: Joseph G. Gerena Fine Art, New York

This complete belt buckle consists of two mirror-image plaques, each one showing a complex animal-combat motif in which a bear and a wolf attack a fallen mythological ungulate. The ungulate's hindquarters are twisted 180 degrees, and its antler tines terminate in raptors' heads that make up the border along the top and inside edge. The back of each plaque displays a woven pattern that indicates that it was cast by the lost-wax and lost-textile process. The pierced hole in the wearer's left-hand plaque shows that it was punched through the cloth-backed wax model from the front. One plaque displays on the reverse two vertical attachment loops that were formed on the model by laying a wax slab on two wax posts and then integrally casting them with the plaque. The loops on the other plaque are broken off, and the front of each is mercury gilded.

Another pair of plaques with the same motif was excavated from a Han antiquarian's tomb near Sandiancun, in the eastern suburbs of Xi'an, Shaanxi Province, where the capital was located during the Western Han dynasty.[1] And an identical right-hand plaque was excavated from a Hun burial at Pokrovka, Kazakhstan, in the southern Urals.[2] Such a discovery, so far from North China, where it originated, suggests that the Pokrovka plaque must have been a treasured heirloom, acquired by trade or warfare, and demonstrates how small objects transported great distances could aid in the transmission of styles and motifs.

This particular animal-combat scene belongs to the iconography introduced into the frontier regions of Northwest China from the Eurasian steppes during the late fourth century B.C. and represented on belt ornaments during the third and second centuries B.C., until the Rouzhi confederacy was driven west by the Xiongnu in the second century B.C.[3] The vigor of the attack scene has been thoroughly Sinicized and almost lost in the manipulation of shapes into pleasing patterns, as in the scene on catalogue no. 67.

Exactly where these plaques were made is hard to determine, since two pairs that are identical but in gold were excavated from an imperial Chu tomb, w1, at Shizishan near Xuzhou, Jiangsu Province.[4] The tomb contained the remains of Prince Liu Wu, who died in 154 B.C. The gold buckles were mounted on silk belts and erroneously attributed to Scythian workmanship from Siberia. Clearly, belt plaques carrying this scene were made in North China, but precisely where is unknown. Whether the Shizishan gold plaques were acquired from the northern herding peoples or, instead, were made in China and reflect a taste for northern exotica among the local Han elite is also unclear. Another bronze buckle that carries the same zoomorphic motif, in the Miho Museum, Shigaraki, was undoubtedly made by Chinese artisans, as it is inlaid with thin gold and silver wire, a technique not used by metalsmiths of the eastern Eurasian steppes.[5]

1. Zhu and Li 1983, p. 24, fig. 1:1, pl. 7:2; Bunker 1989, p. 52, fig. 1.
2. Yablonsky 1994, fig. 81:13.
3. Bunker 1989.
4. Zou and Wei 1998, pp. 37–43, fig. 1.
5. Miho Museum 1997, pp. 216–18.

69.
Belt buckle with kulans attacked by wolves

Southern Siberia, 3rd–2nd century B.C.
Bronze
Each: Height 3¼ in. (8.3 cm); width 5¾ in. (14.6 cm)
Ex coll.: Eskenazi Ltd., London

Each of these openwork plaques portrays two kulans being attacked by two wolves as they sink their fangs into the kulans' necks. The entire scene is enclosed within a rectangular frame embellished by vines with tear-shaped leaves. The kulans can be identified by their upright manes and fringed tails, and the wolves by their bushy tails. The wearer's left-hand plaque bears a hook on its front right edge. The alloy is an arsenical copper with no tin or lead, a characteristic more compatible with the alloys used in eastern and southern Siberia than in North China's frontier regions.[1] The reverse of each plaque is slightly concave, and the presence of flashing in the openings suggests that the plaques were lost-wax cast from a wax model formed in a two-piece mold. The backs are heavily encrusted and retain fragments of textile with which they were wrapped or to which they were attached.

No plaques with this design have been excavated archaeologically, but rectangular plaques with frames decorated with leafy vines and similar tear-shaped cells, such as catalogue no. 105, have been found in eastern and southern Siberia.[2]

1. See analysis tables in Devlet 1980, pp. 32–34.
2. Ibid., pp. 47–48.

70.
Belt buckle with raptors and tigers

Southern Siberia, 3rd–2nd century B.C.
Bronze
Height 3 in. (7.6 cm); width 5 in. (12.9 cm)
Ex coll.: Eskenazi Ltd., London

Two mythological raptors attack two tiger protomes joined at the shoulder in this openwork belt-buckle plaque. The raptor—here, a fantastic creature—is distinguished from the eagle, on which it is based, by its almond-shaped eye. The reverse has two tiny fabric fragments on the lower left. A hook protrudes from the left, and the right side has a horizontal bar in the design. It appears to have been cast by the lost-wax process, probably from a wax model made in a two-piece mold.

Stylistically, the buckle relates to the mirror-image horizontal-B plaques manufactured during the Western Han period that depict a mythological raptor attacking an entire tiger.[1] One such plaque was excavated at Xichagou, Xifeng county, Liaoning Province,[2] and a pair of plaques was discovered near Chifeng, southeastern Inner Mongolia.[3] Another example was found at Urbium, southern Siberia.[4]

The alloy is an arsenical copper with small amounts of tin and lead, suggesting that the plaque was cast in southern Siberia, where such plaques with arsenical copper alloys are confirmed both archaeologically and scientifically.[5]

1. Bunker et al. 1997, p. 260, no. 222.
2. Sun 1960, p. 33.
3. *China Archaeology and Art Digest* 2, no. 1 (1997), pp. 36–37.
4. Devlet 1980, p. 65, no. 117.
5. Ibid., and analysis on p. 32.

71.
Wolf-shaped belt buckle

Southern or eastern Siberia, 3rd–2nd century B.C.
Bronze
Height 3¼ in. (8.3 cm); width 4½ in. (11.4 cm)
Ex coll.: Michael Dunn, New York

This openwork belt buckle takes the form of a mythological walking wolf in profile. All four legs are represented, and the tail, crestlike mane, and antler tines terminate in eared raptors' heads that create a half frame around the central figure. The reverse is concave and displays two vertical loops, one behind the head and the other behind the haunch. On the front, a hook projects from the left edge. The metal is a leaded tin-copper alloy with traces of iron and antimony. There is extensive corrosion with massive crystals of cuprite and considerable intergranular corrosion. The rather clean appearance of the buckle is the result of a recent mechanical cleaning. The wolf is conceived in a planar style, as if the model had been carved in wood. The buckle was cast from a mold-made wax model.

An identically shaped buckle, which appears to have been imported, was excavated at Xichagou, Xifeng county,

Liaoning Province.[1] A plaque depicting the same mythological wolf was collected in the destroyed cemetery at
Dadaosanjiazi, near Qiqihar city, Heilongjiang Province,[2] and
a similar plaque was excavated in Dyrestuy, Transbaikal,
Buryatia, where it was found at the waist of the dead.[3] A third
was collected at Maryasova, in the Minusinsk region of southern Siberia.[4] Because these plaques appear to be exotic at sites
in North China, it is reasonable to suggest that they were manufactured in eastern or southern Siberia and represent the
style of a yet unidentified group.

1. Sun 1960, p. 33, fig. 4.
2. *Kaogu* 1988, no. 12, pl. 3:6.
3. Miniaev 1995a, p. 45, upper right.
4. Devlet 1980, p. 64, fig. 114.

72.
Belt buckle with animal-combat scene

North China, 3rd – 2nd century B.C.
Bronze
Each: Height 3 ¼ in. (8.3 cm); width 4 ¾ in. (12.1 cm)
Ex coll.: Eskenazi Ltd., London
Published: Christie's, New York, sale cat., March 25, 1998.

A mythological scene of animal combat is represented on this
pair of mirror-image belt plaques. On each plaque, a small
carnivore bites the leg of a fantastic ungulate, each of which
has a rapacious beak and raptor's-head antler tines and tail tip.
The wearer's left-hand plaque has a small hook that protrudes
from the front alongside a vertical slit near the ungulate's head.

A nearly identical single plaque was recovered from a disturbed cemetery at Xichagou, Xifeng county, northern
Liaoning Province.[1] The cemetery can be dated numismatically to the second century B.C. Xiongnu may be buried in
some of the graves; Donghu, whom the Xiongnu conquered
early in the second century B.C., appear to be buried in others.

The ungulate with raptor's-head appendages belongs to the
same iconography that governs the tattoos found on the

Mongoloid man buried in kurgan 2 at Pazyryk, which dates from the fourth to the third century B.C. (fig. 37).[2] The same type of fantastic creature adorns the remains of a headdress found at Nalin'gaotu, Shenmu county, northern Shaanxi Province (fig. 36). This iconography has been associated with the nomads who appeared on China's northwestern frontier in the late fourth century B.C. and who introduced mounted warfare.

The horizontal-B motif and animal-combat scene on these plaques are nearly identical to those on a gold plaque collected near Verkhneudinsk, present-day Ulan-Ude, near Lake Baikal in southern Siberia, with one exception (fig. 48). The Verkhneudinsk example has several animal figures superimposed on its body that do not appear on any of the bronze examples. Nevertheless, the similarities suggest a strong connection between the Verkhneudinsk gold plaque and its bronze counterparts from Xichagou, which calls into question the unsubstantiated date of fifth to fourth century B.C. given to the Verkhneudinsk gold plaque in the recent Metropolitan Museum publication *The Golden Deer of Eurasia*.[3]

1. Sun 1960, p. 33, fig. 5.
2. Rudenko 1970, figs. 130, 131.
3. Aruz 2000, pp. 287–89, no. 210.

73.
Belt buckle with wolf and ram

North China, 3rd–2nd century B.C.
Gilded bronze
Each: Height 1⅞ in. (4.8 cm); width 3⅞ in. (9.8 cm)

These mirror-image openwork plaques, each of which depicts a wolf mauling a fallen ram, form a complete belt buckle. The ram's hindquarters are twisted 180 degrees, and its forelegs are placed on either side of the wolf's body. The wolf stands behind the ram and sinks its teeth into the shoulder, and the ram's imminent death is dramatically emphasized by its twisted body and lolling tongue. A single rope frame borders each plaque, giving it a slightly scalloped edge. The reverse of each displays two vertical squared loops that were formed by placing a strip of wax on two wax posts before casting. A woven pattern, characteristic of the lost-wax and lost-textile casting process, is visible on the back. Both plaques are mercury gilded.

The buckle is related stylistically to catalogue no. 103, but the carnivore portrayed in that example is a feline rather than a wolf. The wolf's position, half behind the ram, is an attack pose found on slightly earlier plaques that also have single rope borders,[1] and the lolling tongue is a characteristic of victims that occurs on other third-century B.C. objects, such as catalogue no. 124.

1. So and Bunker 1995, pp. 137–38, no. 56. Such plaques were also found at a slightly later site of Daodunzi, where they appear to predate the other plaques; see Bunker et al. 1997, p. 84, fig. A124.

74.
Buckle with animal-combat scene

Western Inner Mongolia, Ordos region
3rd century B.C.
Gold
Height 2⅝ in. (6.7 cm); width 3⅛ in. (7.9 cm)
The Metropolitan Museum of Art, Gift of J. Pierpont Morgan,
1917 (17.190.1672)
Published: Okladnikov 1946, p. 288, fig. 2; Bunker et al. 1970,
p. 144 and pl. 118; Pirazzoli-t'Sertevens 1982, p. 39, pl. 13;
Bunker (1986) 1988, pp. 222–27; Aruz 2000, p. 5, fig. 3.

Two felines whose hindquarters are rotated 180 degrees sink
their teeth into the necks of two recumbent ibex, each with its
head turned backward, on this animal-combat scene in relief
that adorns the surface of this handsome gold buckle. The animals have been cleverly represented in such a way that they
conform to the shape of the buckle, one of the hallmarks of
steppe art. A hook for fastening purposes projects from the
front of the buckle near the oval opening, and a loop on the
reverse extends from the felines' tails at the opposite end.

The reverse of the plaque displays a prominent woven pattern, which indicates that it was cast by lost wax and lost textile, in which the wax model was backed with a piece of coarse
fabric during the casting process. The wax backing served to
stabilize the model when it was extracted from the mold,
allowing for a thinner finished product and thereby reduc-
ing the amount of gold used.[1] This unusual casting process
was also used to cast many of the gold belt plaques in the

Siberian collection of Peter the Great in the State Hermitage,
St. Petersburg.[2]

When this buckle was donated to the Metropolitan Museum
in 1917, little was known about the culture of the pastoral
peoples on China's northern frontiers. It was not until 1980,
when a bronze buckle of the same shape, discovered in a
Xiongnu grave at Xigoupan, Jungar banner, in the Ordos
Desert in southwestern Inner Mongolia, was published that a
cultural context could be established.[3] The Xiongnu grave
dates to the third century B.C., a time when the Xiongnu were
in control of the Ordos region.

1. For a discussion of this casting technique, see Bunker (1986) 1988;
   and White and Bunker 1994, pp. 41–42.
2. Bunker 1992a.
3. *Wenwu* 1980, no. 7, p. 5, fig. 7.5 and p. 9, fig. 28.

75.
Belt buckle with animal-combat scene

North China, 3rd–2nd century B.C.
Bronze
Height 3 in. (7.6 cm); width 5⅝ in. (14.3 cm)
The Metropolitan Museum of Art, Rogers Fund, 1918
(18.43.10)
Published: Borovka 1960, pl. 70B; Bunker et al., 1970,
no. 114; Jacobson 1984, pl. 22; Bunker 1989, p. 58, fig. 9.

This buckle consists of two mirror-image plaques, each of
which depicts an animal-combat scene in which a wolf and a
tiger savage a fallen ungulate with raptor-headed appendages.
It is essentially the same scene as that depicted on the gilded
bronze plaques that make up another, earlier, buckle in the
Thaw collection, catalogue no. 68. Each of the plaques has
vertical attachment loops on the reverse, and the wearer's
left-hand plaque also has a circular perforation that is part of
the fastening system. The plaques are cast from a wax model
formed in a mold.

These belt plaques are cast in a purely Western Han style
that has transformed a fierce combat scene into a pleasing
rhythmical design of curves and linear patterns. The animals
depicted on the earlier plaques have been subtly altered, so
that the ungulate now has a muzzle instead of a beak, prompt-
ing some scholars to call it a horse, in spite of the fact that the
hooves are cloven.[1] The backs of both catalogue no. 68 and
the present plaques display minor differences, indicating that

they were cast in slightly different ways. An extensive examination of many plaques cast during the third through the first century B.C. reveals that the plain bronze plaques were nearly always cast by a different process than those examples that were gilded, suggesting the existence of separate workshops—one for casting plain bronze ornaments and another for casting those to be mercury gilded. Whether such workshops were in the same metalworking center or in different cities has not been determined.

1. For a detailed discussion of these plaques, see Bunker 1989.

76.
Belt buckle with beaked ungulates

North China, 2nd century B.C.
Gilded bronze
Height 2⅞ in. (7.1 cm); width 4¼ in. (10.8 cm)
Ex coll.: J. J. Lally & Co., New York; Calon da Collection
Published: Rawson and Bunker 1990, no. 225.

Two addorsed beaked ungulates whose hindquarters are rotated 180 degrees and whose tails terminate in eared raptors' heads are depicted on each of these two rectangular plaques, which together form one complete belt buckle. Striated enclosures mark the bodies and lend them texture. A simulated rope border serves as a frame for each plaque. The back of each has two vertical loops. Both plaques have been cast by the lost-wax and lost-textile method and then

mercury gilded. The perforation in the wearer's left-hand plaque is part of the fastening device and was punched through the wax model from the front.

These mythological creatures derive from the glorious ungulate that surmounts the Nalin'gaotu headdress (fig. 36), but the earlier exuberance has been sacrificed to the demands of a design that deliberately orchestrates curves and striated markings. Plaques with this design have been excavated at Xichagou, Xifeng county, Liaoning Province,[1] and at Daodunzi, Tongxin county, Ningxia,[2] and they are included in many collections around the world,[3] suggesting that they were mass-produced for northern consumption.

1. Unpublished.
2. *Kaogu xuebao* 1988, no. 3, p. 344, fig. 9.13, pls. 13:5, 20:12.
3. Rawson and Bunker 1990, no. 225; So and Bunker 1995, pp. 145–46, no. 66.

77.
Belt buckle with recumbent stags

> North China, 2nd century B.C.
> Gilded bronze
> Each: Height 1⅞ in. (4.8 cm); width 4 in. (10 cm)
> Ex coll.: J. J. Lally & Co., New York

This belt buckle takes the form of two rectangular openwork plaques, each of which depicts a recumbent stag with its head turned back toward the hind legs and the antlers extended gracefully over its body. A rope pattern serves as the border for each plaque. The reverse of each displays two loops and

the characteristic lost-wax and lost-textile woven pattern. The pattern on the reverse of one of the plaques must reflect the rumpled state of the textile that served as backing for the wax model during the casting process. The mercury gilding has worn off in places.

No identical plaques are known. The style and rope borders are comparable to features on other belt plaques dated to the second century B.C. Nevertheless, there is a naturalism in the portrayal of the stags that suggests Han Chinese characteristics rather than the zoomorphic symbolism associated with the northern pastoral peoples.

78.
Belt buckle with raptor attacking a goat

> Mongolia or Siberia, 2nd century B.C.
> Bronze
> Height 2¼ in. (5.7 cm); width 3⅞ in. (9.8 cm)
> Ex coll.: Michael Dunn, New York

Each of these mirror-image plaques depicts a scene in which a mountain goat is attacked by a large raptor. The raptor is represented in profile with both wings shown, sinking its beak into the goat's neck while grasping its head with its claws. The goat is male, as indicated by its beard, and is shown in profile, with all four legs represented. A small leafy tree provides a wooded setting. The wearer's left-hand plaque carries a slit and a hook by which to fasten the buckle. The plaques were cast from an alloy of tin and arsenic copper, with a small amount of lead. The presence of arsenic suggests that the buckle may have been cast far north of the Chinese frontier,

like catalogue no. 80. The plaques are lost-wax cast, probably from a wax model formed in a two-piece mold.

Plaques of the same design have been chance finds, but none have been excavated archaeologically.[1] The manner in which the leaves are represented relates the present plaques stylistically to others found in Mongolia and Siberia.[2]

1. Tian and Guo 1986, p. 95, fig. 63.4.
2. Bunker et al. 1997, p. 275, fig. 243; Miniaev 1998, p. 35, fig. 3.

79.
Belt buckle with Bactrian camels

North China, 2nd century B.C.
Gilded bronze
Each: Height 1⅞ in. (4.8 cm); width 4 in. (10.2 cm)
Ex coll.: Eskenazi Ltd., London

Each of these two rectangular openwork belt plaques, which together form one belt buckle, represents two Bactrian camels flanking an Asian elm tree. The camels are shown in profile with naturalistic detail, and the design is framed with a border that imitates braided rope. Each plaque displays two vertical loops on the reverse. The plaques were cast by the lost-wax and lost-textile method from wax models that were made in a mold and backed with a piece of coarse textile and then mercury gilded.

Compositions showing Bactrian camels were very popular among the Xiongnu, who bred and raised camels along with cattle, sheep, and horses.[1] Several versions of these plaques have been excavated at burial sites at Xichagou, Xifeng county, Liaoning Province,[2] and at Daodunzi, Tongxin county, Ningxia,[3] sites that have been dated numismatically to the second century B.C. and associated with the Xiongnu.

The openwork design of a similar but later camel-decorated plaque in the Arthur M. Sackler collections is backed by a piece of soft wood,[4] and several openwork plaques excavated in Buryatia also had backing of some type.[5] Such a backing for an openwork plaque seems contradictory, unless one considers the possibility that the ends of a belt made of brightly colored fabric were inserted between the plaque and the backing to produce a colorful design that would imitate appliquéd felt or gold inlaid with semiprecious stones, both of which were popular among the northern pastoral neighbors of the Han Chinese.

1. So and Bunker 1995, p. 62.
2. Sun 1960, p. 33, no. 3.
3. *Kaogu xuebao* 1988, no. 3, p. 344, fig. 9:5.
4. Bunker et al. 1997, p. 216, no. 233.
5. Sergei Miniaev, conversation with author, 1996.

80.
Belt buckle with a lynx attacking an argali

Eastern Siberia, 2nd – 1st century B.C.
Bronze
Each: Height 3 in. (7.6 cm); width 4¼ in. (10.8 cm)
Ex coll.: Joseph G. Gerena Fine Art, New York; Michael and Henrietta Spink, London

This belt buckle consists of two identical plaques, each of which depicts a lynx about to pounce on an argali. The lynx is shown frontally, amid tree branches, with only its head and four paws shown. The alloy contains a substantial amount of arsenic, typical of plaques made in eastern and southern Siberia.[1] The plaques are slightly concave on the reverse and were cast by the lost-wax process, probably from a model formed in a two-piece mold.

A plaque that bears the same design as this one was found in grave 128 in a Xiongnu burial ground at Dyrestuy, in the southwestern Transbaikal region, 124 miles from Ulan-Ude.[2] According to the excavation report, it was found fastened to a disintegrated piece of wood at the waist of the dead. This further confirms the suggestion that such openwork plaques were originally backed by fabric secured by a piece of wood. (See also cat. no. 79.)

Plaque fragments similar in design to the Thaw and Dyrestuy examples were also found in southern Siberia in the Minusinsk region. The alloys of these bronze fragments also contain arsenic.[3]

The style in which the tree's leaves are rendered on these plaques is the same as that of the tree leaves represented on a plaque fragment discovered in the Gobi Desert by a joint Mongolian–Hungarian expedition, further confirming a northern origin for such plaques in Mongolia, Buryatia, or the Minusinsk region rather than in North China.[4]

1. Miniaev 1998, p. 35; Bunker et al. 1997, pp. 270–74.
2. Miniaev 1998, pp. 34–35, fig. 3.
3. Devlet 1980, pp. 32, 64, no. 110.
4. Bunker et al. 1997, p. 275, fig. 243.

81.
Belt buckle with mounted warrior and demon

North China, 2nd–1st century B.C.
Bronze
Each: Height 2⅞ in. (7.3 cm); width 4⅜ in. (11.1 cm)
Lent by Shelby White and Leon Levy

Each of these two mirror-image plaques, which together form one belt buckle, depicts a narrative scene in which a mounted warrior grabs the hair of a pot-bellied demon that is wrestling with a dog. A second dog points at a bird hidden in the nearby

trees while standing on the canopy of a cart pulled by two reindeer. The landscape setting is indicated by leafy branches. The plaques were each lost-wax cast from a wax model formed in a clay mold.

Belt buckles comprising two plaques that have the same design, as these do, have been recovered from burials at Xichagou, in northeastern Liaoning Province,[1] and at Daodunzi, Tongxin county, Ningxia,[2] sites that can be dated numismatically from the second to the first century B.C.

Reindeer were common draft animals in the Lake Baikal region, where the Xiongnu had their summer campgrounds. The kind of cart represented here was used by the Xiongnu, as well as by other pastoral peoples, in their seasonal migrations to transport both belongings and the elderly.

The warrior brandishes a short sword in his raised hand. This familiar gesture is made also by the warrior on the Western Han belt hook, catalogue no. 130, and by the mounted swordsman on the famous mirror in the Hosakawa collection, said to have come from Jincun, Henan. These similarities would suggest that the gesture was a Han convention used to indicate armed readiness and prowess.[3]

Narrative scenes such as this one undoubtedly illustrate episodes from oral traditions. Most likely, they are translations into metal of scenes represented on textiles, which are perishable artifacts that seldom survive. The transhumant lifestyle of the nomads dictated their mode of habitation. Their tents had to be transportable and easily erected and dismantled. And instead of

walls, textile hangings served to record the heroic tales of their distant past. One such hanging, in felt, was preserved by accident in a frozen tomb at Pazyryk, in the Altai Mountains.[4] There are remarkable similarities between the motifs found on bronze plaques and those found on textiles. Even the stepped triangular design that marks the bottom border of the present plaques reflects motifs found on Pazyryk textiles.[5]

The attempt on the present buckle to integrate the figures into a landscape setting, as well as the foreshortened view of the horse and rider, can be traced back to Hellenistic traditions prevalent at oasis centers in Central Asia following the campaigns of Alexander the Great in the fourth century B.C. Foreshortened views of horses abound in Greek vase painting[6] and later appear in the pictorial traditions of Central Asia found at sites in Sogdiana, along the Silk Road.[7]

1. Sun 1960, p. 30.
2. *Kaogu xuebao* 1988, no. 3, p. 345, fig. 10.6.
3. Umehara 1937, frontis.
4. Rudenko 1970, no. 147.
5. Ibid., no. 160.
6. Bunker 1978a.
7. Azarpay 1981.

82.

Belt buckle with dragon and fantastic creature

China, 1st century B.C.–1st century A.D.
Gold inlaid with quartz
Height 2⅞ in. (7.3 cm); width 4⅝ in. (11.7 cm)
Ex coll.: Eskenazi Ltd., London

Embellished with an extraordinary design in repoussé, this gold belt buckle depicts a crested, lupine dragon entwined with a fantastic creature distinguished by a serpentine body, clawed forepaws, inlaid eyes, and thick bushy eyebrows. The creature faces the buckle's tongue, which represents a beak or nose, lending it an owl-like appearance. Below this dramatic confrontation, in the right-hand corner, is a tiny feline that emerges from behind the creature's body. The buckle tongue, once movable, is now frozen shut.

The plaque is a superbly crafted example of Han goldsmith work. The zoomorphic design was produced by hammering sheet gold over a matrix and then chasing the front surface to enhance the details. Cryptocrystalline quartz in bezels backed by cinnabar to add color is used to form the reddish eyes. The bezels have been fused to the buckle, in an ancient technique using heated glue and copper salts, an elegant way of joining gold without solder. Microscopic examination reveals the use of granulation, producing a border of granules around each

eye, some of which were displaced when the plaque was heated.

Buckles of this type have been found throughout the Far East, from Korea to Xinjiang, at sites contemporary with the Han period, but no identical example has been published.[1] Nevertheless, the wolflike dragon is similar to animals on several Thaw artifacts, such as catalogue nos. 105 and 124, suggesting a tentative Western Han date. A buckle of the same shape embellished by inlay was acquired in 1995 by the Musée Cernuschi, Paris, and given a date of the late first century B.C. to the first century A.D.[2]

1. See Bunker 1997a, figs. 1, 2, for an example found in Xinjiang.
2. *Arts Asiatiques* 50 (1995), p. 119.

83.
Belt buckle with ibex and bear

> Central Asia, 1st century B.C. – 1st century A.D.
> Gold inlaid with amber, carnelian, and turquoise
> Height 2¼ in. (5.7 cm); width 3¾ in. (9.5 cm)
> Ex coll.: James Freeman, Kyoto

An ibex attacked by a bear in a wooded setting adorns this gold belt buckle. The ibex, with sweeping ridged horns that extend to its back, has half fallen to its knees, while the bear, shown standing on its hind legs, bites the ibex's shoulder. A small leafy tree behind the ibex serves as a kind of stage prop to suggest a wooded setting. The bear's husky body is distinguished by a large piece of amber, while a smaller stone, either carnelian or chalcedony, marks the ibex's shoulder. Colored stones also accent each tree leaf. The buckle's gold tongue is fastened by a silver pin, which is now completely mineralized.

The buckle was lost-wax cast, perhaps from a wax model made by pressing a sheet of wax in a mold, and the spaces for the inlay were incorporated into the wax model. There is evidence of considerable post-cast tooling followed by chasing to sharpen the details. The entire surface is burnished. Red powder, possibly cinnabar, is seen under all the transparent cryptocrystalline stones, giving them a deeper brown color. The use of cinnabar to enhance the color of an inlay is observed on many Western Han inlaid artifacts. Fourteen rivet holes, all made by puncturing from inside, are seen on the vertical edge of the plaque.

The animal attack scene on the Thaw buckle is not typical of late Western Han designs. The small tree with tiny tear-shaped leaves is similar to trees depicted on belt plaques cast by warrior-herdsmen living far north of China, such as on catalogue nos. 64, 78, and 80. Amber inlay was not one of the materials favored by Han goldsmiths,[1] and the prominence of amber inlay on the Thaw buckle further suggests that it was not made in China but farther west. The exact location of its manufacture has not yet been determined.

1. For a brief discussion of amber in early China, see Bunker, White, and So 1999, pp. 153–54.

84.
Belt buckle with dragons

China, ca. 1st century B.C. – 1st century A.D.
Gold inlaid with semiprecious stones
Length 3½ in. (9 cm)
Private Collection

This belt buckle, with a curved slit and a movable tongue, is exquisitely worked in repoussé from a single sheet of gold. The central figure is a spirited dragon with two pointed horns, large staring eyes, and a gaping mouth. Six cubs are shown sporting amid spiraling waves. The dragon's sinuous body is densely covered with fine granulation and punctuated by circular bezels that originally held semiprecious stone inlays. The small dragons are also embellished with granules accented by colorful semiprecious stone inlays, and a band of filigree wires meanders along the border.

Three examples are known among archaeologically recovered belt buckles; one from Pyongyang, Korea, a second from Yanqi, Xinjiang Uyghur Autonomous Region, and a third

from Anxiang, Hunan Province, China.[1] The buckles from Pyongyang and Yanqi bear a remarkable resemblance to the present example in both design and in technique, showing extensive use of granulation and filigree on a repoussé surface. The buckle from Anxiang presents a more dramatic design, with a large gemstone set in the middle section of the dragon's body and a finer, denser granulation neatly arranged in rows. It also has more semiprecious stone inlays—forty-four turquoise chips in the bordering frame alone. The highly refined technique points to a more developed stage of Chinese goldwork that coincides with the Western Jin date of the tomb.

The most illustrious feature of this buckle is the granulation, the minute gold granules fused onto the buckle's surface to highlight the design and to create a brilliant texture. The technique was introduced into China in the second half of the first millennium B.C., probably the result of maritime trade with countries in South and West Asia, where the use of granulation dates from the third millennium B.C.[2] Evidence for such transmission is the presence of the granulation found on small gold fixtures excavated from the tomb of the king of Nanyue state, in Guangzhou, Guangdong Province, who was buried in the late second century B.C.[3] A gold crown decorated with fine granules found at Aluchaideng, Hanggin banner, Inner Mongolia, however, points to a northern route of transmission over the steppes, suggesting that the technique may have been brought to China by nomads, who had been a conduit between China and the West since prehistoric times.[4] By the late Western Han and early Eastern Han, Chinese goldsmiths had mastered the technique and put it to extensive use. Goldworks with fine granulation have been found at several Han sites in Hebei, Shaanxi, and Jiangsu.[5] Given the extravagant design and extraordinary craftsmanship, this buckle and those from Pyongyang and Yanqi were most probably made in the imperial workshops and then presented as gifts to the rulers of vassal states and governors of distant provinces.   ZS

1. Machida 1987, pl. 2; Han Xiang 1982, pl. 1:1; Zhongguo wenwu bao 1991, p. 1.
2. Beijing 1991, vol. 1, p. 132, vol. 2, colorpl. 19:3.
3. Ibid.
4. Tian and Guo 1986.
5. Sun Ji 1994, p. 59.

85.
Pair of belt plaques with winged horses

North China, 1st century A.D.
Gilded bronze
Height 2¾ in. (7 cm); width 4⅜ in. (11.1 cm)
The Metropolitan Museum of Art, Purchase, Fletcher Fund,
1924 (24.174.6, 7)
Published: Milleker 2000, fig. 109.

A winged horse in full gallop, its mane and tail streaming in
the wind, is cast in relief on each of these belt plaques. In the
background are distant mountains, represented by small, con-
secutive triangles, and between the horse's head and forelegs
is a narrow rectangular opening through which the belt was
once tied. The worn gilding blends with the brown patina,
lending the plaques a mellow sheen.

Two pairs of buckles that closely resemble the present
example have been found, respectively, in Zhalainoer, Inner
Mongolia, and in Laoheshen, Jilin Province, where early settlements of the Xianbei culture were also discovered.[1] A
nomadic people, the Xianbei originated in the northern range
of the Hinggan Mountains in the far northeast of China during
the first millennium B.C. Beginning in the third century A.D.,
they gradually migrated southward to the vast pasture of what
is today Inner Mongolia. They continued to move southward
in the following centuries, until eventually they controlled
all of North China, establishing the Northern Wei dynasty
in A.D. 386.

Decorative motifs on Xianbei artifacts include horses and
wild animals, which are often represented in groups. The
archaeologist Su Bai has suggested that the winged horse is
probably related to the "heavenly beast in the shape of a horse"
recorded in the *Weishu* (History of the Wei Dynasty) that led
Emperor Shengwu, one of the founders of Xianbei, in the
southward migration.[2] The archaeological data presently
available does not allow us to firmly identify the winged
horse with the "heavenly beast," but the motif is undoubtedly associated with Xianbei art and had its origin in the
Eurasian steppes.   ZS

1. *Yushu Laoheshen* 1987, pp. 63–64, figs. 58–59.
2. Su 1977a, p. 40.

86.

Belt buckle with zoomorphic motif

China, 1st–2nd century A.D.
Gold inlaid with glass and carnelian
Height 3 in. (7.6 cm); width 4⅞ in. (12.4 cm)
Ex coll.: James Freeman, Kyoto

Five animals, both real and mythological, entwined amid undulating scrolls decorate the surface of this gold buckle. The scene is in repoussé and punctuated by inlays of carnelian and colored glass. A red powder, probably cinnabar, is found in and around the stones to enhance their color. The buckle is made from a single sheet of hammered gold, and the edges have been folded back to form a raised border. The fourteen or fifteen small holes just below the border, punched from the inside, were used for nails to fasten the buckle to a support. It would appear that the entire surface was once covered with lacquer, probably one that was clear and transparent. Two textile varieties are embedded in the lacquer at the upper left, one coarser than the other. A mixture of husks and kernels, small quartz pebbles (sand), and clay is used as a backing, with lacquer as an adhesive.

Slightly later in date than catalogue no. 82, the present buckle can be dated from the first to the second century A.D. The lupine dragon is smaller, but the design of entwined animals in cloud scrolls is the same.

Although ornate gold buckles such as this one were probably made by Han craftsmen, the buckle type, without a movable tongue, was first introduced into China during the Spring and Autumn period by the pastoral peoples.[1] By the Han period, the buckle had evolved into the shape represented here and had acquired a movable tongue.

1. Wang Zengshu 1999, pp. 51–52, fig. 3.

87.
Belt buckle with stag

Southern Ossetia, Georgia, and the northern Caucasus, Russia,
1st–2nd century A.D.
Bronze or brass
Height 3 ½ in. (8.9 cm); width 3 ⅝ in. (9.2 cm)
Ex coll.: Ward & Company, Inc., New York

This square belt buckle depicts a stag with its head turned backward and its body in profile with all four legs shown. A small bird beneath the deer, also in profile, perches on one of the back hooves. The design is cast in openwork within a double-string border punctuated by a round boss at each corner. The reverse is provided with a horizontal hook and a horizontal loop on the border next to the stag's neck and rump, respectively.

The stag is highly stylized, with a wasp waist, arched neck, and prominently displayed antlers, all developments from earlier bronze belts produced in the late second to the first millennium B.C. by the Koban culture, in the north-central Caucasus.[1] Belt buckles similar to this one have been excavated in Georgia and the Caucasus, and dated from the first to the second century A.D.[2] One comparable buckle is inexplicably dated from the seventh to the fifth century B.C. in a recent catalogue,[3] and from the second century B.C. to the first century A.D. in another publication.[4]

Many examples of this type are made of cast brass, suggesting contact with the far-reaching Roman Empire, where alloys of this kind were common.[5] It is possible that such plaques were backed with colored cloth or leather, which would have shown through the openwork in the design.

1. Bunker 1981, pp. 182–84.
2. For a list of almost two hundred examples and their sources, see Curtis 1978, pp. 88–114; see also Bunker, Chatwin, and Farkas 1970, pp. 47, 57.
3. Reeder 1999, p. 109, no. 7.
4. Tokyo 1992, p. 40, no. 11.
5. The major constituents of brass are copper and zinc, with minimal amounts of lead and tin; see Curtis 1978, pp. 92–93.

88.

Belt pendant in the shape of a standing stag

Northwestern Iran, 1000–900 B.C.
Bronze
Height 4 in. (10.2 cm); length 2¾ in. (7 cm); width
with antlers 2⅜ in. (6 cm)
Ex coll.: Alberto Ulrich

This standing figure of a stag with oversized antlers is represented in the round to serve as a pendant. It is roughly cast by the lost-wax method, with perforations at the shoulder and haunch. The hooves are cloven, but the facial features are not detailed.

Small bronze stags similar to this one have been found in graves at Marlik, in the southwestern Caspian region of northwestern Iran.[1] Worn on the belt, they were attached by the perforations.[2] Similar small stag figures are included in collections around the world. Like many images of horned ungulates that embodied cultural and spiritual beliefs, their most recognizable characteristics—antlers—are distinguished by their size and beauty.[3]

1. Porada 1965, p. 102.
2. Ibid.
3. For other similar stag images in private collections, see ibid., color-pl. 125.

Whether these tinned bronze ornaments were all made at one Chinese metalworking center or several, or possibly by itinerant Chinese artisans, has yet to be determined.

1. For identification and description of this technique, see Han and Bunker 1993.
2. Bunker et al. 1997, p. 211, no. 150.
3. For the origin of these designs and similar examples, see Tian and Guo 1986, pp. 115, 117, 165, 272–73, figs. 40, 41, 81, 82, 113.

89.
Two belt ornaments with zoomorphic design

> North China and south-central Inner Mongolia, 6th–5th century B.C.
> Tinned bronze
> a. Height 2¼ in. (5.6 cm); width 1⅛ in. (3 cm)
> b. Height 2⅛ in. (5.3 cm); width 1¼ in. (3.2 cm)
> Ex coll.: Calon da Collection
> Published: So and Bunker 1995, pp. 162–63, no. 86a.

Each of these belt plaques is composed of an abstract zoomorphic design in openwork and indented scrolled lines and has a vertical loop behind the central boss. The ornaments are piece-mold cast, and the surfaces have been intentionally tinned by dipping in molten tin without the benefit of mercury.[1]

Tinning was frequently used by the pastoral tribes of northwestern China and southwestern Inner Mongolia as an emblem of status, indicating that the owner of a tinned bronze belt plaque was held in higher regard than the owner of a plain bronze one. Tinning also imitated the appearance of silver.

Belt ornaments similar to these two were cast in large sets, which have been excavated at many burial sites of herding peoples who lived throughout Northwest China beyond the Taihang Mountains during the latter half of the first millennium B.C.[2] The designs ultimately derive from zoomorphic patterns found on early Eastern Zhou carved jade ornaments.[3]

90.
Belt plaque in the shape of a crouching carnivore

> North China and south-central Inner Mongolia, 5th century B.C.
> Bronze
> Height 1⅛ in. (2.9 cm); width 2 in. (5.1 cm)
> Ex coll.: Calon da Collection

This small belt ornament takes the form of a crouching carnivore savaging the head of a herbivore, with anatomical details indicated by intaglio lines. Shown in profile, the carnivore is distinguished by large curled claws. The texture of the fur on the tail is suggested by short parallel lines, and a C-shaped arc marks the shoulder and haunch. The reverse of the plaque displays two heavy vertical loops. Mold marks around the base of the loops show clearly that the plaque and the loops were integrally cast in a multipiece mold.

Eight small belt plaques similar in design to the present example were excavated from a fifth-century burial at Fanjiayaozi, Horinger county, south-central Inner Mongolia.[1] This would suggest that the present ornament was also part of a set of plaques that served to adorn a belt.

The motif of a carnivore attacking a herbivore, here represented only by its head, first appeared in the art of the Near East and was adopted by the pastoral peoples of the Eurasian steppes during the first millennium B.C.[2] The subject appealed because it was drawn from daily life and reflected the harsh experiences of the herdsmen. The image could also confer its power and strength on the wearer. As the motif was transmitted eastward, the West Asian lion was replaced by the East Asian predator—the tiger, the wolf, the leopard—specific to each region. The convention of representing a victim by its head was anticipated on an early-first-millennium B.C. deerstone from Uusgijn üüver, Hovsgöl aimag, in northern Mongolia.[3]

1. Li Yiyou 1959a, p. 79, no. 5; Cheng 1963, p. 134.
2. Bunker et al. 1997, pp. 206–7.
3. Novgorodova 1980, p. 178.

91.
Belt plaque in the shape of a recumbent tiger

North China and south-central Inner Mongolia, 5th century B.C.
Bronze
Height 1½ in. (3.8 cm); width 2½ in. (6.4 cm)
Ex coll.: J. J. Lally & Co., New York

This openwork belt plaque depicts a recumbent tiger with its head turned back and grasping in its jaws the horns of a gazelle's head. The head of another gazelle is shown above the tiger's tail. The tiger's body is decorated with curved lines and C-shaped spirals, and its eyes and those of the gazelles' heads are indicated by unnatural-looking indented circles. A row of parallel lines lends a furry texture to the tiger's tail. The reverse displays two strong vertical loops, and mold marks around the base of the loops, similar to those on catalogue nos. 59, 140, and 141, indicate piece-mold casting.

The linear curves and angles that embellish the tiger's body may relate to patterns on Zhou bronzes of the fifth century B.C. from Liyu, Hunyuan county, northern Shanxi Province.[1] The Liyu bronzes were cast at Houma, the famous Jin state foundry in southern Shanxi, which may have served a far wider market than has hitherto been realized. Conversely, the animal-combat theme appears abruptly in the bronze vocabulary of Jin in the fifth century, suggesting that cultural influence ran both ways.[2]

There are variations of this plaque in both public and private collections.[3] The design of the present example is so pleasing that it was the model for several forgeries cast during the first half of the twentieth century. Such pieces are now easily recognizable because they are cast by the lost-wax method; authentic plaques are piece-mold cast.[4]

1. Weber 1973, p. 232.
2. So 1980a, pp. 267–68, no. 69.
3. Bunker et al. 1997, p. 207, no. 143.
4. Ibid., p. 326, no. F12.

92.
Belt plaque in the shape of a Bactrian camel with rider

Northwest China, Ningxia, 4th century B.C.
Bronze
Height 2⅛ in. (5.4 cm); width 2½ in. (6.4 cm)
Ex coll.: Michael Dunn, New York

This belt ornament is cast in the shape of a kneeling Bactrian camel with a rider sitting between the two humps. The camel's legs are folded beneath it in such a way that the bottom of one hind hoof lies atop that of the front hoof. The eye is a boss within a circular groove, and the shaggy hair is ren-

The two-humped Bactrian camel was native to Central Asia, while the habitat of the single-humped dromedary was the Arabian peninsula and North Africa.[3] Both species were eventually used in trade along the Silk Road but were unknown in China until the fourth century B.C.[4]

1. Yang and Qi 1999, p. 29, fig. 1:1, pl. 6:5.
2. So and Bunker 1995, p. 164, no. 88; Bunker et al. 1997, p. 253, no. 214.
3. Knauer 1998, p. 26.
4. Schafer 1950, pp. 176–77.

93.
Belt plaque in the shape of a standing feline

Northwest China and southwestern Inner Mongolia,
4th century B.C.
Tinned bronze
Height 2¼ in. (5.7 cm); width 4⅝ in. (11.7 cm)
Ex coll.: Michael Dunn, New York

This openwork tinned bronze belt plaque represents a standing feline savaging a fallen gazelle. The feline, enhanced by a lock of hair that extends down the neck, is represented in profile with all four legs shown. Each of the paws displays four front claws and one dewclaw, and the open mouth reveals two rounded teeth and two sharp fangs. The gazelle appears to be in a crumpled heap, its head in profile and ribbed horn pointing toward the feline's mouth. The reverse of the plaque has two tiny vertical loops, one behind the head and one behind the haunches, and the plaque was cast integrally with the loops in a multipiece mold. The front has been tinned by wiping the surface with molten tin without the aid of mercury.[1]

dered by a fringelike strip along the neck. Dressed in a long belted jacket worn over trousers, the rider is shown with his head turned back, perhaps holding a goad in his left hand, and with his right hand high on the camel's neck, presumably holding a rein attached to a nose peg. The reverse of the plaque, slightly concave and with a slanting loop that extends from one hump to the lower rump area, displays turned-up edges, suggesting that it was cast by the lost-wax process.

A plaque that depicts the identical scene was recently unearthed in Pengyang, Guyuan county, southern Ningxia.[1] As late as the twentieth century, herds of wild camels still roamed the area around Etsingol, Ningxia. Like the rider on the present example, the rider on the Pengyang plaque has a prominent nose, identifying him as a foreigner who has arrived in Northwest China via the trans-Asian Silk Road. The existence of similar plaques in mirror image suggests that the present piece once had a counterpart to complete the buckle.[2] Camels appear on a number of belt ornaments, tokens of the owner's wealth.

The artisans who designed plaques representing camels obviously knew their subject well. Camels grind and regurgitate their food, so that it is impossible to place a bit in their mouths as one would with a horse; thus, no bridle is used, and no bridle is represented on the plaque. Instead, a peg is inserted in one nostril, with a single rein attached to it, by which the camel is led. Camels are also notoriously uncooperative and must be encouraged to move with a goad, which the rider on the present plaque may have in his left hand.

A silver plaque excavated at Shihuigou, Eijin Horo banner, southwestern Inner Mongolia, shows nearly the same figures, suggesting that the present example can be associated with the nomadic peoples living in that area.[2] Even the ear on the Shihuigou plaque is spiraled. The entire composition, including the spiral treatment of the ear, can be traced back to the tigers carved on a wooden coffin from Bashadar, in the Altai Mountains of southern Siberia (fig. 32).

1. On this technique, see Han and Bunker 1993.
2. *Neimenggu wenwu kaogu* 1992, no. 1–2, p. 92, fig. 1.5; Takahama and Hatakeyama 1997, pl. 196.

94.
Belt plaque in the shape of a standing wolf

Northwest China, 4th century B.C.
Tinned bronze
Height 2½ in. (6.4 cm); width 4½ in. (11.4 cm)
Ex coll.: J. J. Lally & Co., New York

This bronze belt plaque shows a standing wolf about to annihilate a doe that it holds in its raised left forepaw. The doe's head appears under the wolf's open jaws, which reveal four teeth and two fangs about to sink into the doe's succulent

flesh. The doe's hindquarters, underneath the wolf's left forepaw, are twisted 180 degrees. A tiny wolf pup appears on the ground line between the wolf's front and back legs. The wolf's ear is a distinctive comma shape, and its pelt is marked by a variety of linear patterns that include braided bands, scrolls, dots, and scales. Both the crest and the tail terminate in an eared raptor's head. Shiny patches occur here and there, evidence that the piece was intentionally tinned. A loop with a projecting hook is tangent to the wolf's muzzle, and a vertical loop is placed behind the haunches. The plaque has thick, turned-over edges visible on the reverse, indicating that it was cast by the indirect lost-wax method. In some areas, the joins between sections of the wax model are still visible. It can also be seen that the openings in the plaque were carved through from the front of the wax model.

The plaque originally had a matching mirror-image plate, similar to an example currently in a Swiss collection, that would have completed the buckle.[1] A comparable plaque dating from the fourth century B.C. was discovered in the vicinity of Guyuan county, southern Ningxia.[2] The textured pelt on the present plaque is related to spiral designs found on a bone carving also excavated in Guyuan[3] and to appliqué work from fourth-century B.C. tombs at Pazyryk, in the Altai Mountains. The convention of inverting the victim's hindquarters is seen in the art of southern Siberia, at both Bashadar and

Pazyryk.[4] The rounded form of the teeth derives from a wood-carving tradition, such as that seen on wooden artifacts from Bashadar and Pazyryk,[5] suggesting a distant connection between the Qingyang region and the Altai.[6]

The raptors'-head appendages associate this wolf with the mythological animals tattooed on the man from kurgan 2 at Pazyryk (fig. 37), and the iconography appears on artifacts from Northwest China, in southern Ningxia and the Qingyang region of southeastern Gansu during the second half of the fourth century B.C. It also occurs later, around the late fourth to the third century B.C., in the Ordos Desert region.[7]

1. So and Bunker 1995, p. 131, no. 50. For another example, see Takahama and Hatakeyama 1997, no. 191.
2. Yan and Li 1992, p. 574, fig. 1:10, pl. 8:4.
3. *Kaogu xuebao* 1993, no. 1, p. 7, fig. 5:7–10.
4. Rudenko 1970, pp. 268–69, pl. 139L, fig. 136.
5. Ibid., pl. 138B.
6. Haskins 1988; Rudenko 1970, pp. 268–69, fig. 136.
7. Bunker 1992b, passim.

95.
Belt plaque in the shape of a standing carnivore

Northwest China, 4th century B.C.
Bronze
Height 2 ¾ in. (7 cm); width 4 ¾ in. (12.1 cm)
Ex coll.: J. J. Lally & Co., New York

This openwork belt plaque takes the form of a standing carnivore with an upswept tail. The pointed ear and long muzzle suggest a wolf, a predator often represented on non-Chinese artifacts from Northwest China. Each paw displays four prominent claws that curve forward and a dewclaw that curves in the opposite direction. The pointed ear is an inverted heart, and C-shaped volutes mark the legs and body. The slightly open jaws reveal fangs and teeth with which the carnivore grips a serpentine zoomorph, and a mass of squirming two-legged creatures surrounds the carnivore's legs. Projecting from the front is a hook adjacent to a square perforation in the carnivore's shoulder. The reverse displays a mushroom-shaped stud behind the rump. The plaque was cast by the lost-wax process, and joins in the wax are reproduced in the metal on the back.

The plaque depicts a totally Sinicized version of an animal-combat scene. Originally, it was the left-hand plaque of a mirror-image pair that together constituted one complete buckle.

Plaques of the same shape and similar style were discovered on the Qingyang plateau in southeastern Gansu Province.[1] Additional examples without archaeological provenience are included in numerous collections. A plaque in the Arthur M. Sackler Gallery, Washington, D.C., is nearly identical to the present one.[2]

Like catalogue nos. 62 and 63, this plaque was probably made by Chinese craftsmen specifically for steppe consumption. Such buckles do not appear as personal ornaments in Chinese burials.

1. Liu and Xu 1988, p. 420, fig. 17:3, pl. 4:3, p. 421, fig. 18:5, pl. 4:1.
2. Bunker et al. 1997, p. 244, no. 200.

96.
Belt plaque with mythological creature

Northwest China, ca. 3rd century B.C.
Gilded silver
Height 5 in. (12.7 cm); width 2 in. (5.1 cm)
The Metropolitan Museum of Art, Purchase, Rogers Fund, 1918 (18.43.8)
Published: Jacobson 1985, p. 138; Bunker 1989, pp. 52–59; Milleker 2000, fig. 105.

This openwork plaque features a mythological animal whose hindquarters are rotated 180 degrees. The animal has a horse-like head, body, and hooves, but a beaked muzzle and long antlers. Raptors' heads that grow out of the tail and antlers join with the head and hind legs, forming the rectangular frame, and the fluid lines and modeling that define the physical attributes provide a sense of volume. The surface of the plaque, particularly near the head, antlers, and tail, is moderately corroded, but the flank and hindquarters are largely intact and retain traces of gold, indicating that the metal was once extensively mercury gilded. On the back are three loops, one behind the head and two behind the haunches and hind legs.[1]

A striking image, this composite creature exemplifies the transmission of a motif that the nomads brought from the shores of the Black Sea to the northern border of China in the last centuries of the first millennium B.C. It appears to have evolved from the image of a stag and gradually acquired other attributes. By the fifth century B.C., it had emerged in Scythian art as an ungulate with a prominent beak and elaborate antler tines from which sprout raptors' heads. The earliest evidence of this image in North China is an ornament of a headdress discovered at a mid- to late Warring States site at Nalin'gaotu, Shaanxi Province, where the Chinese had frequent contact with the pastoral peoples.[2] The motif continued in the artistic vocabulary of the area in the following centuries until the Western Han dynasty, as evidenced by a number of ornamental plaques found in North China and Inner Mongolia. The dramatic twist of the animal's hindquarters was a far-reaching characteristic, eventually making its way to the heartland of China. It is found on the cover of a lacquer box, a typical Chinese product, in a Chu tomb of the third century B.C., in Changsha, Hunan Province.[3]   ZS

1. Recent tests have confirmed the antiquity of this buckle. X-ray fluorescence (XRF) analysis indicates that the metal was refined by the traditional method of cupellation and the corrosion on the surface formed under archaeological conditions. Microscopic examination at high magnification reveals fine copper precipitates and disruption at the silver grain boundaries, which are typical of copper-bearing silver of archaeological age. This buckle was published previously as a forgery (Bunker 1989).
2. Dai and Sun 1983.
3. *Changsha Chu mu* 2000, pp. 362–63, fig. 294.

97.
Belt plaque in the shape of a tiger and a kulan

> Northwest China, 3rd century B.C.
> Bronze
> Height 2 ¼ in. (5.7 cm); width 3 ¾ in. (9.3 cm)
> Ex coll.: J. J. Lally & Co., New York

This openwork belt plaque shows the profile image of a tiger walking off with its victim, a kulan, in its jaws. The four paws have powerful arched claws, and the pelt is marked by raised chevrons. Both the eye and the ear are represented by a raised oval. The tail hangs down and terminates in an inward curl.

The kulan is shown hanging limply from the tiger's grasp, its tongue lolling out of its mouth. Its body is represented—unnaturally—in a conventional recumbent pose with folded legs. Visible evidence that the openwork holes were cut through the wax model from the front and a thickened, turned-over rim on the reverse are the result of lost-wax casting.

The plaque is the wearer's left-hand half of a mirror-image pair that originally constituted a complete belt buckle. No identical buckle has been found in archaeological context, but plaques that illustrate the same scene have been excavated at Guoxianyaozi, Liangcheng county, south-central Inner Mongolia,[1] and in Jianghecun, near Yanglang, southern Ningxia.[2] The Guoxianyaozi example even depicts the same victim in the same incongruous leg pose. A mirror-image version of the present plaque was collected in the western outskirts of Xi'an, Shaanxi Province.[3] These discoveries suggest that the present example can be associated with the pastoral nomads of the northwestern frontier of China during the third century B.C.

1. Bunker et al. 1997, p. 61, fig. A83.
2. Zhong 1978, p. 87.
3. Wang Changqi 1991, p. 8, fig. 2:2.

98.
Belt plaque in the shape of a wild boar

> Northwest China, 3rd–2nd century B.C.
> Gilded bronze
> Height 2¾ in. (7 cm); width 4½ in. (11.4 cm)
> Ex coll.: Eskenazi Ltd., London

This gilded bronze plaque represents a standing wild boar shown in profile. The reverse is concave and displays two pairs of tiny horizontal loops, one behind the haunch and the other behind the head. The plaque was cast by the lost-wax process, with the perforations in the design cut through the wax model from the front. The loops were formed by two pieces of wax attached to one another, and integrally cast with the plaque, which was then mercury gilded, creating a new surface enrichment that was often employed to enhance belt ornaments during the third century B.C.[1]

To date, no identical plaque has been found in archaeological context, but the Palace Museum, Beijing, owns a mirror-image pair.[2] A single plaque in the collection of George Ortiz is the mirror image of the present example and may originally have been its mate.[3]

1. For the introduction of mercury gilding into the ancient Chinese and northern pastoral world, see Bunker 1994b, pp. 35–36, 47–48.
2. *Gugong Bowuyuan yuan kan,* no. 1 (1993), p. 20, fig. 18.
3. Ortiz 1994, no. 218.

99.
Pair of belt plaques with ungulate and ram

North China, 3rd–2nd century B.C.
Bronze
Each: Height 1⅞ in. (4.8 cm); width 4 in. (10 cm)
Ex coll.: J. J. Lally & Co., New York

Each of these two mirror-image belt plaques depicts a mythological ungulate with its hindquarters twisted 180 degrees and followed by a half-crouching ram. The series of raptors' heads at the top border append to the tips of the ungulate's antlers. Each plaque originally had two vertical loops soldered onto the reverse, although one plaque is now missing a loop. The plaques are extremely heavy and were probably piece-mold cast.

The wearer's left-hand plaque is not perforated, which indicates that the two plaques do not form a buckle. Instead, they must have served as additional plaques to enrich a warrior-herdsman's belt. On one plaque, textile fragments

are still visible in the corrosion on the back and up the edge, suggesting either that the original belt was made of cloth or that the plaques were wrapped in cloth when buried.

No plaques with identical scenes are known, but both the ungulate and ram figures are represented in similar designs on other belt ornaments cast between the third and the first century B.C., when the Xiongnu were the dominant herding people on China's northern frontier.[1]

1. Bunker et al. 1997, p. 79, fig. A111 (printed from a reversed negative), and cat. no. 76.

100.

Belt plaque with horse and wolf

North China, 3rd – 2nd century B.C.
Bronze
Height 1 ¾ in. (4.4 cm); width 3 ¼ in. (8.3 cm)
Ex coll.: Joseph G. Gerena Fine Art, New York

The animal combat on this belt plaque shows a recumbent horse being attacked by a wolf. The scene is shown within a rectangular frame with a simulated twisted rope border, and striations suggesting fur mark the horse's body. The wolf is represented only by its head and forepaws, with which it grasps the horse's neck and rump. The ornament appears to have been piece-mold cast, with the two vertical squared loops on the reverse soldered on afterward. Originally, it was the right-hand counterpart of a mirror-image pair that together formed one belt buckle.

A plaque in the British Museum, London, is the mirror image of the Thaw plaque and displays a perforation in the horse's shoulder that is part of the fastening device.[1] A similar recumbent horse image occurs among the zoomorphic representations on a pair of plaques in the Therese and Erwin Harris collection.[2]

A bone belt plaque of an earlier date, in the shape of a recumbent horse from Sagli-Bazhi II in western Tuva, has curvilinear carved shoulder and haunch markings that accentuate the musculature, which is not unlike the patterns on the Harris and Thaw horses.[3] These similarities again serve to demonstrate how the artistic motifs and visual symbolism of the pastoral peoples were transmitted from one geographic region to another. Whether this transmission was the result of migration, warfare, or commercial interaction must be determined in each case.

1. Rawson 1978, pl. 5a.
2. So and Bunker 1995, pp. 137–38, no. 56.
3. Aruz 2000, no. 197.

101.

Belt plaque in the shape of a kneeling horse

North China, 3rd – 1st century B.C.
Silver
Height 3 ⅛ in. (8.1 cm); width 5 ¾ in. (14.5 cm)
The Metropolitan Museum of Art, Gift of Ernest Erickson Foundation Inc. 1985 (1985.214.78)
Published: Bunker 1970, no. 116; Hearn 1987, p. 62; Watt 1990, p. 29, ill. p. 30; Milleker 2000, fig. 106.

This handsome silver plaque takes the form of a kneeling horse. While the well-modeled shoulders and haunches display its brawny strength, the pointed ears, staring eyes, and large, flared nostrils describe its lively spirit. The trimmed mane is represented by a row of small rectangles, and the curved tail, indicated by sunken lines, is tucked between the hind legs. The articulated joints and naturalistically modeled torso are characteristic of Chinese metalwork of the third through the first century B.C., but the teardrop-shaped hooves and ears denote the artistic influence of Central Asia. The concave back of the plaque bears the imprint of a textile pattern, the result of using the lost-wax lost-textile technique in the manufacturing process. Developed for the casting of thin plaques, this technique involved the use of fabric to reinforce the wax model.

For the pastoral peoples, the horse was not only the principal means of transportation but a dependable partner in life on the steppes. Their love for the horse is found in its representation on weapons, clothing, and everyday utensils. Ornament plaques decorated with the image of horses are frequently encountered at archaeological sites in North and Northwest China. A bronze plaque with a similar image of a kneeling horse was excavated from a second-to-first century B.C. tomb at Tongxin county, Ningxia, in 1985,[1] and a silver plaque in the British Museum, London, as well as a gilded bronze plaque in the Museum für Ostasiatische Kunst, Berlin, are nearly mirror images of the present example.[2]   ZS

1. *Kaogu xuebao* 1988, no. 3.
2. Rawson 1980, colorpl. 9; Ragué 1970, no. 10.

102.

Two belt plaques with dragon and tortoises

North China, 2nd century B.C.
Gilded bronze
Each: Height 1 ¾ in. (4.4 cm); width 3 ½ in. (8.9 cm)
Ex coll.: Eskenazi Ltd., London; J. J. Lally & Co., New York;
Calon da Collection
Published: So and Bunker 1995, p. 158, no. 80.

An openwork design showing a large figure-eight-shaped dragon wrapped around two tortoises within a simulated rope border constitutes each of these two rectangular plaques. The plaques are not a pair. Rather, each one is the wearer's left-hand plaque of a complete buckle, indicated by the presence on each plaque of an aperture on the edge; on a buckle pair, only one is required. The plaques were cast by the lost-wax process, with loops soldered onto the back.

Many plaques with this design have been excavated from the tombs of local pastoral peoples at Daodunzi, Tongxin county, Ningxia.[1] They have also been unearthed among the grave goods of the king of Nanyue in Guangzhou, Guangdong.[2]

The dragon has a lupine head seen in profile and is startlingly similar to dragons on many Han artifacts,[3] suggesting that some contact with the Eurasian steppe world may have stimulated the development of the Han image.[4] The dragon with a lupine head is comparable to another openwork belt plaque of a type known to have been cast in the north, where in the artistic vocabulary of the region the wolf played a prominent role as a predator. (See also cat. no. 105.)

1. Bunker et al. 1997, p. 83, fig. A123.
2. Beijing 1991, colorpl. 19.1 (right), pl. 96.1, drawing on p. 166, fig. 104.1.
3. Discussed in Rawson and Bunker 1990, p. 303.
4. So and Bunker 1995, pp. 157–58.

103.
Belt plaque with feline and ram

North China, 2nd century B.C.
Gilded bronze
Height 2 in. (5.1 cm); width 4 in. (10.2 cm)
Ex coll.: Michael Dunn, New York

An animal-combat scene between a feline and a ram is depicted on this single belt plaque, which originally must have had a mirror-image mate. The drama of the combat has been suppressed in favor of a pleasing, balanced design. The hindquarters of both protagonists are gracefully twisted 180 degrees, and their tails terminate in eared raptors' heads. Like many other plaques cast during the second century B.C., curved striated enclosures mark the animals' bodies. The reverse is completely flat and displays two soldered vertical attachment loops. The plaque is quite heavy and was probably piece-mold cast.

Numerous plaques with similar scenes are found in several collections. One pair was excavated in a non-Chinese ceme-tery at Daodunzi, Tongxin county, Ningxia,[1] and another was discovered among the exotica in the tomb of the king of Nan-yue in Guangzhou, Guangdong.[2] The raptor's tail terminals relate this scene to the mythology that governs the symbolism on several other plaques in the Thaw collection. The striations are not unlike the markings on a bone cylinder, for example (cat. no. 159), suggesting that such texturing first developed in carving or leatherwork. As with other plaques discussed in this section, the animal-combat scene is enclosed within an imitation rope frame.

1. *Kaogu xuebao* 1988, no. 3, p. 344, fig. 9:12.
2. Huang 1996, p. 55, fig. 1.

104.
Belt plaque with fighting stallions

Southern Siberia, 2nd century B.C.
Bronze
Height 2¼ in. (5.7 cm); width 5 in. (12.7 cm)
Ex coll.: J. J. Lally & Co., New York

This openwork belt plaque depicts two fighting, rut-crazed stallions. They are identified as Przewalski horses by their short, upright manes. A leafy setting at the top and sunken rectangles along the bottom edge and sides serve to frame the scene. The shoulder of each stallion is marked by a tear-shaped depression, and similar sunken areas mark the ears, nostrils, hooves, and leaves. The plaque was originally one of a pair, with identical scenes that together formed a complete belt buckle. It has no hook on the front, which indicates that it was worn on the right-hand side. The reverse is concave and has no loops. The plaque was cast by the indirect lost-wax process.

An earlier version of this scene was excavated in eastern Mongolia.[1] The Mongolian plaque shows a branching, leafy tree behind the two stallions; the tree has been reduced to just a few leaves on the present example, which must be slightly later in date. Numerous examples of this plaque have been found throughout Buryatia and southern Siberia in graves asso-

ciated with the Xiongnu.[2] One example was also found in eastern Xinjiang,[3] and many other similar examples are in both private and public collections.[4]

The composition of this particular scene of combat, in which the stallion on the right bites the leg of the horse on the left, which in turn bites the shoulder of the stallion, appears to have developed many centuries earlier, when it portrayed two fighting camels, a motif that has been found on gold plaques excavated from a fourth-century B.C. kurgan in Filippovka, southern Russia.[5]

1. Askarov, Volkov, and Ser-Odjav 1992, p. 464, fig. 1:c.
2. Devlet 1980, pp. 44–46; Miniaev 1996, p. 75; Bunker et al. 1997, pp. 261–62, nos. 224, 225.
3. Wang Binghua 1986, fig. 2:1, where the two animals are incorrectly identified as a boar and a horse.
4. So and Bunker 1995, p. 95, no. 8.
5. Aruz 2000, p. 160, no. 98.

105.
Belt plaque with tigers and dragon

Mongolia and eastern Siberia, 2nd century B.C.
Bronze
Height 2⅝ in. (6.7 cm); width 5½ in. (14 cm)
Ex coll.: Tony Anninos, California

Two fierce tigers attacking a dragon with a horned, lupine head are shown on this openwork rectangular belt plaque. The scene is framed by a series of tear-shaped depressions. The plaque was cast from a wax model formed in a two-piece mold, indicated by pressure marks on the reverse, which is slightly concave and lacks attachment loops. The alloy is copper with small quantities of lead and a minimal amount of arsenic, an alloy characteristic of plaques found in Mongolia and Siberia.[1]

A mirror-image pair of plaques, each of which carries the same design as the present example, was excavated from a second-century B.C. grave in a Xiongnu cemetery at Ivolga, near Lake Baikal, in Buryatia, a region thought to be the summer camping grounds of the Xiongnu.[2] The plaques were found at the waist of a female and thought to be clan insignia. All three plaques are also identical to the nephrite plaque in a private collection, catalogue no. 106.

The lupine-headed dragon appears to have been important in the iconography of the Xiongnu, as it occurs in a variety of compositions, including two plaques identical to catalogue no. 102 that were excavated at Daodunzi, Tongxin county, Ningxia.[3] The Xiongnu dragon may be one antecedent of the elongated dragon so popular in China during the Han dynasty.[4] A strikingly similar dragon occurs on certain Western Han incense burners.[5]

A source for the design of these dragon-and-tiger combat plaques is provided by an earlier pair of gold plaques discovered in a tomb at Szidorovka, near Omsk, western Siberia, a site dated from the late third to the second century B.C.[6] The three plaques carry the same scene; the only difference between them is that the gold plaques are solid, not openwork, and are inlaid with turquoise, coral, and amber (fig. 45). The gold examples were found at the waist of a thirty- to thirty-five-year-old man of mixed Europoid-Mongoloid type.

This stunning new find clearly demonstrates that a tradition of inlay work lies behind the tear-shaped cells that mark the tigers' pelts and the border of the present example, as well as

many other similar plaques. Another important discovery is the identification of a woven pattern on the back of the Szidorovka gold plaques, indicating that they were cast by the lost-wax and lost-textile process.[7]

1. Devlet 1980, pp. 32–33, plaque nos. 43–45.
2. Davydova 1971, p. 96.
3. Bunker et al. 1997, p. 83, fig. A123.
4. For a discussion of this possibility, see Rudenko 1958, pp. 119–21; and So and Bunker 1995, p. 78.
5. Lally 1986, no. 13.
6. Matiushchenko and Tataurova 1997, p. 148, fig. 27; Bunker et al. 1997, p. 88.
7. M.P. Zavitukhina, The State Hermitage, St. Petersburg, letter to author, 1998.

106.
Belt plaque with tigers and dragon

Eastern Siberia, 2nd century B.C.
Nephrite
Height 2⅞ in. (7.3 cm); width 6½ in. (16.4 cm)
Private Collection
Published: Watt 1980, p. 38, no. 6; Keverne 1991, chap. 3, no. 26; Rawson 1995, p. 311, no. 23:1; Bunker et al. 1997, pp. 274–75, no. 242.

A sinuous dragon with a horned, wolflike head being attacked by two fierce tigers is depicted on this openwork nephrite plaque. The dragon's body is marked by longitudinal parallel grooves, and the tigers' bodies have irregular indented tear shapes within raised rims that suggest a striped pelt. More regular tear-shaped marks embellish the rectangular frame. Like the other nephrite plaque in the exhibition (cat. no. 114), this one may once have been fitted into something of metal, with the two semicircular cuts at either edge used as an attachment device. A reddish substance identified as cinnabar is visible in some of the indented areas.

The combat scene is virtually identical to that on a belt buckle excavated from the second-century B.C. Xiongnu cemetery in Ivolga, Buryatia, and to catalogue no. 105.

The plaque is carved from a dark green nephrite of a type found in Mongolia and eastern Siberia, suggesting that it was carved locally rather than in China.[1] It has not been determined whether the Xiongnu had developed the intricate technique of carving nephrite, but Chinese artisans are known to have been employed at the Xiongnu northern stronghold in Ivolga, and they may well have carved this plaque. That it may have been carved in China does not seem plausible, since plaques with this design have never been found there or in the nearby frontier regions.

1. *Mongol Messenger,* June 12, 1996, p. 6, and personal communication from Janet Roberts when she was working in Irkutsk.

107.
Belt plaque with dragon

North China, 2nd century B.C.
Gilded bronze
Height 2 ⅛ in. (5.4 cm); width 3 ⅝ in. (9.2 cm)
Ex coll.: Throckmorton Fine Art, Inc., New York

A feline dragon, its body twisted into a figure eight, is shown on the surface of this belt plaque. Originally one of a mirror-image pair that together formed a complete belt buckle, it is rectangular in shape, with a simulated double-rope border. A loop tangent to the left side is part of the closure device, and two vertical loops that project from the back are provided for attachment. The plaque was cast by the lost-wax process and then mercury gilded, and the loops appear to be soldered on.

The plaque is an interesting mixture of northern and Chinese elements. Buckles formed by two mirror-image plaques are an invention of the eastern Eurasian steppes, while the feline dragon is an auspicious Han Chinese motif. It is depicted on many Western Han artifacts, especially jades dating to the second and first centuries B.C.[1] Such an unusual combination suggests that the buckle may have been made for elite Chinese consumption, perhaps for someone with a taste for northern exotica.[2]

1. Rawson 1995, pp. 301–2, nos. 21:14, 21:16.
2. See So and Bunker 1995, chap. 5.

108.
Two belt plaques with three ibex

Northwest China, 2nd – 1st century B.C.

Bronze

Each: Height 2⅝ in. (6.7 cm); width 5½ in. (13.9 cm)

Ex coll.: Eskenazi Ltd., London

Published: Hôtel Drouot 1996, no. 38.

Each of these openwork belt buckles takes the form of two frontal ibex in a wooded setting, their bodies in profile and the foreleg of each raised and hooked over a branch or tree trunk. Between the two ibex stands a third, shown frontally. One tree rises behind each flanking ibex, and two trees, one on either side of the plaque, serve as the frame. The slightly concave reverse has no attachment loops. Each plaque was cast by the lost-wax process from a wax model formed in a mold.

The two plaques do not constitute one complete belt buckle. Rather, they are both left-hand plaques belonging to different buckles. Each has the characteristic curved hook that protrudes from the right side of the plaque, although the hook on the right plaque has been filed off.

No plaque with three ibex has been archaeologically excavated, but such ornaments are included in several private collections.[1] A similar plaque with only two ibex shown was unearthed from a Xiongnu tomb at Lijiataozi, Tongxin county, Ningxia, along with *wuzhu* coins of a type not minted before 118 B.C.[2] Plaques such as the present examples reflect the new emphasis on real animals in naturalistic settings that characterizes the design of belt ornaments made during the late first millennium B.C. for the Xiongnu.

1. Potratz 1963, no. 67; Artamonov 1973, p. 158, no. 209; Hôtel Drouot 1996, no. 38; Bunker et al. 1997, p. 265, no. 231.
2. *Kaogu yu wenwu* 1988, no. 3, p. 19, fig. 6:2.

109.
Plaque in the shape of a grazing kulan

> Northwest China, 2nd–1st century B.C.
> Gold
> Height 1 ⅜ in. (3.5 cm); width 1 ¾ in. (4.3 cm)
> Ex coll.: Michael Dunn, New York

This sensitively designed and beautifully cast openwork gold plaque is made in the shape of a grazing kulan shown in profile. Naturalistically represented, it has an almond-shaped eye, articulated muscles, and a long tail marked by ridges. The reverse has two flat attachment straps behind the shoulder and haunches, and there is ample evidence of wear. The plaque was cast by the lost-wax process.

No gold plaques similar to this one have been excavated, but a bronze example that is nearly identical in shape was discovered in a Xiongnu grave at Daodunzi, Tongxin county, Ningxia.[1] Many plaques that depict two confronted grazing horses in a similar pose have been discovered in the Minusinsk region of southern Siberia, an area that was once occupied by the Xiongnu during their period of expansion in the last few centuries of the first millennium B.C.[2]

1. Duan 1995, p. 54, no. 169.
2. Devlet 1980, p. 43.

110.
Plaque in the shape of a grazing ibex

> Eastern Siberia and Mongolia, 2nd–1st century B.C.
> Gold
> Height 1 in. (2.5 cm); width 1 ½ in. (3.8 cm)
> Ex coll.: Joseph G. Gerena Fine Art, New York

This small openwork plaque takes the form of a grazing ibex. Characterized by arching ridged horns, a beard, and a conventionalized round eye, the ibex is shown with its body in profile and with all four legs represented. Tiny triangular cells, perhaps derived from an earlier inlay tradition, mark the hooves. There are no attachment loops on the reverse, but the circular aperture in the shoulder and the loop formed by the short tail perhaps served the same purpose. The plaque was made by casting and hammering.

Numerous plaques cast in bronze in a shape similar to this one have been found throughout Transbaikal, Buryatia, and Mongolia,[1] where they can be associated with the Xiongnu. The Ordos Desert attribution frequently given to such plaques cannot be confirmed.[2]

1. Tsultem 1987, fig. 1; Bunker et al. 1997, p. 277.
2. Andersson 1932, pl. 22.7; Rudenko 1969, fig. 54:f.

1 1 1.
Belt plaque with Bactrian camel

> North China, 2nd – 1st century B.C.
> Gilded bronze
> Height 2¼ in. (5.7 cm); width 3½ in. (8.9 cm)
> Ex coll.: Ariadne Galleries, Inc., New York

A Bactrian camel shown in a half-crouching position within a simulated rope frame constitutes this openwork belt plaque. Highly naturalistic, the representation includes such anatomical details as fur and a shaggy mane. The horns of a bovine mask placed sideways under the camel's head form an open vertical slot that is part of the fastening device. On the reverse is a vertical loop behind the camel's rump that appears to be soldered on. The plaque is lost-wax cast from a wax model formed in a mold.

No plaques similar to this one have been found in archaeological context. The mask is far more Chinese than steppe in conception. The rounded ridges at the base of the horns are characteristic features of small bovine-headed ornaments found in elite Western Han tombs, such as those in Mancheng, Hebei Province,[1] and Guangzhou, Guangdong Province.[2] These similarities suggest that the plaque was made for the northern market at a Han metalworking center but not based on northern imagery.[3]

1. Beijing 1980a, vol. 1, p. 205, fig. 138:9.
2. Beijing 1991, vol. 1, p. 100, fig. 17:8, vol. 2, pl. 54:3.
3. Bunker et al. 1997, pp. 294–95, no. 270.

1 1 2.
Casting model

> North China, 2nd – 1st century B.C.
> Clay
> Height 3 in. (7.6 cm); width 4 in. (10.2 cm)
> The Metropolitan Museum of Art, Rogers Fund, 1918 (18.43.2)
> Published: So and Bunker 1995, pp. 142–43, no. 62; Milleker 2000, fig. 108.

A crouching camel in high relief within a herringbone-patterned frame is represented on this clay casting model. Such models were used by artisans to form mother molds in which wax models were made for use in the lost-wax process. The models could be used to mass-produce bronze plaques and could be made of metal, clay, or stone, such as a steatite example in the British Museum, London.[1]

Few casting models have survived, or they are not recognized as such,[2] which makes the existence of this plaque crucial to our understanding of China's ancient casting processes. A few casting models are found in Western museum collections, but, to date, no similar models have been published in Chinese excavation reports.[3]

1. Rawson 1995, p. 311, fig. 1. The date given of fourth to third century B.C. is too early for the animal-combat scene portrayed, which has a metal counterpart excavated at Xichagou, Xifeng county, Liaoning, and is dated numismatically no earlier than the second century B.C.; for a discussion of this plaque, see Bunker et al. 1997, p. 260, no. 222.
2. Rawson 1995, p. 311, fig. 1. The function of the British Museum steatite model was not understood when it was published in 1995.
3. See So and Bunker 1995, p. 143, fig. 62.1, for an example in the Freer Gallery of Art, Washington, D.C. (16.8).

113.
Belt plaque with confronted bovines

> Southern Siberia, 2nd–1st century B.C.
> Bronze
> Height 2⅛ in. (5.4 cm); width 4⅝ in. (11.7 cm)
> Ex coll.: Michael Dunn, New York

This openwork belt plaque depicts two bovines with frontal heads and profile bodies showing all four legs and set within a narrow rectangular frame. The reverse is slightly concave and without loops. The alloy has small amounts of tin, arsenic, and lead, and the plaque was cast by the lost-wax process, while the wax model was probably formed in a two-piece mold.

Several versions of this plaque have been found throughout North China, Mongolia, and southern Siberia, wherever the Xiongnu expanded their rule during the early Western Han. One example was excavated at Xichagou, Xifeng county, Liaoning Province,[1] and others at sites in southern Siberia.[2] The presence of arsenic in the alloy is characteristic of plaques cast in southern Siberia.[3]

1. Sun 1957, p. 53.
2. Devlet 1980, pls. 1–6.
3. Bunker et al. 1997, p. 270.

114.
Belt plaque with ox

> North China, 2nd–1st century B.C.
> Nephrite and gilded bronze
> Height 1¾ in. (4.5 cm); width 2⅞ in. (7.2 cm)
> Private Collection
> Published: Rawson 1995, pp. 312–13, no. 23:3.

Carved with the figure of an ox, this openwork nephrite plaque is set within a gilded bronze frame embellished with two sinuous felines whose frontal masks appear at opposite corners. The frame was made expressly to fit the irregular shape of the plaque. The back of the piece is flat and displays two vertical loops for attachment.

The figure of the ox is very similar to the oxen on catalogue no. 65, two mirror-image belt plaques in the Thaw collection. The present plaque, in a private collection, is an excellent illustration of an exotic steppe motif's having been adopted as a *xiangrui* (an auspicious omen) by the Chinese during the Western Han dynasty and then carefully Sinicized by enclosing it within a typically Chinese gilded bronze frame.

With its blend of steppe and Chinese motifs, this ornament clearly demonstrates the close cultural contact between the herding and the agricultural worlds that had developed by the end of the third century B.C. Whether it was intended to be worn by an elite Chinese antiquarian with a taste for the exotic or was an elaborate gift for an elite Xiongnu herdsman cannot be determined, but it is an important visual reminder of the intercultural relationship that existed between the two peoples.

115.
Belt plaque with fallen stag

> Western Eurasia, 2nd–1st century B.C.
> Gold inlaid with semiprecious stones
> Height 3 in. (7.6 cm); width 4⅝ in. (11.7 cm)
> Lent by Shelby White and Leon Levy

This gold openwork belt plaque depicts an animal-combat scene in which a raptor and a feline savage a fallen stag. The animals' bodies and the tear shapes on the frame are accented with turquoise inlays placed in bezels, and the eyes are perhaps inlaid with opaque calcite or shell. The buckle was formed by casting and hammering, and the edges appear to have been chisel cut. The reverse displays the remains of four attachment loops, one in each corner, that were attached by soldering.

The palmate-shaped antlers of the stag identify it as a fallow deer, a species known to have inhabited Northwest Asia in antiquity. A similar animal-combat scene, with the same cast of zoomorphs, decorates an ointment container excavated at Novocherkassk, a major Sarmatian site in the Rostov region of southern Russia, dated to the second century B.C.[1] The raptors on both the present plaque, in the Shelby White and Leon Levy collection, and the Novocherkassk container have round

birds' eyes and should thus technically be identified as eagles rather than as mythological griffins, which traditionally had almond-shaped eyes.[2]

The White–Levy plaque exemplifies the so-called Sarmatian polychrome style, which preceded and may have influenced the development of the superb plaques and buckles produced during the Migration period (ca. A.D. 400–800) throughout most of Europe.

1. Schiltz 1995, pp. 53, 57, no. 80.
2. Mayor 1994.

116.
Belt plaque with animals in a landscape

North China, 1st century B.C.
Gilded bronze
Height 2¼ in. (5.7 cm); width 4⅜ in. (11.1 cm)
Ex coll.: Ariadne Galleries, Inc., New York

A complex landscape scene is shown on this gilded bronze plaque. Two camels stride past Asian elms and mountains, behind which are six wild boars, three facing right and three facing left. Two horses are seen diving headfirst down the sides of the plaque, and the entire scene is enclosed within a simulated rope border. The reverse displays two vertical loops and the characteristic woven pattern resulting from the lost-wax and lost-textile casting process.

No identical plaques have yet been archaeologically excavated, but several similar pieces in private collections are known.[1] The present example is the wearer's right-hand plaque of a matched pair, as it has neither hole nor hook. Each camel holds a branch of the Asian elm in its mouth, just like the camels on catalogue no. 79.

The scene on this ornament is quite perplexing. Belt plaques are associated primarily with the northern pastoral peoples, but a landscape scene on such a plaque is highly unusual. If the plaque was made for a Chinese aristocrat with a taste for exotica, it might be interpreted as representing animals living in harmony with nature, a favorite *xiangrui* (auspicious) design characterized by a fantastic mountain landscape teeming with animals. Such a scene could reflect the "correlative thinking" of the early Chinese, which was frequently expressed in terms of animals and mountains, as in the following passage from the *Shiji* (Records of the Grand Historian): "As . . . wild beasts congregate in the most secluded mountains, so benevolence and righteousness attach themselves to a man of wealth."[2]

If, on the other hand, the plaque was made by Han Chinese craftsmen for northern, pastoral consumption, we may be ascribing Chinese ideas to a landscape scene made only to appeal to nomadic taste. This interpretive dilemma is one that continually faces scholars who deal with artifacts from the steppes, since the pastoral peoples left no written records to explain the meaning of their designs.

1. So and Bunker 1995, p. 74, fig. 32; Ariadne Galleries 1998, no. 108.
2. Quoted in So and Bunker 1995, p. 72.

117.
Belt plaque with confronted rams

North China, 1st – 2nd century A.D.
Bronze
Height 3⅛ in. (7.9 cm); width 4⅛ in. (10.5 cm)
Ex coll.: J. J. Lally & Co., New York

This openwork belt plaque, which may originally have been one of a matched pair, shows two confronted rams within a rectangular frame and wheel-shaped forms that fill the spaces beneath and between the two animals.[1] On the reverse, the animals' bodies are concave and the border areas flat. The plaque has a very high copper content and is lost-wax cast.

A plaque of gold that carries the same scene of confronted rams and wheel shapes was found at a Xianbei site in Tianmiliang, eastern Inner Mongolia,[2] and other bronze examples are in public and private collections.[3] A plaque with a similar zoomorphic design was found in Huachi county, Gansu Province, an area once part of the vast territory under the control of the Xianbei.[4] The back of the Huachi plaque is technically similar to the present example, having been cast with the animal bodies concave and the rest of the design flat.

1. Ariadne Galleries 1998, no. 89, in which the animals are misidentified as deer.
2. Qi 1999, p. 241, fig. 2-84.
3. Salmony 1933, pl. 28:4; Barbier 1996, pl. 55.
4. Huang and Liang 1985, p. 40, figs. 1, 2.

118.
Garment hook in the shape of a feline

North or Northwest China, 6th century B.C.
Bronze
Height 2⅛ in. (5.4 cm); width 4⅛ in. (10.5 cm)
Ex coll.: J. J. Lally & Co., New York; Calon da Collection

This garment hook was cast in the form of a feline with its head turned back 180 degrees. Only one front leg and one hind leg are shown, each ending in a small three-clawed paw. The feline's body is marked by raised chevrons that suggest its striped fur pelt, and its open mouth reveals sharp, menacing canines. A collar encircles the throat, and a long plain hook extends sideways from the neck. The reverse has a button that projects on a stem from behind the neck. Crescent-shaped mold-join seams flanking the button indicate that the garment hook and button were integrally cast in a multisection mold.

The collar around the feline's neck indicates that it is a trained hunting animal. References abound in both art and literature to trained falcons, dogs, leopards, and cheetahs used in hunting throughout history.[1] Feline-shaped garment hooks similar to the present example are represented in collections around the world, but none have been found in archaeological context. The type of multisection mold that would have been needed to cast this hook integrally with its button is related to casting traditions found at Houma, the Jin state foundry site in southern Shanxi.[2] It is possible that hooks of this type, which are rather roughly cast, may have been made

by the pastoral nomads on China's northwestern frontier using section-mold techniques borrowed from their Chinese neighbors to the south.

1. Andersson 1932, pp. 304–6.
2. For another garment hook cast in a similar multisection mold, see White and Bunker 1994, no. 7.

119.
Belt hook in the shape of an ungulate

Northwest China, 5th century B.C.
Bronze
Height 2½ in. (6.4 cm); width 3⅞ in. (9.8 cm)
Ex coll.: J. J. Lally & Co., New York

This belt hook takes the form of a fantastic ungulate with only two legs shown and its head turned backward. The actual hook is created by the tail of another, smaller creature that grasps the ungulate's neck in its jaws and foreclaws. Large surface spirals mark the ungulate's shoulder and haunch, while pebbling lends a furry texture to the pelt. A pendant ring hangs from the mouth of each long-necked feline below the ungulate's leg. The back is flat and displays a button on a stem that projects outward behind the haunch. Flashing visible in the openings indicates that the belt hook was piece-mold cast and the precast rings cast on.

No identical garment hook has been found in archaeological context, but a feline-shaped hook with a chain was discovered

in Xietuncun, Ansai county, northern Shaanxi Province, in an area known to have been inhabited by pastoral peoples.[1] The complex casting technology required to make belt hooks with pendant rings and the pebbled surface texture relate such hooks to personal ornaments that may have been cast at the Jin state foundry at Houma, southern Shanxi Province.[2] The smaller creature on the present example is duplicated by the hook on one of the garment hooks associated with Houma, further confirmation for this association.[3] It is even possible that such garment hooks were manufactured by Chinese craftsmen expressly for trade with their northern pastoral neighbors.

1. Ji 1989, pl. 4:4.
2. So and Bunker 1995, pp. 174−75. The Houma foundry is discussed in So 1995b, intro. sec. 4.2.
3. So and Bunker 1995, pp. 174−75, no. 101.

120.
Belt hook in the shape of a carnivore

Northeast China, 5th−4th century B.C.
Bronze
Height 2 in. (5.1 cm); width 4½ in. (11.4 cm)

A standing carnivore shown in profile forms the body of this small belt hook. Marked by a band of raised chevrons that extends down the tail and legs, the carnivore has an almond-shaped incised eye, turned-up snout, pointed ear, and a curl at the base of the jaw. The hook itself emerges from the carnivore's open mouth and ends in an animal's head. The reverse has an attachment button with crescent-shaped mold marks on either side, indicating that the hook was cast integrally with the attachment button in a multipiece mold.

Small animal-shaped hooks with similar chevron body markings have been found at numerous sites in northern Hebei Province and are associated with the Shanrong hunting peoples who inhabited the area about the middle of the first millennium B.C.[1] The blunt way in which the feet terminate also occurs on Eastern Zhou jade carvings,[2] especially on examples found in northern Hebei dated to the fourth century B.C.[3] With its pointed ear, the carnivore is neither a tiger nor a leopard, but most likely a dog, a popular asset among the hunting peoples of Northeast China.[4]

1. So and Bunker 1995, p. 168, fig. 95.1.
2. Rawson 1995, p. 261, fig. 5.
3. Ibid., fig. 6.
4. Bunker et al. 1997, pp. 67, 69, fig. A103.

121.
Belt hook

Central China, ca. 5th–4th century B.C.
Iron inlaid with gold and silver
Length 10⅝ in. (26.8 cm); width 1¼ in. (3.2 cm)
The Metropolitan Museum of Art, Purchase, Joseph Pulitzer
Bequest, 1965 (65.170.2)

This unusually large belt hook is made of iron. The sumptuous pattern on its broad, arched shaft is composed of seven
square forms and numerous spirals set in gold and silver inlay.
The hook terminates in a small, partially corroded feline head,
and on the back of the shaft is a round stud decorated with
circular designs.

Nearly all large belt hooks with a broad, arched surface
have been found in tombs from the state of Chu in southern
Henan and northern Hubei Provinces. They seem to have
been common in the Chu area during the fifth and fourth centuries B.C., after which they gradually went out of use.[1] Belt
hooks of this size are not practical; rather, they are objects
that reflected the wealth and status of the owner, for their
broad surface afforded the artist ample space to display extravagant, embellished designs. Among archaeologically recovered examples, three iron belt hooks from Xinyang, Henan,
bear the closest resemblance to the present example; they are
almost as large and have an equally luxurious surface inlaid
with gold and silver.[2]   ZS

1. Wang Renxiang 1985, pp. 274–75.
2. Henan 1959.

122.
Belt hook in the shape of a monkey

North China, ca. 4th–3rd century B.C.
Gilded bronze inlaid with turquoise
Height 2⅜ in. (6 cm); length 6 in. (15.2 cm)
Private Collection

The bowed shaft of this bronze belt hook is cast in the form of a monkey. Balancing its weight on the right arm, the lively and spirited monkey flexes its legs as it stretches its left arm and curls its hand to form a hook. Two round staring eyes, originally filled with semiprecious stone inlays, gaze out defiantly at the viewer. And thin ribbons and curls of bright turquoise inlay flow along the torso and limbs, creating an appealing contrast against the gilded surface. The back of the hook is also decorated with a curved linear design that is highlighted with silver. Judging from a comparable example in a private collection, the monkey may have held a ring, now lost, in its left hand.[1]

A popular motif of late Eastern Zhou and early Western Han art, the monkey is frequently encountered on decorations in bronze, and belt hooks with the image of a monkey are represented in both private and public collections. A close example is the aforementioned belt hook in a private collection, which is nearly a mirror image of the present hook but with slightly more curl motifs. Another comparable example is a silver belt hook excavated at Qufu, Shandong Province, the site of the ancient capital city of the state of Lu, which dates to the fourth century B.C.[2]   ZS

1. Eskenazi 1996, pl. 7.
2. *Qufu Lu guo* 1982, pp. 159–60, figs. 106, 107.

123.
Feline-shaped belt hook

North China, 4th – 3rd century B.C.
Tinned bronze
Height 2 in. (4.9 cm); length 4⅜ in. (11.1 cm)
Ex coll.: Susan Chen & Company, Hong Kong

This tinned bronze belt hook is cast in the shape of a feline with its head turned backward. Its body is marked by small spirals framed by two longitudinal bands of raised dots to suggest the textured pelt. A hook terminating in another feline head projects sideways from the chest. The reverse displays a protruding button in the middle that shows extensive wear around the stem. The belt hook has been piece-mold cast and the front surface tinned.

Hooks that project to the wearer's right, as it does here, rather than to the left, are unusual. They occur chiefly on pieces intended for China's northern neighbors, such as those who inhabited northern Hebei Province during the second half of the first millennium B.C.[1] The surface markings and tin plating relate the Thaw belt hook to Jin and Qin artifacts, suggesting that it may have been made at one of these northern Warring States metalworking centers expressly for the herding peoples beyond their frontiers.[2]

1. So and Bunker 1995, p. 169, fig. 95.1.
2. Ibid., pp. 174–76, nos. 101, 102; Bunker et al. 1997, p. 249, no. 208.

124.
Belt hook with wolf and dzo

Northwest China, 3rd century B.C.
Bronze with traces of gilding
Height 2¾ in. (7 cm); length 8 in. (20.3 cm)
Ex coll.: Eskenazi Ltd., London

This unusual belt hook depicts an animal-combat scene between a wolf and a dzo. Cast in openwork within a plain rounded rectangular border, it tapers to a hook, now broken off, on the wearer's right side. The wolf is shown biting the dzo in the neck while holding it down by the horn with one paw. In return, the dzo has pierced the wolf's throat with the other horn. The wolf has a long muzzle with a sharp fang, strong clawed paws, and a tail curled between the hind legs, and the dzo is characterized by a tufted tail and the shaggy fur on its belly and upper legs. The belt hook is lost-wax cast and once had mercury gilding, the remains of which are only faintly visible. Root marks from burial surroundings are embedded in the corrosion on the back.

In many lower regions where yaks are found, they are often interbred with the local cattle, resulting in a hybrid known as a dzo. The hybrids can surpass their parents in strength, are less stubborn, and can survive in lower altitudes than yaks, all of which makes them more useful as domesticated animals.[1]

The way in which the dzo's horn in this plaque pierces the wolf's throat is similar to that in which a yak pierces the tigers' ears on a gold belt buckle dated to the third century B.C. that was excavated at Aluchaideng, Hanggin banner, southwestern Inner Mongolia.[2] This close association suggests that the Thaw belt hook and the Aluchaideng plaques are roughly contemporary.

The present example belongs to a group of similar hooks that all depict animal-combat scenes between a wolf and a dzo. One is in the Osaka Municipal Museum of Art;[3] another, in the Stoclet collection, was published by Umehara;[4] and a third is in the Museum of Far Eastern Antiquities, Stockholm.[5] All these scenes display similar compositions and use the same narrative devices, showing the victim with its tongue lolling out, for example, and the wolf holding down the dzo's horn with one paw, suggesting that all four plaques may have been cast at the same foundry.

1. Clutton-Brock 1981, p. 140.
2. Shanghai 2000, p. 83.
3. Osaka Municipal Museum 1991, p. 113, no. 179.
4. Umehara 1933, pl. 80.
5. Ardenne de Tizac 1923, pl. 18A.

125.
Hook with horned feline

North China, 3rd century B.C.
Gilded bronze
Length 4¼ in. (10.8 cm); width 2¼ in. (5.7 cm)

A mask of a fierce-looking horned feline with comma-shaped ears is represented on the shield of this garment hook. The eyes and forehead were once embellished with inlay, now missing. The hook is lost-wax cast and gilded on both sides, and a button protruding from the slightly concave back displays a character or linear design, partially hidden by incrustation.

Garment hooks cast in the shape of animal masks similar to this one, dated to the third century B.C., are included in many collections.[1] The comma-shaped ears with a small

sphere at the inside base are stylistic features found on earlier belt ornaments associated with the pastoral peoples of the northwestern frontiers, such as catalogue nos. 63 and 94, further confirming the cultural interaction between the Chinese and their herding neighbors.

1. W. Watson 1963, p. 70, fig. 19.c; Brinker 1975, no. 114.

126.
Hook with raptor-headed ungulate

North China, 3rd–2nd century B.C.
Gilded bronze
Height 1¾ in. (4.4 cm); max. width 1¼ in. (3.2 cm)
Ex coll.: J. J. Lally & Co., New York

The body of this coiled, raptor-headed mythological ungulate, its hind legs slung over its neck, has been ingeniously manipulated to fit into a small circular space. The single horn that sprouts from its head forms the shaft for the actual hook, which takes the shape of another animal's head. The reverse is concave and has a wide flat attachment button that was affixed by soldering after the garment hook was lost-wax cast. A clay model, similar to an example in the study collection of the Freer Gallery of Art, Washington, D.C., was probably used to form a mother mold for the wax model used in the final lost-wax casting process.[1] In this way, such artifacts could be easily mass-produced.

A garment hook in the form of a camel, with its body manipulated in the same way as the ungulate on the Thaw hook, is in the collection of Therese and Erwin Harris.[2] The camel's body is marked by the same striated enclosures found on the bodies of numerous animals represented on artifacts associated with the China's pastoral neighbors, such as catalogue nos. 67, 76, 100, 103, and 159. The creature on the Thaw hook is also very similar to the one on a Qi state *se* string anchor from Linzi, Shandong Province, which is identical to catalogue no. 180. Again, these similarities illustrate the cultural ebb and flow that must have existed between ancient China and their herding and hunting neighbors to the north.

1. So and Bunker 1995, pp. 142–43, fig. 62.1.
2. Ibid., p. 171, no. 97.

127.
Belt hook in the shape of a dragon

North China, 3rd–2nd century B.C.
Gilded bronze
Height 1¾ in. (4.4 cm); length 7⅛ in. (18.1 cm)

An elongated dragon with a wolflike head twisted into a figure eight forms the body of this belt hook, and an animal's head with a long neck extending from the side forms the hook. A round button on a stem projects from the back for attachment to a belt. The belt hook was cast by the lost-wax process and enhanced by mercury gilding, most of which has worn off.

Belt hooks cast in the shape of a figure-eight dragon similar to the present example are represented in numerous collections.[1] One hook was collected in Yulin, northern Shaanxi, indicating that such hooks were produced in the Xi'an area.[2]

Comparison between the dragon on this belt hook and the wolves on several plaques made for the neighboring pastoral peoples, such as catalogue nos. 63 and 105, illustrates their similarities, suggesting that the northern lupine-headed dragon may well have been part of the ancestry of the Chinese dragon image which evolved during the Western Han period. Another pair of northern plaques, catalogue no. 102, was certainly made by Han craftsmen for northern consumption, providing further evidence of Chinese access to and familiarity with northern zoomorphic motifs.

1. W. Watson 1963, p. 70, fig. 19a; Rawson and Bunker 1990, p. 196, no. 109; Uldry, Brinker, and Louis 1994, pl. 54; Ariadne Galleries 1998, p. 158, no. 175.
2. Lu 1988, inside back cover, no. 4; Li Hong 1995, pp. 43–44, pl. 159.

128.
Belt hook in the shape of a fantastic creature

North China, 3rd – 2nd century B.C.
Bronze inlaid with gold and silver
Max. height 1 ¾ in. (4.4 cm); length 5 ½ in. (14.1 cm)
The Metropolitan Museum of Art, Gift of Ernest Erickson
Foundation Inc. 1985 (1985.214.61)
Published: Hearn 1987, p. 56.

This belt hook takes the form of a serpentine creature with a round face, a beaked mouth, and enormous pointed ears. The clawed arms grip the fins that project from its sides, and from the hind legs extends a straight, tapering shaft that terminates in a feline-headed hook. Lavish gold and silver inlays arranged in striated bands, complex geometric patterns, and dense simulated granulation create an unusually ornate surface.

Although fantastic animals and creatures are common decorative motifs in late Eastern Zhou and Western Han art, images closely comparable to the present example are rare. A gilded bronze figure with similar facial features is in the Shumei collection in the Miho Museum, Shigaraki. Apparently a fragment of a larger object, it too has a beaked mouth and large pointed ears, and a slightly broader face.[1] The pointed ears are also found on a kneeling figure on a bronze screen stand that was excavated from the tomb of the king of Nanyue of the Western Han.[2] The present example was most likely made in the late years of the Warring States period, since the rich gold and silver inlays on the surface point to a connection with the sumptuous bronzes reportedly from the Eastern Zhou royal tombs at Luoyang, Henan Province.   ZS

1. Arnold et al. 1996, pp. 128 – 29.
2. Beijing 1991, vol. 2, colorpl. 28.

129.

Belt hook in the shape of a sinuous creature

China, ca. 3rd–1st century B.C.
Silver with gold foil
Length 6⅛ in. (15.6 cm)
The Metropolitan Museum of Art, Gift of Ernest Erickson
Foundation Inc., 1985 (1985.214.69)
Published: Hearn 1987, p. 58.

The gold sheathed end of this slender belt hook is modeled into a large animal head that has an unusually long snout, staring eyes, pointed ears, and a ringed horn. The crocodilian snout is characterized by fluid, wavy lines with sharp, raised edges. The hook itself, also covered with gold foil, is cast in the shape of a smaller animal's head, and a round stud is set on the back of the arched shaft.

A common type during the late Eastern Zhou and Western Han, belt hooks with a slender shaft, such as this one, are generally made of bronze and often decorated with precious metal and semiprecious stone inlays. Comparable examples have been found in Warring States and Han tombs, from the northeastern coast to deep in the southwestern highland. While their shapes remain largely the same, their sizes vary to a considerable degree, the longest being twelve inches and the shortest merely four to five inches. Belt hooks in silver, especially those with gold-sheathed embellishment, are rare, although silver as a metal seems to have become more available by the Han period. The finest was found in a late Warring States tomb at Guwei village, Hui county, Henan Province. Decorated with animal motifs raised in high relief, it is partially sheathed in gold and inlaid with jade and glass.[1]   ZS

1. Beijing 1956.

130.
Belt hook in the shape of a warrior and a leopard

North China, 3rd – 1st century B.C.
Gilded bronze inlaid with turquoise
Height 1 ¼ in. (3.2 cm); width 3 in. (7.6 cm)
Ex coll.: Eskenazi Ltd., London

A warrior with distinctly Mongoloid features is shown fending off a leopard that sinks its teeth into his side as it grabs him with both paws. The warrior holds a short sword in his raised right hand, as if to strike the leopard. He has long hair and wears a short, belted jacket that fastens on the left. The hook, which would have taken the form of the warrior's left arm and hand, is broken off. Lost-wax cast, the hook is inlaid with turquoise to imitate leopard spots and two-tone gilded on the front and back.[1]

A belt hook that depicts a similar combat between a Mongoloid warrior and a leopard is in the Danish Museum of Decorative Art, Copenhagen.[2] The warrior wears the same apparel as the warrior on the present plaque, a tunic reaching to the knees, and also has bare legs and feet. His appearance identifies him an inhabitant of the northern frontier of China during the last centuries of the first millennium B.C., but his clothes are not those of a hunter or a mounted warrior-herdsman. Rather, they identify him specifically as a contestant in the ritual combats between men and animals staged by the Chinese emperor to demonstrate the cosmic character of imperial rule.[3] A late Warring States bronze oil lamp in the Miho Museum, Shigaraki, is cast in the shape of such a wrestler dressed in similar attire.[4]

1. For an explanation of two-tone gilding, see Bunker 1994b.
2. Leth 1959, no. 32; for an illustration in color, see Miniaev 1996, p. 79.
3. For a discussion of these complex displays of ritual violence, see Lewis 1990, pp. 150–63.
4. Miho Museum 1997, pp. 186–87.

131.
Belt hook in the shape of a horned dragon

North China, 3rd–1st century B.C.
Gilded bronze and glass
Height 1¾ in. (4.4 cm); length 7⅛ in. (18.1 cm)
Ex coll.: Joseph G. Gerena Fine Art, New York

This belt hook takes the form of a serpentine horned dragon. The hook itself represents an animal's head with a long neck. Four oval glass inlays adorn the dragon's body, and a small piece of glass backed by gilding marks the eye. The belt hook was piece-mold cast and the button on the back soldered on.

Examples of this type of hook are included in many collections.[1] The interesting feature here is the use of glass for inlay, a new practice that appeared in China during the late Eastern Zhou and Han periods.[2] Early glass eyebeads made in the west have been found in many burials associated with the pastoral peoples, who may have participated in their transmission eastward across the Eurasian steppes. The inlays on the present hook are not actual eyebeads but probably glass ovals with stems designed to fit into sockets, such as the inlays with eye designs that adorn a belt hook in the Miho Museum, Shigaraki.[3]

1. W. Watson 1963, fig. 18:d; Eskenazi 1995, p. 24, no. 9.
2. Bunker 1994b, p. 37, n. 98.
3. Miho Museum 1997, pp. 190–92, no. 91.

132.
Belt hook with dragons

North China, 2nd century B.C.
Gilded bronze
Length 6⅜ in. (16 cm); width 1½ in. (3.8 cm)

Two entwined dragonlike creatures are represented on the body of this belt hook, and an animal's head on a long neck or shaft extends from the wearer's left side to form the hook itself. The hook is mercury gilded on both sides, and the eye of the smaller dragon appears to be inlaid with some type of stone. The reverse is flat and has a button on a stem.

Western Han tombs for the elite abound with richly adorned belt hooks, such as the example seen here. Chinese garment hooks were luxury items designed for show and prestige; they were not intended to indicate clan and rank, as were the belt ornaments of the northern pastoral peoples.

During the Eastern Han dynasty (A.D. 25–220), belt hooks declined in popularity, and they were not listed as an appropriate accoutrement in an official edict of A.D. 59.[1] By the Western Jin (A.D. 265–317), elaborate belt hooks had gone out of fashion altogether and were replaced by sectioned belts formed by a series of plaques with a matching buckle.[2]

1. White and Bunker 1994, p. 21.
2. Ibid., p. 22, no. 50.

5. GARMENT PLAQUES

The majority of these artifacts served the same purpose as belt buckles, visually reinforcing the power and prestige of their owners. Some plaques functioned as additional belt ornaments, and some were appliquéd on clothing. A hierarchy of metals, gold, silver, gilded bronze, tinned bronze, and plain bronze proclaimed the status of the wearer. A reconstruction of the lavishly decorated clothing of an elite male buried at Issyk-Kul, near Almaty, in Kazakhstan, suggests how such plaques may have been worn (see fig. 54).

133.
Bird-shaped garment plaque

Northeast China, 8th–7th century B.C.
Bronze
Height 1 5/8 in. (4.1 cm); width 1 3/4 in. (4.4 cm)
Ex coll.: Michael Dunn, New York

This small garment plaque takes the form of a bird with outspread wings and prominent claws. Raised striations suggest feathers on the wings and tail, and raised chevrons mark the long neck. A vertical loop for attachment is placed behind the head on the reverse, and a mold mark that runs along the length of the loop and down the back indicates that the loop was cast integrally with the plaque in a multipiece mold.

Two bird-shaped ornaments similar to the present one were discovered in Northeast China at Zhoujiadi, Aohan banner, southeastern Inner Mongolia, a site that has been dated from the eighth to the seventh century B.C.;[1] two more were excavated at Nanshan'gen, Ningcheng county, southeastern Inner Mongolia, another eighth-to-seventh-century B.C. site.[2] The bird on this plaque is very similar to a bird depicted on a mirror excavated at Shangcunling, near Sanmenxia, Henan, a site dated from the late Western Zhou to the early Spring and Autumn period, about the eighth century B.C.[3] The Shangcunling mirror was not made in China but appears to be an exotic object acquired from farther north or northeast, presumably through trade.[4]

The bird that constitutes the present plaque, the excavated examples, and the bird on the Shangcunling mirror all have unusually long necks. This feature suggests that the bird por-

trayed is a vulture, a bird of prey and scavenger common to Northeast China and the Eurasian steppes.

1. *Kaogu* 1984, no. 5, p. 422, fig. 10:1–2.
2. *Kaogu xuebao* 1975, no. 1, pl. 7:11–12.
3. Beijing 1959, p. 27, fig. 21; Song 1997, p. 152, fig. 3:1.
4. Song Xinchao (1997) emphasizes the similarity between the zoomorphic motifs on the Shangcunling mirror and those represented on artifacts excavated at sites in Northeast China.

134.
Pair of tiger-shaped plaques

Northeast China, 7th–6th century B.C.
Bronze
Each: Height 1 ⅜ in. (3.5 cm); width 1 ¾ in. (4.4 cm)
Ex coll.: Michael Dunn, New York

Each of these two mirror-image plaques is cast in the shape of a crouching tiger with its tail terminating in a stylized raptor's head. The body, tail, and legs are marked by raised diagonal ridges. A ribbed, rounded triangle accentuates the tigers' shoulders, and a concentric oval, the haunches. The eyes of both the tigers' and the birds' heads are round and perforated, and each tiger's mouth is indicated by an indented X-shape. The reverse of each plaque is flat and has two vertical loops for attachment that have been soldered on. Flashing in the openings indicates that each of the ornaments was cast in a two-piece mold.

Several plaques excavated at Xiaoheishigou, Ningcheng county, southeastern Inner Mongolia, have body markings and perforated eyes similar to those seen here.[1] One Xiaoheishigou tiger-shaped plaque also has an X-shaped mouth.[2] The Xiaoheishigou burials have been redated here from the seventh to the sixth century B.C.[3] The body markings and raptor-headed tails relate these plaques to catalogue nos. 26 and 27, harness jingles of the same period.

1. Xiang and Li 1995, p. 16, figs. 19:9,11, and 23:3.
2. Ibid., p. 18, fig. 23:1.
3. See discussion in catalogue no. 45.

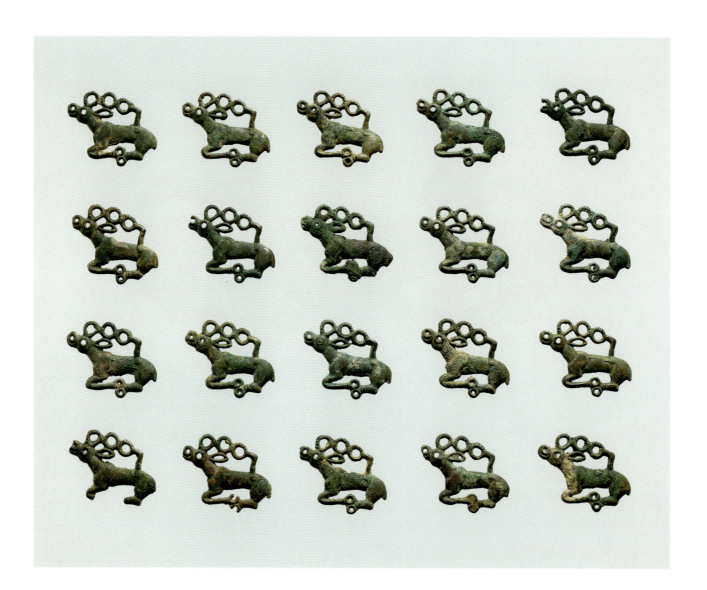

135.
Set of twenty ornamental plaques

Northeast China, 6th century B.C.
Bronze
Average height 1 ¼ in. (3.1 cm); width 1 ¾ in. (4.3 cm)
Lent by Shelby White and Leon Levy
Published: So and Bunker 1995, pp. 160–61, no. 83.

These twenty bronze deer once served as personal ornaments for one of the pastoral peoples inhabiting the Dongbei (Northeast China) about 600 B.C. Each deer is shown in profile, with its legs folded in such a way that the forelegs overlap the hind legs and with the hooves indicated by pierced circles. The antlers have been transformed into a series of tangent circles that terminate in a strut attached to the deer's hindquarters. Each plaque has a long horizontal loop on the

back extending from the chest to the rump for attachment and appears to have been mass-produced by piece-mold casting.

The pose in which the deer are shown is characteristic of that which developed throughout the Eurasian steppes during the first half of the first millennium B.C.[1] Similar images of deer have been found in various frontier regions east of the Taihang Mountains, but never in northern regions west of the Taihang. An attribution of such images to the Ordos region was made by art dealers in Beijing in the 1920s,[2] but in fact deer images produced in the Ordos seldom have horns and are shown recumbent, whereas the Dongbei figures are shown with horns and in motion (see cat. no. 35). Excavations made during the last decade, in northern Hebei Province and the Dongbei, have provided a more accurate provenience for such motifs. Burials dating to about the sixth century B.C. at Ganzibao, Huailai county, northern Hebei, have revealed graves in which the dead were literally covered with animal-shaped ornaments, just as they were at related sites at Jundushan, Yanqing county, north of Beijing.[3] Deer with folded legs and with their antlers transformed into a series of tangent circles have also been found in tomb 3, at Ganzibao.[4]

Five similar gold deer in the Carl Kempe collection in Stockholm reinforce the observation that status was partially expressed by the choice of metal from which personal ornaments were cast.[5]

1. Chlenova 1963, pp. 66–67, tables 1, 2.
2. Ibid., p. 67, table 2, nos. 21–27.
3. *Wenwu*, no. 2 (1989), p. 23, fig. 9.
4. He and Liu 1993, p. 31, fig. 9.4.
5. Bunker, Chatwin, and Farkas 1970, p. 138, no. 129 and p. 148.

136.
Deer-shaped garment plaque

Pamir Mountains, Kazakhstan, 6th–5th century B.C.
Bronze
Height 3 in. (7.6 cm); width 3 ¾ in. (9.5 cm)
Ex coll.: Ward & Company, Inc., New York

This elegant garment plaque is cast in the form of a mythological deer with raptor-headed antler tines and folded legs. The body, from which two buttons project, is concave on the reverse, and the horns are flat. The plaque was cast by the lost-wax process, but the wax model may have been mold made.

Garment plaques in the shape of mythological deer with two attachment buttons on the reverse have been found among grave goods from Saka burials in the Tamdinskii cemetery, tentatively dated from the sixth to the fourth century B.C., in the Pamir Mountains of Central Asia.[1] A pointed muzzle similar to that of the present deer appears to be a characteristic specific to the Saka ungulate figures of the eastern Pamirs.[2] The presence of brow tines indicates that the deer is based on a reindeer image that must have remained in the collective memory of the Saka, since reindeer never lived as far south as the Pamirs.

The transformation of horns and antler tines into raptors' heads is an iconographic phenomenon that first developed

among the pastoral peoples during the first millennium B.C. The earliest known example of this image was discovered in a seventh-to-sixth-century B.C. Saka grave at Chilikta, in eastern Kazakhstan,[3] and from there transmitted west to the Black Sea area and ultimately eastward to southern Siberia and the borders of Northwest China.[4]

1. Litvinskii 1984, p. 53, fig. 12, pp. 71–72; Yablonsky 1995, p. 236, fig. 102.
2. Jettmar and Thewalf 1987, photo. 10–pl. 7.
3. Artamonov 1973, p. 37, no. 41; Aruz (2000, p. 248, no. 170) gives Chilikta a seventh-century B.C. date.
4. For a more extensive discussion of this iconography, see Bunker 1989, passim.

137.
Garment plaque with two raptors

      Kazakhstan, 6th–5th century B.C.
      Bronze
      Height 1⅝ in. (4.1 cm); width 1¾ in. (4.4 cm)
      Ex coll.: Joseph G. Gerena Fine Art, New York

Two raptors swirl around a central circle on this small plaque. Such raptor images are based on the eagle, a predator that threatened the herds, was used in falconry, and was credited with magical powers. The plaque is flat on the reverse and has a projecting button on a stem that shows considerable wear. The piece is lost-wax cast.

A similar design, which adorns a wooden roundel from Tuekta, kurgan 1, in the Altai Mountains of southern Siberia, is dated to the sixth century B.C.,[1] suggesting a common ancestry

for the motif in the distant past. The only difference between the raptors on the present plaque and those on the Tuekta roundel are the eyes, which on the former are naturalistically round, as birds' eyes should be, while on the latter they are almond-shaped, like those of the mythological griffin.

1. Aruz 2000, no. 107.

138.
Garment plaque in the shape of a coiled panther

      Eastern Kazakhstan, 6th–5th century B.C.
      Bronze
      Diameter 2⅝ in. (6.7 cm)
      Ex coll.: Ward & Company, Inc., New York

Shaped as a stylized coiled panther, this plaque has two attachment buttons on stems on the reverse and a loop formed by the tail tip touching the tiger's haunch. Considerable wear marks are visible on the loop, which appears to have been rubbed by a leather strap, and the panther has a scooped-out back with a thick outside edge. The plaque appears to have been lost-wax cast.

Coiled panthers are a characteristic motif of the Saka people and have been found at several Saka sites in eastern Kazakhstan, among them the Uigarak cemetery[1] and the Saka-Charga Hills burials,[2] both situated south and east of the Aral Sea. Other sites in Kazakhstan include the Chilikta burial ground, dated from the seventh to the sixth century B.C.[3]

The Saka coiled-panther motif is a slightly later version of the coiled carnivores represented on steppe ornaments, such as the paws of a seventh-century B.C. gold panther from Kelermes, in the Black Sea region[4] and a seventh-to-sixth-century B.C. harness breastplate from Arzhan, in Tuva, southern Siberia (fig. 34).

1. Litvinskii 1984, fig. 28 B:8, 10.
2. Yablonsky 1995, p. 228, fig. 82.
3. Aruz 2000, p. 250.
4. Schiltz 1994, pl. 8.

139.
Garment plaque with kulan

Northern Hebei Province, 6th–5th century B.C.
Bronze
Height 1⅞ in. (4.8 cm); width 1⅛ in. (2.9 cm)
Ex coll.: J. J. Lally & Co., New York; Calon da Collection

Two pairs of kulan protomes with heads turned back and both ears shown are enclosed within a rectangular frame on this openwork plaque. Each pair features only the forequarters, as if the first animal overlapped the adjacent animal that in turn is overlapped by the frame. The round eyes are each surrounded by a circular ridge, and slight depressions mark the ears, nostrils, and mouth. The reverse of the plaque is slightly concave and has no attachment devices, suggesting that it was affixed through the openings in the design. Mold marks around the edge of the frame indicate casting in a two-piece mold.

A small ornament decorated with the same kulan protome was recently excavated from tomb 3 at Ganzibao, Huailai county, northern Hebei Province, with other artifacts tentatively dated from the sixth to the fifth century B.C.[1] Another plaque similar to the present example was collected in Chongli county, northwestern Hebei Province.[2]

1. He and Liu 1993, p. 37, fig. 16:10; Duan 1995, p. 104, pl. 151.
2. Zheng Shaozong 1991, p. 9, fig. 32.

140.
Garment plaque in the shape of a raptor's head

North China and south-central Inner Mongolia, 6th–5th century B.C.
Bronze
Height ⅞ in. (2.2 cm); width 1 in. (2.5 cm)
Ex coll.: Calon da Collection

A prominent curved beak, round eye, and tiny round ear characterize the stylized raptor's head that constitutes this garment plaque. The eye is indicated by a wide circular groove surrounding the pupil, and sunken areas mark the beak and ear. The reverse of the plaque is flat and displays a vertical rounded loop that was piece-mold cast integrally with the plaque. Mold marks are visible around the base of the loop.

Small garment ornaments similar to this one abound in Liangcheng county, south-central Inner Mongolia, especially at Maoqinggou[1] and Guoxianyaozi,[2] in graves dating to between the sixth and the fourth century B.C. Another example was found in a fifth-century B.C. grave at Xigoupan, Jungar banner, in the Ordos Desert region of Northwest China and southwestern Inner Mongolia.[3]

The entire plaque is a representation of the head alone, and the design is made by a pattern integrated into rather than

superimposed on the anatomical form. These are both features characteristic of Chinese birds' heads seen on Western Zhou chariotry equipment, and they became popular throughout the Eurasian steppes during the first millennium B.C.[4] Stylized birds' heads are also represented on wood carving in the Altai region of southern Siberia (fig. 30).

It is possible that ancient bird's-head designs were carried from southern Siberia by the Scythians, after which they moved into northwestern Asia in the seventh century B.C. Such designs first appear in Northwest Asia together with the coiled feline, another eastern motif, on material from the seventh-century B.C. Ziwiye hoard found in northwestern Iran.[5] These birds' heads should not be confused with griffins' heads, which have almond-shaped animal eyes and can be traced back through the Pontic steppes to the Hellenic world and ultimately to the ancient Near East.[6]

1. Höllmann and Kossack 1992, pls. 37:B, 29:2, 11:B4, fig. 16:8.
2. *Kaogu xuebao*, no. 1 (1989), p. 566, fig. 11:2–3, pl. 11:8.
3. Tian and Guo 1986, p. 361, fig. 9:3.
4. W. Watson 1971, p. 115; Barkova 1987.
5. Godard 1950, pp. 5–12 and p. 30, fig. 29. For a discussion of the problems associated with the Ziwiye hoard, see Muscarella 1977, pp. 169–70, 184–85.
6. Toshio 2000.

141.
Garment plaque with raptors' heads

> North China and south-central Inner Mongolia, 6th–5th century B.C.
> Bronze
> Height 2 in. (4.9 cm); width 1¾ in. (4.4 cm)
> Ex coll.: Emma C. Bunker

A medley of four stylized raptors' heads that together form one large head adorn this garment plaque. The heads are all similar to that on catalogue no. 140 and cast in the same style. And like catalogue no. 140, the reverse of the present plaque displays two heavy vertical loops. It was cast in a multi-piece mold.

Although no exact duplicate has been excavated, there is no doubt that the plaque shares the same style and was made in the same geographic region as the other south-central Inner Mongolian examples in the Thaw collection (cat. nos. 59,

140). The smooth surface has a dark, shiny tin-oxide patina, indicating that the alloy is a high-tin leaded bronze.[1]

1. Bunker et al. 1997, p. 206, no. 142, shows a bronze with a similar patina that was identified as a high-tin leaded bronze by X-ray fluorescence.

142.
Deer-shaped garment plaque

> Pamir Mountains, Kazakhstan, 6th–4th century B.C.
> Bronze
> Height 2 in. (5.2 cm); width 2¼ in. (5.7 cm)
> Ex coll.: Ward & Company, Inc., New York

This garment plaque is cast in the shape of deer with flowing antlers and folded legs. Like catalogue no. 146, the eye, shoulder, and haunch are marked by round depressions. The reverse is flat and displays two buttons on stems; and the plaque is lost-wax cast.

The deer has the same pointed muzzle and round body markings as those on catalogue no. 136, both stylistic characteristics seen on Saka artifacts excavated in the Pamirs.[1] The rounded loop of the front leg is also a stylistic trait found on such plaques (cat. nos. 136, 144–146).

1. Litvinskii 1984, p. 53, fig. 12:6,14.

This plaque depicts a deer with flowing antlers and folded legs. The reverse is flat with two stemmed buttons. Although similar to the other deer plaques associated with the Pamir Saka in the Thaw collection, the image here is less stylized, with more naturalistically rendered antlers and a less pointed muzzle, suggesting that it may be slightly earlier in date. In other respects, such as the attachment buttons and the method of casting, it is quite similar and must come from the same general area.

143.
Garment plaque in the shape of a deer

Pamir Mountains, Kazakhstan, 6th–4th century B.C.
Bronze
Height 2¼ in. (5.7 cm); width 3¼ in. (8.1 cm)
Ex coll.: Joseph G. Gerena Fine Art, New York

144.
Deer-shaped garment plaques

Kazakhstan, 6th–4th century B.C.
Bronze
a. Height 1½ in. (3.8 cm); width 1⅝ in. (4.1 cm)
b. Height 1½ in. (3.8 cm); width 2 in. (5.1 cm)
Ex coll.: Joseph G. Gerena Fine Art, New York

Each of these small garment plaques comprises two deer protomes joined at the midsection. Each deer has an extended muzzle. The presence of brow tines indicates that the images are based on the reindeer, suggesting that the original homeland of the Pamir Saka may have been far to the north. Because both male and female reindeer have antlers, it would be risky to identify these deer as stags. A large button on a stem projects from the concave back of each ornament. The two plaques were lost-wax cast.

While no similar plaques have been published in scientific excavation reports, the present examples are stylistically and technically similar to the other Pamir Saka plaques in the Thaw collection (cat. nos. 136, 142).

145.
Deer-shaped garment plaque

> Pamir Mountains, Kazakhstan, 6th–4th century B.C.
> Bronze
> Height 1¾ in. (4.5 cm); width 2⅜ in. (6 cm)
> Ex coll.: Ward and Company, Inc., New York

This garment plaque takes the form of a deer with flowing antlers and folded legs. The reverse is flat and displays a broad horizontal loop for attachment. The plaque is lost-wax cast.

As on the other three Saka plaques in the Thaw collection (cat. nos. 136, 142, 143), the deer's muzzle is slightly pointed and the antlers are shown as a graceful series of tangent circles, both features associated with Saka artifacts excavated in the Pamir Mountains.[1] Whether the present plaque and other examples were cast at one metalworking center or several different ones can not be determined from the evidence available.

1. Yablonsky 1995, p. 236, fig. 102.

146.
Garment plaque in the shape of a Przewalski horse

> Pamir Mountains, Central Asia, 6th–4th century B.C.
> Bronze
> Height 1½ in. (3.8 cm); width 2½ in. (6.4 cm)
> Ex coll.: Joseph G. Gerena Fine Art, New York

This garment plaque is cast in the form of a Przewalski horse, the wild Asian horse that roamed the Eurasian steppes in ancient times. Sandy beige in color, it has a short black upright mane and short legs. The shoulder, haunch, and eye are each marked by a round depression, but such marks were not intended for inlay. The back of the ornament is concave, with a rim that turns inward and an attachment button on a bent stem behind the horse's midsection. The plaque was cast by the lost-wax process and displays extensive wear.

Although no identical plaques have been published from a controlled excavation, this horse-shaped example relates stylistically to catalogue no. 142. Both animals have slightly pointed muzzles, typical of Saka artifacts found in the Pamirs, and presumably can also be dated from the sixth to the fifth century B.C. Several plaques similar to the present horse-shaped ornament have appeared on the art market in the last five years and were attributed to the Pamir Saka.[1]

1. Hôtel Drouot 1999, nos. 87, 90.

on a sixth-century B.C. wooden coffin from Bashadar, in the Altai Mountains (fig. 32).

1. For the technique of tinning bronze, see Bunker 1994b, pp. 48–49, and Bunker 1994a, pp. 75–76.
2. *Wenwu* 1995, no. 2, p. 46, fig. 16; *Orientations* 25 (November 1994), p. 11. See also extensive discussion of the present plaque in So and Bunker 1995, p. 113, no. 28.

148.
Garment plaque in the shape of a wild boar

Northwest China, 5th–4th century B.C.
Bronze
Height 1 in. (2.5 cm); width 1⅝ in. (4.1 cm)
Ex coll.: Peaceful Wind, Santa Fe

147.
Leopard-shaped garment plaque

Northwest China, 5th century B.C.
Tinned bronze
Height 1⅜ in. (3.5 cm); width 2¾ in. (7 cm)
Ex coll.: J. J. Lally & Co., New York; Calon da Collection
Published: So and Bunker 1995, p. 113, no. 28.

This tinned-bronze plaque is cast in the shape of a standing leopard in profile with only two legs showing. The pelt is indicated by striated circles of sunken line relief, and indented diagonal lines mark the tail. The ear is formed by a spiral that begins at the interior. The leopard's fierceness is accentuated by open jaws revealing pointed fangs and teeth and two paws that display four prominent claws. The back of the ornament has a smooth concave surface with a small round vertical attachment loop at the midsection, and the front has a silvery-looking surface produced by wiping with molten tin.[1] The plaque is lost-wax cast, and the openings in the design appear to have been cut through a wax model from the front.

The ornament displays an intriguing combination of northern and Chinese characteristics. The indented, striated circles are associated with the Jin state foundry at Houma, in southern Shanxi Province, which produced animal motifs and animal-shaped vessels that also carry striated circle decoration.[2] The emphasis on sharp fangs and claws is a northern characteristic that derives ultimately from the wood-carving traditions of southern Siberia, exemplified by the tigers carved

This small plaque takes the form of a standing wild boar with a bristly mane and curly tail. A wide ridge suggests a tusk, raised volutes mark the legs, and the eye is described by a circle surrounding a boss. The reverse displays a long wide horizontal loop that extends from the shoulder to the haunch, and mold marks are visible at the base of the loop ends and along the edges, indicating piece-mold casting.

No similar plaques have been found in archaeological context, but a nearly identical example was collected in the early twentieth century in Fenyang, northern Shanxi Province.[1] Similar boars occur on small plaques associated with the northwestern frontier region of China that have been traditionally dated to the fifth century B.C.[2]

1. Andersson 1932, p. 269, pl. 25:6.
2. Wu En 1981, p. 53, fig. 4:4; Bunker et al. 1997, p. 226, no. 173.

149.
Garment plaque with animal motif

Northwest China, 5th–4th century B.C.
Bronze
Height 1 ¾ in. (4.4 cm); width ¾ in. (1.9 cm)

This elongated S-shaped plaque features at each end the fore-quarters of a carnivore with the head of a herbivore in its jaws. At the midsection is a standing wild boar similar to catalogue no. 148. The animals' heads at each end have round conventionalized eyes, while the boar's eye has a more naturalistic almond shape. The carnivores' paws each display four claws. The reverse of the plaque has pronounced hollows and a vertical attachment strap at the top, behind one of the carnivore's heads. Mold marks are visible along the edges.

Several ornaments similar to this one are included in the Arthur M. Sackler collections.[1] Plaques of this type often include tiny hedgehogs among the animal motifs.[2] These images were often represented on artifacts of the pastoral peoples in northern Shaanxi Province and the Ordos Desert region, where one species of hedgehog flourished.[3]

1. Bunker et al. 1997, p. 227, no. 175.
2. Salmony 1933, pl. 16:11–12.
3. For a zoological discussion of hedgehog species and their range in North China, see catalogue no. 52.

150.
Garment plaque with leopard and bear

Northwest China, 5th–4th century B.C.
Bronze
Height 2 ¼ in. (5.7 cm); width 2 ¼ in. (5.6 cm)
Ex coll.: Michael Dunn, New York

This plaque depicts a coiled leopard with slightly open jaws menacing a small bear. The eyes of both animals are represented by intaglio circles and the ears by small depressions within rounded rims. The leopard's claws are marked by indented lines, and the tail is textured by diagonals. The reverse of the plaque is slightly concave and displays two small vertical loops at the midsection, one at each edge. Flashing in the openings suggests that the object was piece-mold cast.

A plaque with an almost identical design was excavated at Dabeishan, Yanglang, in Guyuan county, southern Ningxia. The animals have been described as a mother leopard and her cub,[1] but the short tail and long muzzle are characteristic of a bear rather than a leopard. The paws are represented in a style that may ultimately derive from styles prevalent in the Minusinsk region of southern Siberia.[2]

1. Zhong and Han 1983, p. 205, fig. 2:2 and pl. 1:2; Tokyo 1988, p. 33, no. 10.
2. Zavitukhina 1983, no. 196.

The ibex can be readily identified by the regular anterior ridges that mark the length of the horn. Ibex have physical attributes that enable them to thrive in mountainous regions, such as those which exist in northern Hebei Province, where examples of this plaque have been found in Luanping county.[1] Such plaques have also been discovered in the Manhan Mountains in Liangcheng county, south-central Inner Mongolia.[2] Another example was found far to the west, in the Hanqigou cemetery, near Hami, in Xinjiang, where it was probably carried through trade.[3]

1. Seen by the author at the Luanping County Museum in 1993.
2. Tian and Guo 1986, p. 90, fig. 59:4,5.
3. *Kaogu* 1997, no. 9, p. 36.

151.
Plaque with ibex and kid

> Northern Hebei Province, 5th–4th century B.C.
> Bronze
> Height 1½ in. (3.8 cm); width 1⅜ in. (3.5 in.)
> Ex coll.: J. J. Lally & Co., New York; Lord Cunliffe Collection; Calon da Collection
> Published: Rawson and Bunker 1990, no. 209.

This small flat plaque represents an ibex with a suckling kid. The eye is marked by a circular ridge with an interior depression, a conventional treatment found on many representations of animals associated with the pastoral peoples. There are two tiny attachment loops, a vertical one beneath the kid and a horizontal one between the ibex's neck and horn. The plaque is flat on both the front and back and was cast in an open mold that resulted in minimal flashing.

152.
Garment plaque with three stags

> Northeast China, 1st–2nd century A.D.
> Gold
> Height 2⅛ in. (5.4 cm); width 3 in. (7.8 cm)
> Ex coll.: J. J. Lally & Co., New York

This gold openwork Xianbei plaque, which is very similar in design to catalogue no. 154, depicts three standing stags with their heads turned back toward their hindquarters. The stags' bodies are concave on the reverse, while the rest of the design is flat. The plaque was cast by the lost-wax process, the openings in the wax model having been cut through from the front.

Numerous Xianbei ornaments that carry this design have been found throughout North China. A very handsome gold example comes from a burial at Jingtan, Qahar Youyi Hou banner, Ulanqab league, southeastern Inner Mongolia.[1] Some examples are cast in gold; some in bronze covered with thin gold sheet, such as catalogue no. 154; and others are in plain bronze, depending on the status of the owner.

1. Desroches 2000, p. 159, no. 147.

153.
Garment plaque in the shape of two horses

North China, 1st–3rd century A.D.
Bronze
Height 1⅝ in. (4.1 cm); width 2⅜ in. (5.9 cm)
Ex coll.: Michael Dunn, New York

This plaque is cast in the shape of a small horse on top of a larger horse. The bottom horse's folded legs are so abstracted that they form a straight line. The reverse of the plaque is slightly concave and carries no loops. The plaque is lost-wax cast.

Plaques cast in similar shapes depicting horses have been found throughout North China and are associated with the Xianbei people.[1] The Xianbei were among the Donghu people conquered by the Xiongnu during the formation of their extensive empire in the late third century B.C. By the first century A.D., the Xianbei had succeeded the Xiongnu as the dominant pastoral people on China's northern frontier.

Plaques in the shape of a large horse surmounted by a smaller horse appear to have been one of the Xianbei's most distinctive visual motifs. Similar examples have been excavated at a Xianbei cemetery in Houbaoshi, Da'an, Jilin.[2] Those found in Qinghai Province with geometric designs on the body and with recognizable Xianbei decoration are later in date[3] and can be associated with a breakaway Xianbei group better known as the Tuyuhun.[4]

A less stylized version of this design on a plaque cast in gold was excavated in Horqin Zuoyi Zhong banner, Jirem league, Inner Mongolia, and shows how the legs of the bottom horse were originally depicted before they were abstracted into a straight line.[5] The legs on the gold example are folded under the horse but do not overlap, as they do on catalogue nos. 32 and 135. This folded-leg pose is quite different from that of the recumbent ungulates portrayed in earlier artifacts made in North China.

1. Bunker et al. 1997, pp. 279 and 283, no. 253; Kessler 1993, p. 76.
2. Guo Min 1997, p. 86, fig. 1:1–4.
3. Feng Zhou 1983, p. 104.
4. Tony Anninos, unpublished manuscript, 2001.
5. Kessler 1993, p. 76.

154.

Garment plaque with three stags

> Northeast China, 1st–3rd century A.D.
> Bronze wrapped with gold sheet
> Height 1 ⅞ in. (4.8 cm); width 3 in. (7.6 cm)
> Ex coll.: Joseph G. Gerena Fine Art, New York

Three standing stags within a stylized ropelike border are represented on this openwork Xianbei plaque. The area above the stags' heads suggests vegetation, continuing a scheme used on earlier ornaments cast for the Xiongnu. The plaque is lost-wax cast and wrapped with gold sheet. On the reverse, the stags' bodies are seen to be concave, like those on catalogue no. 117.

Similar ornaments depicting stags in an openwork design have been found throughout Northeast China, in areas controlled by the Xianbei.[1] Although the designs on many Xianbei plaques became increasingly abstracted, the message they imparted was understood as well as if the scene had been more easily recognizable.[2]

Mercury gilding was seldom used by the Xianbei, who gilded their artifacts by applying gold sheet to the bronze surface. A gold version of the present design was excavated at Sandaowan, Qahar Youyi Hou banner, Ulanqab league, southeastern Inner Mongolia.[3]

1. Bunker et al. 1997, pp. 281–82.
2. For a less abstracted example of this Xianbei symbol, see Su 1977, p. 46, fig. 6, where the stags are misidentified as ibex. See also Qi 1999, p. 245, fig. 2.95.
3. Li and Wei 1994, p. 419, fig. 14:5.

6. PERSONAL ORNAMENTS

Personal ornaments included in this section are pectorals, shoe buckles, amulets, circular plaques, and one bone bead. The pectorals were as important as belt decorations among the pastoral peoples of northern Hebei and the Dongbei. For the ancient Chinese, nephrite (jade) was the symbol of excellence long before the introduction of metal. The initial inspiration to wear metal next to the skin had priority among ancient China's pastoral neighbors, but the custom was soon adopted in nuclear China and became a major indication of status and rank by the first millennium A.D.

155.
Kulan-shaped pectoral

> Northeast China, 6th century B.C.
> Gold
> Height 2⅝ in. (6.7 cm); width 3⅜ in. (8.4 cm)
> Ex coll.: J. J. Lally & Co., New York

This gold plaque, in the form of a standing male kulan, signified the status of the owner who wore it as an emblem on his chest. The kulan is shown in profile with only two legs but both ears depicted, and the mane is represented by raised striations. The overly large ears and tassel at the end of the tail confirm its identity. Two vertical V-shaped loops for attachment are placed on the reverse, one behind the muzzle and the other behind the haunch. The plaque has rather jagged edges and appears to have been cast in a two-piece mold. It has not been overly cleaned and still retains a bit of red cinnabar on the head from burial rituals. The tail appears to have been reattached in antiquity, as it is not a recent mend.

The wild ass roamed over a good part of North China and beyond in ancient times. The prominent emphasis on sexuality associates this ornament with the hunting cultures of Northeast China, where genitals were frequently depicted in representations of both humans and animals. One of the tombs unearthed in 1963 at Nanshan'gen, Ningcheng county, yielded two bronze ladles with handles in the shape of male genitals.[1] They are also displayed on a bronze stag unearthed at Longtoushan, Hexigten banner, southeastern Inner Mongolia, as is the unusual combination of only two legs but both ears in profile.[2] Gold appears to have been far more popular among the peoples of Northeast China during the earlier part of the first millennium B.C. than it was among the pastoral groups inhabiting the northern grasslands west of the Taihang Mountains.

Hunting was a major factor in the local economy of the pastoral peoples of Northeast China and the adjacent area of southeastern Inner Mongolia,[3] and the need for visual symbols of fertility to assure the proliferation of wild game may explain the widespread representation of this pronounced sexual image. Scenes of wild animals copulating were also popular subjects on grave goods found in Northeast China.

1. Shanghai 2000, p. 119.
2. So and Bunker 1995, pp. 64–65.
3. Bunker et al. 1997, p. 166.

156.
Horse-shaped pectoral

> Northeast China or Hebei Province, ca. 6th century B.C.
> Gold
> Height 2 in. (5 cm); width 3½ in. (8.9 cm)
> Ex coll.: Ariadne Galleries, Inc., New York

This handsome gold pectoral represents a standing horse in profile. Perforations mark the eye, shoulder, and haunch, as well as the nostril, ear, and mouth. The mane is notched and protrudes from the surface. Red powder, probably cinnabar, can be seen in crevices both on the front and back of the plaque, which also displays two small vertical loops along the top edge. A clear wear pattern on the loops suggests that a cord was passed through both loops, running through two notches worn into the top rim and then farther upward around the owner's neck, to form a V-shape. The loops were integrally cast with the plaque by the lost-wax process.

The horse shown here is a Przewalski, identifiable by the upright mane and fringed tail.[1] Horses played a major role in

the culture of the hunting peoples in the mountain regions of northern Hebei Province, and they are depicted on many excavated artifacts associated with these peoples.[2] The pierced anatomical features relate this plaque to catalogue no. 157, a leopard-shaped pectoral, suggesting that it was used for the same purpose, serving a function that is consistent with the wear patterns on the loops.

1. Bökönyi 1974; Clutton-Brock 1981, pp. 81–84.
2. Bunker et al. 1997, nos. 115, 118, 132.

157.
Leopard-shaped pectoral

> North China, Hebei Province, ca. 6th century B.C.
> Gold with turquoise inlay
> Height 1¾ in. (4.4 cm); width 4⅛ in. (10.5 cm)
> Ex coll.: Joseph G. Gerena Fine Art, New York

This gold pectoral takes the form of a crouching leopard shown in profile. Turquoise inlays once marked the tail tip, shoulder, haunch, paws, eye, and mouth, but only two inlays now remain. A short strut between the tail and hind leg acts as a support. The reverse is hollow and displays two vertical attachment loops, one behind the neck and the other behind the

haunch. The plaque is lost-wax cast. The back leg and tail were previously broken off; they have recently been reattached.

Several gold plaques very similar in shape and design to this one have been found in Tang county, northern Hebei Province.[1] Another superb gold example was discovered in a male burial at Yuhuangmiao, Jundushan, Yanqing county, Beijing, worn high on the chest as a pectoral to indicate clan and rank.[2] The use of gold proclaimed the wearer's status, which was higher than that of someone with a plain bronze pectoral.

1. Beijing 1980b, p. 96, pl. 170.
2. Jin Fengyi 1990, p. 6; So and Bunker 1995, p. 50, fig. 18; Bunker et al. 1997, fig. 91A.

158.
Deer amulet

Northeast China, 5th century B.C.
Bronze
Height 1 ⅜ in. (3.5 cm); width 1 ¼ in. (3.2 cm)
Ex coll.: J. J. Lally & Co., New York; Calon da Collection

This amulet takes the form of a deer with folded legs and abstracted antlers surmounted on a short twisted shaft with an attachment loop. Both the antlers, a series of three tangent circles and ribbed to suggest texture, and the eye, rendered by a raised circle with an indented center, are conceived as highly stylized, a characteristic feature of Eurasian steppe art. A mold mark along the edges and in the openings indicates that the amulet was cast in a two-piece mold.

No amulets of this type have been found archaeologically, but numerous collected—rather than excavated—examples

are included in the collections of the Inner Mongolia Museum, Hohhot, and the Arthur M. Sackler collections.[1] A set of twenty plaques in the Shelby White and Leon Levy collection (cat. no. 135), each in the shape of a deer similar to the present one, has been dated to the sixth century B.C. and associated stylistically with the art of Northeast China.[2] Similar deer-shaped plaques, but no amulets, have also been excavated at Ganzibao, Huailai county, north of Beijing.[3] The White-Levy deer and the Ganzibao deer have the same stylized antlers represented by tangent circles, a feature that also occurs on the deer-shaped harness jingle in the Thaw collection (cat. no. 29).

The stag's pose, in which the legs overlap, is a characteristic leg position for representing ungulates that had developed throughout the Eurasian steppes by the early first millennium B.C.[4] Such a pose can be seen on many deerstones found throughout southern Siberia and Mongolia[5] and on the seventh-century B.C. gold belt fragment from the Ziwiye hoard, from northern Iran (cat. no. 168).

1. Tian and Guo 1986, p. 133, fig. 97:2–4; Bunker et al. 1997, p. 172, no. 83.
2. So and Bunker 1995, p. 160, no. 83; Takahama and Hatakeyama 1997, pl. 149.
3. He and Liu 1993, p. 31, fig. 9:4.
4. For a discussion of the deer motif with flowing antlers, see Bunker et al. 1997, p. 171.
5. Chlenova 1963, pp. 66–67, tables 1, 2.

159.
Cylinder-shaped bead

Northwest China, 4th–3rd century B.C.
Bone
Height 1 ¾ in. (4.4 cm); diameter ⅝ in. (1.6 cm)
Ex coll.: Anthony Hardy; Calon da Collection
Published: So and Bunker 1995, p. 138, fig. 56.1.

This small carved bone cylinder is decorated with a mythological ungulate with an eared, raptor-headed tail flanked by two striated bands. The ungulate has a rapacious beak rather than a muzzle, its hindquarters are twisted 180 degrees, and carved striated enclosures give texture to the body. Such features may have originated in stamped leatherwork and in wood and bone carving, surface markings that were then translated into bronze on belt plaques such as catalogue no. 63.

Another silver ornament similar to this one is included in the collection of Therese and Erwin Harris.[1] Several similar objects cast in gold were excavated from tomb 30 at Xinzhuangtou, near Yi county, Hebei Province, the southern capital of the Yan state during the late fourth and third centuries B.C. Evidence for Chinese manufacture of the Xinzhuangtou plaques is provided on the back of each ornament by inscribed characters indicating the weight of the gold in the Yan weight system.[2] How this ornament was worn is not known

1. So and Bunker 1995, p. 139, no. 58.
2. Shi Yongshi 1980, pp. 172–75; Li Xueqin 1985a, p. 335, fig. 150.

To date, no identical objects have been excavated archaeologically, but the raptor-headed appendage relates the image to certain mythological creatures represented on the tattooed man from Pazyryk, kurgan 2 (fig. 37). Surface patterns that are similar also embellish belt plaques cast during the second and first centuries B.C., as can be seen on numerous examples in the Thaw collection (see, for example, cat. nos. 99, 100).

160.
Ornament with goat

> North China, 3rd century B.C.
> Silver
> Diameter 1½ in. (3.8 cm)
> Ex coll.: Michael Dunn, New York

A wild goat with its inverted hindquarters slung over its head embellishes this small silver ornament. Striated enclosures mark the goat's body, which has been ingeniously manipulated to surround the central opening. The ornament is lost-wax cast from a wax model formed in a mold.

161.
Ornament with fantastic creature

> North China, 2nd century B.C.
> Gilded bronze
> Diameter 2⅛ in. (5.4 cm)
> Ex coll.: J. J. Lally & Co., New York; Calon da Collection; Eskenazi Ltd., London
> Published: So and Bunker 1995, p. 159, no. 82.

A fantastic creature with a beak, long ear, cloven front hoof, hindquarters twisted 180 degrees, and clawed hind paw is coiled to fit within a thick, ropelike frame on this circular gilded-bronze ornament. One of three curved hooks projects from the edge of the ornament; the other two have broken off. A small attachment loop is located in the center of the concave underside. The ornament is cast by the lost-wax process, and inlay may once have filled the eye socket.

Fantastic, composite animals with twisted hindquarters appeared in the art of the steppes around the middle of the first millennium B.C. Creatures with twisted hindquarters are seen on a carved wooden sixth-century B.C. coffin from Bashadar in the Altai Mountains (fig. 32) and later were represented on artifacts belonging to the pastoral peoples bordering Northwest China, such as catalogue nos. 63 and 94. The elegance of the present ornament represents a characteristic steppe motif that has been Sinicized to suit the exotic princely tastes of the Western Han elite. The plaque may also have served as a *xiangrui*, a symbol of auspicious portent in Han culture.[1]

1. So and Bunker 1995, p. 159, no. 82.

162.
Pair of buckles with recumbent boars

> Rostov and Volgograd regions, Russia, 2nd century B.C.–
> 1st century A.D.
> Gold inlaid with glass and turquoise
> Each: Height 1¼ in. (3.1 cm); width 1¾ in. (4.5 cm)
> Lent by Shelby White and Leon Levy
> Ex coll.: von Bothmer 1990, pp. 63–64, no. 46.

A recumbent boar in high relief is represented on each of these gold buckles. The boar is shown with a hind leg overlapping one foreleg, while the other foreleg extends forward. A heart-shaped inlay cell, now empty, is placed behind each animal. The hooves, shoulder, and rump are distinguished by inlays, mostly turquoise, while glass inlays that are badly crizzled mark the eyes and ears.

The buckles were formed by hammering sheet gold into a matrix from the back, and the details were made by chasing on the front of each buckle. On the reverse, at the end opposite the hook, is a silver loop attached by solder. A small upright pin, visible on the underside, has been inserted just in front of the oblong opening to serve as the hook with which to fasten the buckle. The plaques are essentially mirror images with minor differences, which suggests that they may have been made at the same time in the same workshop but by two different goldsmiths.[1]

No buckles similar to the White-Levy buckles have yet been discovered, but several Sarmatian ornaments display stylistic characteristics similar to those on the buckles. Only one hind leg and both forelegs of each boar are depicted, a typical artistic convention present in Sarmatian art of the first century B.C. For example, a gold belt plaque from the Rostov region, east of the Black Sea, depicts deer with only one hind leg but both forelegs.[2] The deer on the Rostov belt plaque are shown in profile like the boars on the White-Levy buckles, but, like the boars, the deer are shown with two ears. On both the Rostov plaque and the buckles the animals' hooves are

identified by tear-shaped inlays. The dot-and-comma motif on the hindquarters of each boar is another Sarmatian trait and distinguishes the animal depicted on a gold belt buckle excavated in the Volgograd region.[3]

The two White-Levy buckles may have been intended to be shoe buckles, like catalogue no. 163, which has a similar fastening hook. The fact that each plaque has a hook precludes their being part of the same buckle, as each is made to function separately. On the basis of the stylistic and technical similarities, the two buckles can be tentatively attributed to the Sarmatians, the major horse-riding people who succeeded the Scythians as masters of the western Eurasian steppes by the second century B.C.

1. For a more detailed technical and stylistic analysis, see Karen Rubinson's excellent entry in von Bothmer 1990, pp. 63–64, no. 46. I would also like to thank Dr. Rubinson for her help with this entry.
2. Schiltz 1995, p. 91, no. 113.
3. Ibid., p. 44, no. 62.

163.
Shoe buckle in the shape of a recumbent ram

Bactria, 1st century B.C. – 1st century A.D.
Gold and turquoise
Height 2¼ in. (5.7 cm); width 2⅛ in. (5.4 cm)
Ex coll.: Michael and Henrietta Spink, London

This heavy gold buckle takes the form of a recumbent ram whose frontal head with arching horns is placed in the center of a profile body. Tool marks are still visible on the reverse, where the wax used to form the model was pushed into the mold. The back once had loops, now missing. A button for fastening purposes, above the ram's head, was positioned by being pushed through a perforation, and is still movable. The turquoise inlays appear to be original. There are several mends to the gold visible from the back that were done in antiquity. The buckle is cast by lost wax.

Small gold buckles similar in type have been excavated at Tillyatepe, in what was ancient Bactria, a site located in present-day Afghanistan.[1] The site was occupied by pastoral peoples who had fled western China after their defeat by the Xiongnu in the second century B.C. The present plaque was originally one of a matched pair of shoe buckles, similar to a pair excavated at Tillyatepe. Even the tips of the ram's horns turn up at the ends the same way as they do on the Tillyatepe artifacts, which date from the first century B.C. to the first century A.D.[2]

1. Sarianidi 1985, p. 246, site 4, fig. 4.2.
2. Ibid., pl. 164.

7. MIRRORS, TOOLS FOR MUSICAL INSTRUMENTS, AND CEREMONIAL PARAPHERNALIA

Section seven includes mirrors, tools for tuning and tightening strings on musical instruments, and a few objects whose functions have not yet been determined. Many of these, such as the tools for musical instruments, are considered traditional Chinese objects. However, the decoration frequently reflects a northern stylistic element. The presence of mountain forms on one example (cat. no. 179) suggests that three-dimensional landscape representation in early Han and later Chinese painting may have been inspired, in part, through contact with the steppe world.

164.
Implement with curved blade

> North China, ca. 13th–11th century B.C.
> Bronze
> Length 12¼ in. (31.1 cm)
> The Metropolitan Museum of Art, Purchase, Fletcher Fund, 1923 (23.226.6)
> Published: So and Bunker 1995, pp. 99–100, no. 13.

This implement has a slender, blunt blade that broadens to a rounded end. The handle, separated from the blade by a double-spiraled guard, terminates in a playful-looking animal's head with goggly eyes and a moveable tongue in an open mouth. The creature's flat body merges with the shaft of the handle, while its pointed tail extends into the ridge of the blade. A rectangular opening pierces through the shaft near the guard.

Several similar implements have been found on the northern frontiers of China, where the Shang had frequent contact with the nomadic cultures. The example excavated at Gaocheng, Hebei Province, is similar in design but decorated on the handle with an ibex.[1] Three other examples, found in Shanxi Province—two at Shilou and one at Suide—have the same animal's head with a moveable tongue on the handle.[2] Among the three, the two from Shilou have a hollow handle with an openwork design that was once inlaid with turquoise.[3]

The function of this implement remains unknown. Chinese archaeologists generally refer to it as a *bi,* implying that they regard it as a utensil for scooping up food, but its shape differs so significantly from that of *bi* found at late Shang sites that it could not possibly have served the same function. Moreover, the blade is too narrow to scoop up food effectively. It has also been suggested that the implement served as a wand for a shaman, but there is no evidence to support this argument,[4] and we have yet to look to future discoveries for help in solving this puzzle.   ZS

1. Lin Yun 1986, p. 249, fig. 50:6.
2. Tao 1985, p. 63, fig. 5:9.
3. Bunker et al. 1997, p. 115.
4. So and Bunker 1995, pp. 99–100; Bunker et al. 1997, p. 115.

165.
Ornament with six bells

North China, early first millennium B.C.
Bronze
Length 6⅞ in. (17.5 cm)
Katherine and George Fan

This ornament is formed by two hollow tubes placed parallel to each other and joined by two struts, one near each end. Both the tubes and the three bells suspended from loops on the outer sides are embellished with a medley of designs based on triangles, zigzags, and hatched lines. Each bell is crudely cast in the shape of a cone, with four triangular perforations and a clapper. The clapper of each bell was cast first, then the bell, and finally all six bells were placed in the mold and the double-tube object cast onto them.[1]

Small bells with clappers, frequently suspended from the underside of vessels or associated with horse and chariot equipment, have been found at numerous northern sites dating to the late second and early first millennium B.C.[2]

Noisemakers that jingled when the objects to which they were attached were moved figure prominently in cultures in which shamanism played a major role. They are unrelated to the development of Chinese musical bells, which were actually percussion instruments played by striking specific areas on the bells rather than by moving them.

Although no jingles identical to this one have been found in archaeological context, objects decorated with similar linear geometric forms have been found throughout the Dongbei.[3] Traditionally, scholars have given more attention to zoomorphic motifs than to geometric decorations and linear patterns, a tendency no longer adequate in the light of recent archaeological finds. Similar designs in various combinations adorn the belts of male figures carved on deerstones found in northern Mongolia.[4] Such patterns must originally have had specific symbolic meanings: since their distribution, as on the present jingle, is intentional not just random.

1. On the casting of similarly shaped bells, see Bagley 1987, p. 43.
2. So and Bunker 1995, pp. 34–35.
3. Jin 1982, figs. 4–5.
4. Novgorodova 1989, p. 131.

166.
Drum

     Northeast China, 7th century B.C.
     Bronze
     Height 9 in. (22.9 cm); max. diameter 5 in. (12.7 cm)
     Katherine and George Fan

The larger open end of this one-sided, waisted drum was originally covered with a membrane of thin skin that served as the tympanum. Below the area where the membrane would have been attached, the surface is decorated by three bands of raised running triangles that alternate with two bands of raised lines. These reflect the original stitching that would have affixed the membrane to the body of a wooden or pottery drum. Two mold seam marks that have been filed down are barely visible on the sides of the drum.

Two similar drums were excavated in the Dongbei, but their musical function was not recognized and they were referred to simply as drum-shaped objects. One bronze example was unearthed at Xiaoheishigou, Ningcheng county, southeastern Inner Mongolia, and in 1992 another similar example made of red pottery was discovered.[1]

The identification of this object as a drum was recently confirmed after discussions with the music archaeologist Bo Lawergren. Several waisted drums made of horn, with shapes similar to the present bronze drum, were excavated from tombs at Pazyryk, in the Altai Mountains in Siberia, dating to the fourth and third centuries B.C.[2]

Ceramic drums with similar waisted shapes have been identified at Neolithic sites in North China, from present-day Shandong Province in the east to Gansu in the west.[3] Many of these examples predate the earliest evidence for this type of drum in northwestern Eurasia at Beycesultan, an Anatolian site in Turkey dated to 1900–1550 B.C.[4] Whether there is a relationship between eastern and western waisted drums is yet to be determined, as the intermediary links, if they ever existed, have not been discovered. The Beycesultan skin stitching seems to be the same as the stitching that once attached the skin membrane to the present drum.

It is worth mentioning that waisted drums were completely alien to Zhou ritual orchestras and do not occur in China again until the first millennium A.D., when they were reintroduced by foreign orchestras associated with Buddhism by way of the Silk Road.[5]

1. Duan 1995, p. 63, pl. 200.
2. Rudenko 1970, pp. 277–78, fig. 138.
3. Gao 1991, p. 127, fig. 2; Rawson 1996, pp. 42–43. The suggestion that the membranes of such drums may have been made from crocodile skin should be amended to alligator skin, as the crocodile was never native to North China; see Bunker 1979; Bunker et al. 1997, pp. 114–15.
4. Lawergren 1997, p. 166.
5. Lawergren 1995–96, fig. 2.

167.
Mirror with ungulates

Volga River region, Russia, 8th–7th century B.C.
Bronze
Height 7 in. (17.8 cm); width 7½ in. (19.1 cm)
Published: Sotheby's, New York, sale cat., December 8, 2000.

This oval mirror with two finlike projections on the flanged rim is decorated in relief with four standing ungulates: an ibex, a horse, a bovine, and a Bactrian camel. The mirror is lost-wax cast and was once highly polished.

A mirror of this type, but missing one fin, was discovered at Selitrennoye Gorodhishiche, near Volgograd, Russia.[1] Another example, also missing a fin, is in the Ortiz collection.[2] It has been suggested that the Ortiz mirror once had a handle attached through the holes now visible where the break occurred. In antiquity, it may have been provided with a handle after it was damaged, but such mirrors in their original form did not have fixed handles, as demonstrated by the present example.

It would appear that mirrors of this type were cast in western Eurasia. To date, such mirrors have had little scholarly attention, and traditionally they have been associated with the circular mirrors with zoomorphic decoration in raised thread relief found in eastern Eurasia.[3] With the appearance of this undamaged example, further investigation into the history of this unusual type of mirror is now indicated.

1. Takahama and Hatakeyama 1997, p. 89, fig. 89.2.
2. Ortiz 1994, no. 213.
3. Takahama and Hatakeyama 1997, p. 168, figs. 89–1, 89–3.

168.
Plaque fragment with zoomorphic motif

Northwestern Iran, Ziwiye, 7th century B.C.
Gold
Height 5⅝ in. (14.3 cm); width 2¼ in. (5.7 cm)
The Metropolitan Museum of Art, Purchase, Joseph Pulitzer Bequest, 1950 (50.196a, b)
Published: Wilkinson 1955, p. 219; Amandry 1966, fig. 4:9; Goldman 1974–77, pp. 55–57, figs. 1–4.

This gold fragment is embellished with images in repoussé of ibex and deer placed within alternating ribbon-framed spaces linked together by frontal lions' heads. The ibex and deer are shown in profile, their legs drawn in under the body, with the legs overlapping.

The design of the plaque was most likely produced by hammering sheet gold over a wooden matrix. Remnants of the borders reveal perforations punched through from the front that must have served to attach the plaque to a larger object.

The numerous extant sheet-gold fragments that carry the same decoration must once have comprised an object excavated from the remains of the ancient citadel on Ziwiye, a hill in Iranian Kurdistan about twenty-five miles east of Saqqiz.[1] Known as the Ziwiye Treasure, the artifacts from this find have been dated to the seventh century B.C. by stylistic comparison with objects from the ancient Near East that were excavated under controlled conditions.[2]

A projected reconstruction of these fragments suggests that they once formed the sheathing of a belt, presumably backed by leather or cloth.[3] But the fact that similar bronze sheathing, once also associated with a belt, is over seventy-eight inches in length calls into question the identification of the

Metropolitan's fragment as belt decoration.[4] Under the circumstances, its original function must remain open, until further information becomes available.

The motif of a deer with flowing antlers and folded legs, with the hooves pointing forward and backward, has traditionally been associated with the Scythians, who were already in the Black Sea region by the seventh century B.C.[5] Although reindeer are not known among the fauna of northwestern Eurasia, the animal must have remained in the collective memory of this people, remnants of their earlier homeland in southern Siberia. Images of deer with flowing antlers occurred earlier on deerstones in southern Siberia and Mongolia and were then modified in northwestern Asia, where the image was combined with Near Eastern and Greek elements to form what was to become a hallmark of Scythian art.[6]

1. For descriptions of the site and the Treasure, see Godard 1950; Porada 1965, pp. 123–36; Amandry 1966; and Jettmar 1967, p. 220.
2. Goldman 1974–77, pp. 56–57.
3. Amandry 1966, where the Metropolitan Museum fragment is shown in the reconstruction as fig. 4:9.
4. Goldman 1974–77, pp. 66–67.
5. Chlenova 1963, for a discussion of cervid images.
6. Amandry 1966, pp. 149–50; Bunker et al. 1997, pp. 170–71.

169.
Fitting with two horses' heads

> Northeast China, 6th–5th century B.C.
> Bronze
> Height 4¼ in. (10.8 cm); length 13¾ in. (34.9 cm)
> Ex coll.: J. J. Lally & Co., New York

Two superb horse's heads in the round adorn this fitting. Each horse is shown with alert, upright ears, round eyes indicated by circular raised rims with sunken centers, and slightly open mouths outlined with indented lines. The fitting itself is a long bar with thirteen circular perforations. The horse's heads were first lost-wax cast and then cast onto the fitting. Both the heads and the fitting are made of a lead, tin, and copper alloy, and corrosion extends over the cast-on parts.

To date, nothing similar is known from a controlled excavation, but stylistically the piece appears to conform to the artistic vocabulary of the hunting and pastoral peoples who inhabited Northeast China. A plain bar of similar shape with thirteen perforations in the David-Weill collection was published as a chariot ornament, but confirmation must await future archaeological evidence.[1]

1. David-Weill sale 1972, no. 67.

170.
Figure of a young man

North China, Shanxi Province, 5th century B.C.
Bronze
Height 4 in. (10.2 cm)
The Metropolitan Museum of Art, Gift of Ernest Erickson
Foundation, 1985 (85.214.48)

This small bronze sculpture, in the Metropolitan Museum, represents a young man in a lively pose with upraised arms. He stands on his right leg with his face turned to the right, while his left knee is bent, suggesting that he is about to move forward. He wears a short jacket belted at the waist with a sash and shoes and appears to be barelegged. A short sword in a scabbard is secured to his sash at the back by a scabbard slide, and indented lines mark the details of his costume. The pres-

ence of mold seam marks indicates that the figure is piece-mold cast.

The young man's attire and bare legs and the short sword that he carries suggest that he is not Chinese but a northerner from beyond the frontiers of China. A virtually identical counterpart to this figure in mirror image is in the Freer Gallery of Art, Washington, D.C.[1] At some point, the Freer figure was transformed into an acrobat by attaching a *qin* tuning key surmounted by a bear to his raised right hand. The tuning key was later removed.[2] Excavations at the Jin state foundry site at Houma, Shanxi Province, have yielded several clay models and mold fragments for casting figures in similar dress and wearing short swords at the back. The swords are secured by scabbard slides dating to the fifth century B.C., suggesting that both the Freer and the Metropolitan figures were cast at Houma.[3]

To date, the original function of these two figures has not been determined, but they must represent foreigners at the court of a northern Eastern Zhou principality, as does the figure of a wrestler that serves as a lampstand in the Miho Museum, Shigaraki.[4] A careful examination of the Metropolitan figure suggests that it may once have been part of a much larger assemblage. The palm of the right hand reveals a filed-down stump, and the sole of the right shoe has been drilled. The Metropolitan and Freer figures are so similar that it is reasonable to consider that they may once have served as decoration at the opposite corners of some larger object.

These figures display one of the earliest Chinese representations of a scabbard slide. This accoutrement was invented in an equestrian culture that matured in the Ural steppes of southern Russia from the seventh to the sixth century B.C. It was not introduced into China, however, until the fifth century B.C. When it first appeared in China, it was associated with bronze short swords, and only later with a long sword, which did not develop until late in the Warring States period.[5]

1. Lawton 1982, no. 37.
2. So and Bunker 1995, pp. 97–98; Bunker 1997, pp. 67, 69, fig. 4.
3. Li, Liang, and Bagley 1996, pp. 484–88, belonging to phase v, dated to the fifth century on p. 81.
4. Bunker 1997, fig. 1.
5. Trousdale 1975; for a summary of Trousdale's thesis, see Bunker 1978b.

171.

Mirror with ibex

Northwest China, Xinjiang region, 5th–4th century B.C.
Bronze
Height 4⅝ in. (11.7 cm); diameter of mirror 3¼ in. (8.3 cm)
Ex. coll.: J. J. Lally & Co., New York

A standing ibex with gracefully curved, ridged horns shown in profile serves as the handle of this mirror. The ibex is highly stylized, with a round depression marking the eye and muzzle. The legs, which are attached to the rim of the mirror, are abstracted into two cone shapes. A circular, slightly convex disk, the mirror has a highly polished reflecting surface on one side, while the reverse is left unfinished and encircled by a turned-up rim. A small but sturdy horizontal loop, which was piece-mold cast integrally with the figure and by which the mirror could be suspended, is placed behind the ibex's body. The mirror appears to have been cast separately and then the ibex handle soldered onto the rim. The smooth, silvery surface indicates that the alloy is a high tin bronze.

A mirror of similar design was excavated in 1965 at Weizixiaxiang, Yiwu district, Xinjiang,[1] and mirrors with similar tangentially attached zoomorphic handles have been excavated from Scythian tombs in the Black Sea region, where they were produced between the sixth and the fourth century B.C.[2] A sixth-to-fifth-century B.C. mirror of similar design but with a much larger animal-shaped handle was excavated in the Minusinsk region of southern Siberia,[3] suggesting that this type of mirror was probably introduced into the Xinjiang region from elsewhere in the Eurasian steppes.

1. Mu, Qi, and Zhang 1994, p. 219, no. 109. The first-century A.D. date given for this excavated example is far too late, unless the mirror was retained as an heirloom for a long period of time.
2. Jacobson 1995, fig. 72.
3. Zavitukhina 1983, no. 148.

bisected by a mold mark, indicating that the doe and socket were cast integrally in one pour.

The intertwined serpents display stylistic features usually associated with artifacts cast at the Jin state foundry at Houma, in southern Shanxi Province, such as scaly texturing that enhances their reptilian bodies. Similar interlaced designs are also seen on artifacts excavated from Qin tombs in southern Shaanxi. It is unclear what these fittings were originally attached to, but they exhibit a curious combination of both Qin and northern elements, suggesting that they may have been made by Qin craftsmen expressly for their herding, non-Chinese neighbors.[2]

1. Bunker et al. 1997, p. 250, no. 210; see also catalogue nos. 32–34.
2. For a discussion of these two fittings and their stylistic relationships, see So 1992, fig. 8.

173.
Bird's head finial

Northwest China, Ningxia and Gansu, ca. 4th century B.C.
Bronze
Height 1 1/2 in. (3.8 cm); width 1 in. (2.5 cm)
Ex. coll.: Michael Dunn, New York

This small finial is cast in the shape of the head of a bird of prey. Each of the bird's eyes is represented by a boss surrounded by a circular depression, and the mouth by a long indentation with a raised central strip that follows the curve of the beak. The socket is rectangular, with a hole on either side for attachment. The piece is hollow cast, and a mold mark bisects it longitudinally.

172.
Pair of horse fittings with does

Northwest China, Ningxia and Gansu, 5th–4th century B.C.
Tinned bronze
Each: Height 4 3/4 in. (12.1 cm); width 1 5/8 in. (4.1 cm)
Ex. coll.: J. J. Lally & Co., New York; Calon da Collection; R. H. Ellsworth, Ltd., New York
Published: Rawson and Bunker 1990, pp. 352–53, no. 230; So 1992, fig. 8.

Each of these two rectangular sockets is surmounted by an alert-looking doe with a turned head. The socket is adorned on two sides with three intertwined serpents, their bodies marked by longitudinal, scale-textured bands. Each doe has a hollow, open-ended muzzle, a characteristic of deer-shaped yoke ornaments from the Ningxia–Gansu region.[1] The silvery colored surface is the result of intentional tinning and the reddish patches, of corrosion. The sockets have two large oval holes in each side for attachment, and the entire fitting is

Eagles and other birds of prey are often represented on artifacts associated with the pastoral peoples on the northwestern frontier of China. Several small finials similar to the present one have been excavated at burial sites in Ningxia, at Wangjiaping, Touying township,[1] and at Langwozikeng, Zhongwei county.[2] In a herding economy, eagles were dangerous predators, as they could carry off the young animals that were so vital to survival. They were also used in falconry, which even today is popular in certain regions of the Eurasian steppes (fig. 35).

1. Zhong and Han 1983, p. 205, fig. 3:6–7.
2. Zhou 1989, p. 976, fig. 6:4.

This unusual ornament is cast in the shape of a donut and surmounted by a recumbent ibex. A raised spiral marks the shoulder and haunch, and a raised circle describes the eye. The back of the ornament is flat and has a horizontal loop behind the shoulder. The plaque was piece-mold cast with flashing left here and there in the openings.

Whether this ornament was purely decorative or had some specific function is as yet unknown, but it was certainly attached to something by the loop on the reverse. No identical artifact has been found in archaeological context, but the object is characteristic of the type associated with the pastoral peoples of the eastern Eurasian steppes.

174.
Ornament with ibex

Eastern Eurasian steppes, ca. 4th century B.C.
Bronze
Height 4½ in. (11.4 cm); width 3⅜ in. (8.6 cm)
Ex. coll.: Michael Dunn, New York

175.
Two carved bone finials

Northwest China, 4th–3rd century B.C.
Bone
Left: Height 1¾ in. (4.3 cm); width 1½ in. (3.8 cm)
Right: Height 1½ in. (3.7 cm); width 1 in. (2.5 cm)
Ex. coll.: Joseph G. Gerena Fine Art, New York

These two bone finials are beautifully carved with spiral designs in broad, graceful lines accentuated by sunken curvilinear spaces. Following the carving of the bone, the finials were given a smooth, highly polished surface. A circular socket drilled into the base of each finial would have enabled it to be attached to some as yet unidentified object.

Bone artifacts with curvilinear designs similar to those seen here have been recovered from pastoral burials in

southern Ningxia, in the Guyuan region. Several were found at Yanglong,[1] and others in burials at the Yujiazhuang cemetery, Pengpu township.[2]

Objects of bone were not uncommon among the pastoral peoples, but they rarely survived and are not always accorded the same attention as that given to bronze artifacts. An easily available animal product, bone could readily be made into buckles, ornaments, and other fittings, even when people were on the move. To produce the polished surface and gracefully carved designs that occur on these finials took a highly accomplished craftsman.

1. *Kaogu xuebao* 1993, no. 1, p. 45, fig. 26:2, 4, 5.
2. *Kaogu xuebao* 1995, no. 1, p. 99, fig. 18:6.

176.
Raptor's-head finial

Northwest China, Ningxia, 3rd century B.C.
Tinned bronze
Height 5½ in. (14 cm); width ⅞ in. (2.2 cm)
Ex. coll.: R. H. Ellsworth, Ltd., New York

This finial is cast in the shape of a stylized raptor's head with a long neck. The eyes are each represented by a bulging, oval-shaped boss and the beak by a sharp, curved triangle. The neck terminates in a long tubular socket with a ridged ring that may imitate an earlier mechanical coupling join which has been retained as a decorative element. Two holes are visible, one behind each ear, but their function or what they once held is unknown. The finial is hollow, with wood fragments remaining inside. It is a lost-wax-cast leaded, tin bronze, with a surface that has been enriched by tinning. The finial is further distinguished by splashes of vermilion cinnabar, a red substance often used as a ritual preservative in burials.

The extreme stylization of this finial is quite unusual, but a smaller finial excavated at Wangjiaping, Ningxia, is similar enough to suggest that it can also be associated with the Ningxia region of Northwest China during the second half of the first millennium B.C.[1] The raptor represented is a mythological creature with almond-shaped eyes rather than more naturalistic round birds' eyes. Such creatures ultimately derive from Greek and Iranian iconography and were introduced into the eastern Eurasian steppes sometime during the fourth century B.C.[2]

This finial is very different from another raptor-headed finial, catalogue no. 173, which represents a real bird rather than a mythical creature. The type of ring-shaped coupling seen on this example occurs frequently as a decorative feature on garlic-neck *hu* vessels that have been excavated at Qin sites dating to the third century B.C.[3] Such similarities suggest that it may have been made in a Qin foundry during the third century B.C. for trade with the nomadic peoples north of the Great Wall.

1. Zhong and Han 1983, p. 205, fig. 3:5.
2. Toshio 2000.
3. *Kaogu xuebao* 1976, no. 2, p. 125, fig. 13:3; *Kaogu xuebao* 1986, no. 4, p. 501, fig. 15:3.

177.
Finial in the shape of a tiger's head

> North China, 3rd century B.C.
> Tinned bronze
> Diameter 2 in. (5.1 cm)
> Ex. coll.: Richard Kimball Designs, Denver

This tiger's mask once surmounted the curved top of a tinned bronze finial. The tiger's features are shown in relief and skillfully articulated. The presence of a woven pattern on the underside of the mask indicates that it was cast by the lost-wax and lost-textile process. After casting, the mask was enhanced by tinning, much of which has worn off.

Similar finials cast in the shape of an animal's head have been found in numerous late Warring States and early Western Han burials. A very handsome example inlaid with silver was exhibited in Hong Kong in 1990.[1] The use of tinning suggests that the present example was made in a northern Chinese metalworking center west of the Taihang Mountain range, as tinning was seldom employed in Northeast China.

1. Rawson and Bunker 1990, no. 104.

178.
Tuning key for a qin

> North China, 3rd – 2nd century B.C.
> Bronze
> Height 3¼ in. (8.3 cm)
> Published: Christie's New York, sale cat., Sept. 21, 2000.

A bear balanced atop a tall squared shaft is represented on this tuning key for a a type of zither called a *qin*. The shaft ends in a square socket that would have fit over the square tip of a tuning peg. The center of the bear's arched back is cut out to fit a hinged crescent-shaped blade with a triangular cross section. The body is pierced through for a peg to keep the blade open, and both the body and the shaft are cast integrally by the lost-wax process.

Long a puzzle to archaeologists, this type of object has recently been identified as a tuning key for a Chinese *qin*, a plucked string instrument that is tuned by tightening each string around a tuning peg.[1] Remains of the earliest known *qin* were found in South China, in the late-fifth-century B.C. tomb of the marquis of Zeng in Sui county, Hubei Province.[2] By contrast, the earliest known bronze tuning keys, which are decorated with zoomorphic motifs that relate to traditions found beyond the frontiers of China,[3] appear to have been cast in North China.

The crescent-shaped blade on the back of the bear, which may originally have been sharper, has been described as a plectrum,[4] but, according to the music archaeologist Bo Lawergren, such usage would have damaged the string and thus cannot be substantiated. Instead, as Dr. Lawergren has convincingly suggested, it was a tool used to cut the thin silk

strings of the *qin* when they snapped and had to be repaired.[5] Such a blade attached to the tuning key would have been a very handy gadget in a *qin* player's toolkit.

The persistence of northern motifs on tuning keys, as well as the *qin*'s portability, suggests that plucked string instruments may have been introduced into China through contact with peoples to the northwest. The remains of a harp recovered from a fourth-century B.C. grave at Pazyryk, in the Altai Mountains, are ample evidence for the existence of plucked string instruments among the herding peoples of the eastern Eurasian steppes, where gut and sinew strings were more common.[6]

A tuning key similar to the present example, but without the tiny flick knife, was recovered from a late Warring States burial site at Luoyang, Henan Province.[7] It would seem that the addition of the tiny knife to the *qin* players's toolkit was a Western Han innovation.

1. So and Bunker 1995, pp. 148–50.
2. Beijing 1989, pl. 47.1, p. 93, fig. 62.1.
3. So and Bunker 1995, pp. 148–50; Lawergren 2000, pp. 77–79.
4. Christie's New York, September 21, 2000, lot 175.
5. Bo Lawergren, telephone conversation with author, January 28, 2001.
6. Lawergren 1990, pp. 111–18; Bunker et al. 1997, p. 293, fig. 267.2.
7. White 1934, pl. 69, no. 167.

179.
Se string anchor (se rui)

China, 3rd–2nd century B.C.
Gilded bronze
Height 2½ in. (6.4 cm)
Lent by Shelby White and Leon Levy

This spectacular gilded-bronze mountain with jagged peaks inhabited by wild beasts surmounts the square socket of a *se rui*, or zither string anchor. The mountain is solidly cast, with a dragon and a tiger in high relief climbing around the sides. The dragon's and the tiger's bodies are entwined around and partially obscured by the undulating, stylized cliffs. The dragon, with its head outstretched toward the summit, is flanked by a bear that stands on its hind legs and a crouching monkey with its paw to its mouth. The piece is lost-wax cast integrally with the square socket, which has beveled edges.

During the Han period, *se rui* were usually cast in sets of four but could have as few as two or as many as five. The *se*

normally had from twenty-three to twenty-six strings that were gathered into four bundles, each wound around one of four anchors with identical decoration.[1] A similar mountain-shaped anchor with traces of string still wrapped around it was discovered among the burial goods found at Shouzhou, Anhui Province.[2] Shouzhou was the capital of the state of Chu from 241 B.C. until 223 B.C., when it was conquered by the Qin. During the early Western Han, its fortunes fluctuated, and Shouzhou was, off and on, a provincial Chu capital during the early part of the second century B.C., when this small mountain-shaped anchor was probably cast.

Excavations in Guangdong Province confirm the function of these zither string anchors. Four similar mountain-shaped anchors were discovered in Guangzhou, in the second-century B.C. tomb of the king of Nanyue.[3] According to the excavation report, wood fragments were found inside the sockets, suggesting that they were designed to fit over the wooden pegs used to anchor the strings. The mountain-shaped anchors served also as knobs with which to turn the pegs. This motion would then produce the tension that would determine the pitch and the scale.[4]

The recent suggestion that stringed instruments in ancient China may possibly have had a northern origin hints at an interesting new interpretation of the Han image of the mountain inhabited by wild animals.[5] This theory is supported by the innumerable mountain-shaped censers and jars that display such imagery which appeared at a time when the Han Chinese were in close association with the nearby pastoral world (fig. 52).

The cosmic mountain as the most prominent image of the cosmic pillar that connects heaven, earth, and the underworld was a fundamental concept of shamanism, the ancient religion of nature that was practiced by most of the herding and hunting peoples throughout northern Eurasia.[6] During the fourth and third centuries B.C., these symbolic mountains inhabited by wild animals were represented in vertically integrated landscapes portrayed on headdresses associated with the steppe peoples. The headdresses, such as the late-fourth-century B.C. example from Issyk-Kul, near Almaty, Kazakhstan, describe the steppe and mountain pastures that dominated the nomadic world and display motifs of tigers and other animals among the mountain peaks (fig. 54).

It is this concept that is reflected in the Han censers and in the mountain landscapes on the small zither string anchors. The strong parallels between early Han landscapes in the round and pastoral imagery may have been a major catalyst to the integrated development of pictorial Chinese landscape representation rather than the art of the ancient Near East, which is frequently cited but exhibits no parallels.[7]

With its newly recognized northern heritage, a small mountain teeming with wildlife seems quite appropriate for a fitting on an instrument that has also been considered to have a northern pastoral ancestry. In this way, the present anchor fits easily with the other two *qin* and *se* fittings, catalogue nos. 178 and 180, which also display distinctly northern subject matter.

1. So 2000, pp. 69–70, 72–73, figs. 2, 3.
2. Karlbeck 1955, pl. 41:4.
3. Beijing 1991, vol. 2, pl. 48:1.
4. Ibid., vol. 1, pp. 92–93, fig. 62:3.
5. So 2000, p. 31; So and Bunker 1995, pp. 148–50.
6. Eliade 1964; Munakata 1991, p. 7.
7. For an in-depth study of this interpretation, see Jacobson 1985 and parts of Munakata 1991.

180.
Zither string anchor (se rui)

North China, 3rd–2nd century B.C.
Gilded bronze
Diameter 2 in. (5.1 cm)
Ex. coll.: Michael Dunn, New York

A mythological ungulate with inverted hindquarters is here ingeniously manipulated to embellish the domed cap for the square socket of a *se* string anchor. It has a beaked head, a single antler, a bifurcated crest, and a long tail, with striated enclosures on the body. The piece is lost-wax cast.

A nearly identical *se rui* was excavated at the Shangwang cemetery in the Linzi district of Zibo city, Shandong Province, the capital of the state of Qi during the late Warring States and Han periods.[1] Such fittings were cast in sets of four to serve as anchors for the strings of a *se* zither that were gathered together and wound around them.[2]

Like the bear motif on the *qin* tuning key, catalogue no. 178, the mythological ungulate has strong associations with the art of the north and was a popular symbol on artifacts dating to the latter half of the first millennium B.C. (see cat. nos. 72, 76, 99, 159). The possibility of northern influence on the development of early plucked string instruments in ancient China is supported by these findings and warrants further investigation.[3]

1. Jinan 1997, pl. 29:2, p. 38, fig. 29:1.
2. So and Bunker 1995, pp. 250–51, fig. 72.1.
3. For a discussion of plucked instruments in ancient China, see So 2000.

181.

Pair of fittings in the shape of carnivores

North China, 3rd – 2nd century B.C.
Tinned bronze
Left: Length 4½ in. (11.4 cm); width 1⅞ in. (4.8 cm);
diameter of ring 1¼ in. (3.2 cm)
Right: Length 3½ in. (8.9 cm); width ⅞ in. (2.2 cm)
Ex. coll.: R. H. Ellsworth, Ltd., New York

Each of these two fittings terminates in a small carnivore's head with a long muzzle and with its ears laid back. A ring is suspended from the mouth of the carnivore on the left, while the ring for the fitting on the right is missing. The opposite end of each fitting has an open socket into which an object was once inserted. The ridged rings around each socket imitate an earlier mechanical coupling join that has been retained as a decorative element, similar to that on catalogue no. 176. Each fitting is lost-wax cast onto a precast ring. The surface has been intentionally tinned to give it a burnished appearance.

Two fittings of a similar type with animal-head terminals were excavated at the Qi state cemetery near Shangwang, in the Linzi district of Zibo city, Shandong Province.[1] Such fittings probably embellished the wood pole ends of a litter-bearer frame or platform and held tassels appropriately colored for those occasions when the litter was in use. Bits of wood are still visible inside the sockets.

1. Jinan 1997, pl. 32:3, fig. 30:7.

182.
Incense burner lid with stag

Western Pakistan, ca. 1st century B.C.
Bronze
Height 4¼ in. (10.8 cm); diameter 2⅞ in. (7.3 cm)
Ex. coll.: James Freeman, Kyoto

A stag with gathered feet stands atop a hill with eight petals at the base. The hill, in turn, surmounts a dome decorated in openwork with three registers of floral and zoomorphic motifs. The bottom register appears to depict either a floral motif or some kind of winged insect seen from above, and the second register shows recumbent lions and standing, horned ungulates that may be sheep. Above this parade of animals is a register with double-ended spirals. The entire piece is lost-wax cast.

The function of this interesting object, said to have come from western Pakistan, is not readily apparent, but the openwork and the object's similarity to lids used for incense burners suggest that it may have served the same purpose. Several Indo-Scythian bronze incense burners have lids of similar shape with openwork decoration,[1] and there is a significant parallel to the lid of a first-century B.C. Indo-Scythian covered vessel, also said to come from Pakistan, that is now in the Miho Museum, Shigaraki.[2] The Miho lid is surmounted by an ibex, also with gathered feet, in a pose very similar to that of the stag seen here.

1. Carter 1993, fig. 10.1a. I am very grateful to Dr. Martha Carter for bringing this reference to my attention.
2. Salomon 1997, fig. 1.

8. VESSELS AND IMPLEMENTS

The eighth and final section includes bronze vessels, some of which can be attributed to the pastoral groups bordering ancient China. Other examples were cast in China but exhibit design features taken from the pastoral world (cat. nos. 184, 185). Although the pastoral peoples never practiced the complex ceremonies that produced the ritual vessels of ancient China, some utilitarian vessels appear also to have served ceremonial purposes on certain occasions.

183.
Spoon

> Northwest China, 13th–11th century B.C.
> Bronze
> Length 5⅞ in. (15 cm)
> Katherine and George Fan

This spoon is distinguished by an elliptical bowl and a long handle terminating in an animal's head. On the upper side of the handle, which bears a series of raised dots, is a suspension loop, while three loops, one of which retains its small oblong pendant, depend from the underside. Originally, the other two underside loops would have also had pendants that would have made a jingling sound when the spoon was in motion. Longitudinal mold marks along the side of the handle suggest production in a piece mold. Each pendant was cast separately and then placed in the mold when the spoon was cast. The handle of the spoon was originally straight, but has become bent through usage.

Similar spoons with pendants have been excavated from the graves of China's northern pastoral neighbors west of the Taihang Mountains at Chujiayu, Shilou county, Shanxi Province.[1] A similar spoon was also found at the waist of a

dead male in a grave excavated at Shangdongcun, Ji county, Shanxi, contemporaneous with the late Shang period—from the thirteenth to the eleventh century B.C.—but non-Shang in character.[2] Spoons in the sedentary Chinese world were used for cooking and eating and were not carried on one's person, as they were in the more mobile, pastoral world.[3]

Spoons with suspension loops were probably introduced into eastern Asia from northwestern Siberia and eastern Europe, where both men and women habitually carried them.[4] The noisemaking jingles appear to have been an eastern addition, like the rattles on other artifacts belonging to China's northern neighbors. (See also cat. nos. 26, 28, 29.)

1. Yang Shaoshun 1981, p. 52, fig. 23.
2. Yan Jinzhu 1985, p. 848, fig. 2.
3. Wang Renxiang 1990.
4. Gimbutas 1965, p. 289.

184.
Wine container (hu)

North and Northwest China, late 11th–early 10th century B.C.
Bronze
Height 16⅛ in. (41.1 cm)
Katherine and George Fan
Published: So and Bunker 1995, pp. 105–6, no. 19.

This tall slender wine container has a smooth, undecorated surface and a fitted lid that serves, when inverted, as a small drinking vessel. Like a modern-day Thermos bottle, it was designed to be portable. A cord or leather strap by which it could be suspended was run through the two holes in the flared foot, up through the two small handles on each side, and finally through the two holes in the flared top of the lid. When all the holes were aligned, the lid was secured and the vessel could be carried.

Wine containers similar to the present *hu* in shape and design have been found at numerous archaeological sites in North China, which have yielded evidence for active contact between the Chinese and the northern pastoral peoples during the late eleventh and tenth centuries B.C., such as at Baifu, Changping county, outside Beijing,[1] and at the Yu family cemetery at Rujiazhuang, Baoji county, southern Shaanxi Province.[2] During the tenth century B.C., vessels of this shape

continued to be produced in dynastic China, where they represented a new type and were decorated with typical Western Zhou designs.[3]

1. *Kaogu* 1976, no. 4, pl. 2:4
2. Lu and Hu 1988, pl. 160.2.
3. Rawson 1990, pp. 74–75, figs. 15.4, 95.

185.
Stemmed food container (fu)

Northwest China. 8th century B.C.
Bronze
Height 8⅝ in. (21.9 cm); diameter 7⅜ in. (18.7 cm)
Katherine and George Fan
Published: So and Bunker 1995, p. 108, no. 22.

This cauldron, or *fu*, is distinguished by a deep rounded U-shaped bowl on a short flared stem foot and two upright handles placed opposite each other on the rim of the bowl. The handles are marked by slanting parallel lines so that each resembles a twisted rope. The bowl is decorated with two horizontal registers separated by a twisted rope band. The top register displays a typical Western Zhou running design of S-shaped motifs and the bottom register, two rows of U-shapes that encircle the bowl. The presence of a sooty black substance in the grooves is evidence that the vessel was once subjected to fire. A casting sprue projects beneath the *fu* within the flared stem foot, suggesting that the vessel was cast integrally with the foot and handles upside down in a multi-piece mold.

A smaller example of this type of *fu*, with similar Western Zhou decoration, was recovered near Xi'an, Shaanxi Province.[1] The vessel has no Chinese antecedent, which suggests that the shape was based on a non-Chinese example made in another material.

Vessels of this shape became a diagnostic artifact of the pastoral peoples, serving both ceremonial and mundane functions. Unlike Chinese ritual vessels, the steppe cauldrons have, until recently, received little scholarly attention.[2] The Chinese may have been the first to cast this type of vessel in bronze. Before the eighth century B.C., they were probably made in hammered metal or carved wood, with real twisted-rope handles. Vessels such as the hammered bronze stem-footed cauldron from the Trialeti cemetery in Transcaucasia, Georgia, may have preceded the eastern Eurasian type.[3] By the seventh or sixth century B.C., cast *fu* occur in burials in northern Hebei[4] and also in burials in the Black Sea region associated with the Scythians.[5]

1. Wang Changqi 1991, pl. 7, fig. 1:13. Four plainer examples were also discovered in the same vicinity, ibid., figs. 1:2–3, 6–7. See also So and Bunker 1995, p. 108, no. 22.
2. Takahama 1994; Érdy 1995.
3. Gimbutas 1965, p. 94, fig. 52:3; Bunker et al. 1997, p. 178, fig. 93.
4. So and Bunker 1995, p. 108, fig. 22.1.
5. Jacobson 1995, pp. 188–92.

186.
Cauldron (fu)

Northwest China, 3rd – 2nd century B.C.
Bronze
Height 7 in. (17.8 cm); width 4½ in. (11.4 cm)
Katherine and George Fan
Published: Érdy 1995, p. 92, fig. 6.3, no. 2; So and Bunker 1995, pp. 96–97, no. 10.

This bronze cauldron is typical of the vessels used by the hunting and herding peoples who lived beyond China's northern frontiers. Primarily utilitarian, they have a cone-shaped base that was pierced in three places to allow heat to escape when they were placed over a fire. The handles are rectangular in shape with three points on the top. A pendant casting sprue

within the base and mold marks that bisect the vessel indicate that it was cast upside down integrally with the handles in a multipiece mold. (See also cat. no. 185.)

Similar cast cauldrons occur at numerous pastoral sites dating to the latter half of the first millennium B.C., but they have minor differences in design. Cauldrons with rounded handles are considered to be earlier than cauldrons with rectangular handles, like the example seen here, and cauldrons with an openwork foot appear to be of later date than those with a solid walled foot.[1]

A very similar but smaller cauldron, with the same rectangular handles with three points on the top, was found in the Qingyang region of southeastern Gansu Province, suggesting that the present cauldron, in the Fan collection, may come from the same vicinity.[2] Érdy dates both and the Qingyang example from the third to the second century B.C.[3] The rough casting of the present *fu* suggests that it was made locally and not at a Chinese metalworking center.

1. Érdy 1995, p. 38; see also Bunker et al. 1997, pp. 178–79, 239–40.
2. Egami and Mizuno 1935, p. 180, fig. 106.2; Érdy 1995, p. 92, fig. 6.3, no. 1.
3. Érdy 1995, pp. 47–48, 92, fig. 6.3, no. 2.

187.
Cauldron with lid (fu)

North China, 2nd–4th century A.D.
Bronze
Height 14¾ in. (37.5 cm); width 8¾ in. (22.3 cm)
Katherine and George Fan
Published: Érdy 1995, p. 92, fig. 6.3, no. 3; So and Bunker 1995, p. 97, fig. 10.1.

This cauldron, from the Fan collection, is distinguished by a bulging, almost hemispherical bowl on a conical foot with four openings, and two handles that are each surmounted by three mushroom shapes on stems. It is provided with a lid that has a handle also surmounted by three mushroom shapes on stems, like those on the handles.

The cauldron is the same type as, but far more complete than, a cauldron excavated from a tomb at Lingpi village, Horinger county (Hohhot) municipal district, Inner Mongolia.[1] The foot of the Lingpi cauldron is broken off, and the lid is missing. Consequently, the Fan cauldron is crucial in demonstrating how the Lingpi example looked originally. The Lingpi vessel has been associated with the Xianbei people, who succeeded the Xiongnu as rulers of the eastern grasslands north of the Great Wall of China.[2]

The mushroom-shaped decoration suggests that *fu* developed into ritual vessels, acquiring symbols that are little understood today. Later cauldrons, with more prominent mushroom-shaped projections, have been found in Xinjiang, Northwest China, and may mark the route taken by mobile horse-riding groups who ultimately carried such vessels into Eastern Europe, where they became important objects among the early inhabitants of Hungary.[3]

1. Kessler 1993, p. 21.
2. Ibid.; So and Bunker 1995, p. 97, fig. 10.1.
3. Zhang and Zhao 1991.

Frontispiece: Detail of figure 69

THE LEGACY OF NOMADIC ART IN CHINA AND EASTERN CENTRAL ASIA

JAMES C.Y. WATT

THE XIONGNU AND THE ORDOS REGION

The northern provinces of China from early historical times were inhabited by a mixture of races and ethnic groups with no clear-cut boundaries until the time of the Eastern Zhou (770–256 B.C.). At this time various states in the north that shared a common culture with those in the Central Plains (along the middle and lower reaches of the Yellow River) began to build walls on their northern frontiers as a defensive measure against nomadic tribes, who were probably becoming more persistent in raiding and in their demand for trade. The walls were more or less joined together in the Qin dynasty (221–206 B.C.), which saw the first unified empire in China. At the same time, a powerful confederation of nomadic tribes was being formed to the north, under the leadership of the Xiongnu. The sheer scale of the political entities thus created on either side of the walls engendered a new mode of interaction between the sedentary civilization in China and the nomadic world to the north, with the Great Wall standing for the line of demarcation.[1]

An essential precondition for forming a confederation of nomadic tribes was the establishment of a "court" (Chinese historians called it a *ting*) as a command center and supply base. Early in the process of confederation under Xiongnu leadership, the area of the Selenga River drainage in the Transbaikal became the seat of power. This region provided ideal pasture and could also be irrigated for agriculture, creating the conditions for settlements—at least for most of the year—where necessities for daily use and for warfare could be produced. Agriculture was particularly important at this stage of political development for the nomads to gain minimal economic independence, removing the constant need to trade or raid for grain from agrarian neighbors—as

no people, including nomads, can survive solely on animal products. A number of fortified settlement sites in the Transbaikal associated with the Xiongnu have been excavated and studied by Russian archaeologists in recent years.[2] At one of the sites in the Selenga River valley, known as the Ivolga complex, the finds "demonstrate that the inhabitants of the site were engaged in agriculture, cattle breeding, hunting and fishing, and that their occupations included metalwork in iron, bronze, and precious metals."[3]

Another area that served similar military and economic purposes, though it was not necessarily a political center, was the Ordos region in Northwest China. As a geographic term, the Ordos denotes the northern part of the area surrounded by the great loop of the Yellow River (see the map on pp. xii–xiii). It is a land of mixed ecology, with grassland and desert; but in the northernmost part, south of the Yinshan Mountains, the river flows from west to east through a fertile plain that provides excellent pasture and arable land. Other regions in the Ordos can be irrigated by the waters of the Yellow River. During those periods in history when the Ordos was occupied by a Chinese population, systems of canals were built to serve this function.[4] It appears that in earlier times, there was more grass cover in the Ordos than in later centuries. In the early fifth century B.C., it was the territory of the state of Xia (A.D. 407–31), founded by an unregenerate Xiongnu by the name of Helian Bobo, who made his capital, Tongwan, in an area that is now pure desert but was lush with vegetation at the time.[5]

The Ordos became strategically important to the Xiongnu from about the third century B.C., when they emerged as the leading tribe in the confederation of nomads in the Mongolian steppes and when the region served as a supply base and forward position in their economic and military dealings with China. For the Chinese, the same region represented a frontier that guarded the approach to the Guanzhong area, at the center of which were the capitals of the Qin and Han empires (near present-day Xi'an). From time to time, the Xiongnu would be driven out of the Ordos and a wall would be built well to the north—by the short-lived Qin dynasty and during the reign of Emperor Wudi (r. 140–87 B.C.) of the Han. However, the periods of Han occupancy were never long and, after Wudi, the region basically remained in the dominion of the Xiongnu for several centuries, until they disappeared from the scene as an identifiable ethnic group and other nomads from Mongolia moved in. These cycles of occupation would recur throughout Chinese history, and the region would witness many drastic changes, resulting from forced movements of large populations, preparations for massive military campaigns, and battles. The events are recorded indifferently in historical writings, and the human dimension associated with the changes are brought to life only in Chinese literature—especially in poetry—and in the songs of the nomads. For the agricultural Chinese, the Ordos is a land of sorrows. But the nomads sing of the joy of life under the Yinshan Mountains, where their flocks and herds multiply, and of their sadness at the loss of the land they have from time to time had to abandon.

In recent centuries, as the desiccation of the Ordos advanced, large numbers of metal objects became exposed on the surface of the earth, including utilitarian objects such as knives and axes and ornamental plaques with animal designs. It is difficult to estimate what proportion of the ornamental objects was made of gold, as they would have been put to good use by the peasantry who found them. But some of the bronze plaques, starting in the nineteenth century, would eventually find their way into antiquarian collections. In the twentieth century, as more objects were found either on the surface of the earth or by archaeological excavation, the type of bronze ornaments known to have come from the Ordos region gave rise to the term "Ordos bronzes" and attracted wide attention. Most Ordos bronzes date from the third to the first century B.C. and can be associated with the Xiongnu.[6] Unfortunately, the term has been applied rather indiscriminately to all "animal style" objects found in the vast northern border areas of China, irrespective of place of discovery or dating.[7] This is a pity, as the term Ordos bronze, with its multiple associations of place, history, and cultural interaction, can be a useful term in archaeological and historical writing when properly defined.

The Xiongnu were not the only nomads the Chinese had to contend with in the Han period, nor was the Ordos the only region of interaction between nomadic tribes and the settled population of North China. But the Xiongnu were the paramount power in the Mongolian steppes during this time and the Ordos the most important theater for acts of cultural exchange. The interaction between the Chinese and the nomads in other areas on the northern border would follow similar lines on a lesser scale.

In the following section, an attempt will be made to outline the aftermath of the increased contact between the nomadic peoples and the settled population of North China beginning in the Western Han (206 B.C.–A.D. 9) in the last two centuries B.C.

THE LEGACY OF NOMADIC ART IN CHINA

The Great Wall, from the beginning, did not so much create a dividing line between ethnic groups as between different ways of life. As peoples from a nomadic background migrated south, whether as conquerors or as captives or fleeing from natural disasters or hostile tribes, they would sooner or later acculturize to a way of life and to a sociopolitical organization on the Chinese model. At the same time, the northerners would bring with them customs and beliefs that would be absorbed to varying degrees into the Chinese system or eventually discarded. The horse sacrifice, for example, brought into North China by the Xianbei confederation in the late fourth century A.D. was being discontinued by the mid-sixth century. There is a telling passage in the biography of Lei Shao, a military leader who in the 530s supported the establishment of the Western Wei dynasty (A.D. 535–56) in today's Shaanxi Province, that records his instructions in his will to his sons: "The funeral practice in my home district [Wuchuan, north of present-day Hohhot, in Inner Mongolia] entails the sacrifice of a big horse. It is of no benefit to the deceased and you should discontinue it."[8] Lei Shao, to judge from his name, was probably an ethnic Qiang but an acculturized Xianbei—as were all military officers guarding the frontier fortress at Wuchuan. Whatever the original or religious significance

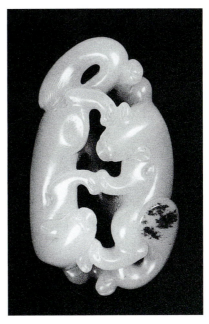

Figure 55. Gilded bronze mat weight with animal-combat scene, Western Han. 2nd-1st century B.C. The Metropolitan Museum of Art, Rogers Fund, 1918 (18.39)

Figure 56. White jade double-cat pendant, Qing dynasty. 18th century (after Watt 1980, pl. 20)

attached to the horse sacrifice, by this time it was obviously lost in the collective memory of the peoples in North China who inherited the tradition.

A similar course was followed in exchanges in the visual arts. Certain styles and motifs, once introduced into China, would remain as part of the permanent language and vocabulary of the decorative arts, devoid of their original connotation and, in most cases, modified so as to be intelligible in terms of Chinese sensibility. In other instances, the popularity was short-lived and the style or motif would fade away, leaving only the faintest trace.

The "animal combat" motif is a chief example of the persistence and transformation in China of a popular theme in the art of the steppe world. A common article in affluent households in the Western Han period was the mat weight, used on the corners of sitting mats. Most of the examples that have survived to this day are in the form of a bear and a tiger in combat, of solid cast bronze, often gilded, or hollow cast and filled with lead (see, for example, fig. 55). There are also versions in jade.[9] Objects featuring the theme of animal combat had appeared earlier in China, in the fourth century B.C.[10] However, these were the products of a state established in northern Hebei Province by a nomadic tribe

known as the Xianyu, or Baidi, rather than objects made by the Chinese—despite the fact that inscriptions on Xianyu ritual vessels demonstrate that they had thoroughly assimilated Confucian systems of political and ethical thought.[11] Moreover, the combatants in the Chinese version of this motif in the Western Han are conventionalized and restricted to the bear and the tiger.

The animal-combat motif persisted in Chinese art, taking various unexpected forms. The eleventh-century artist-collector Mi Fu recorded a Tang (A.D. 618–907) painting he had seen of two horses biting each other,[12] and there are jade carvings probably of the Tang period of paired animals biting and clawing.[13] In carvings of later periods, however, the animals seem to be locked in a friendly embrace. The ultimate adaptation of this motif in Chinese art is manifested in eighteenth-century jade carvings of a pair of playful animals clutching at each other (fig. 56). This type of carving was known as *shuanghuan,* literally "double jackal," but a rebus for "mutual delight."

Other aspects of Chinese art in the late centuries B.C. that were likely to have been inspired by contact with nomads had a limited duration. One example is the predilection for gilding. There are spectacular examples of gilded objects in

Figure 57. Gilded bronze horse, Western Han. 2nd–1st century B.C. Museum of Maoling Mausoleum (after Tokyo 1986, pl. 72)

the early Han period, such as the horse (fig. 57) and the incense burner from a tomb that dates to the early reign of Emperor Wudi.[14] The sheer scale of the Chinese objects (the horse is nearly twenty-five inches high) would have made it impracticable to cast them in pure gold, but the thickness of the gilding must have created an impression of solid gold. It should be noted that the animal patterns on the lower part of the bowl of the incense burner are entirely nomadic in style (see fig. 50 on p. 34).

The inscriptions on the incense burner indicate that these objects were made in the imperial workshops. The fashion for gilding large objects declined after the Western Han, for economic and/or cultural reasons. It was revived in the first half of the Tang dynasty, when the Chinese empire extended far into Central Asia, and less commonly employed thereafter.

Chinese contact with the nomadic world during the Western Han was not confined to Mongolia, which was dominated by the Xiongnu confederation. There are unmistakable indications of exchanges farther to the west along the Eurasian steppes. It has been observed for some time that there is a striking similarity between a certain image seen on gold ornaments found in the Almaty region of southeastern Kazakhstan, north of the Tianshan Mountains in Central Asia, and Chinese decorative art of the same period. This image is the "feathered man" with flowing hair, riding on a winged chimera or dragon. It appears, for example, on an openwork gold diadem dating from the second century B.C. to the first century A.D. found in the Kargali valley in the Almaty region (fig. 58).[15] The image is described in Chinese literature of the Han dynasty[16] and seen on Chinese painting, pottery, and jade carvings of the same period.[17] One of the jade carvings is in the Arthur M. Sackler Gallery, Washington, D.C. (fig. 59). The fact that the feathered man is known to represent an immortal (*xian*) in Han China and that its significance, if any, in the nomadic world is not

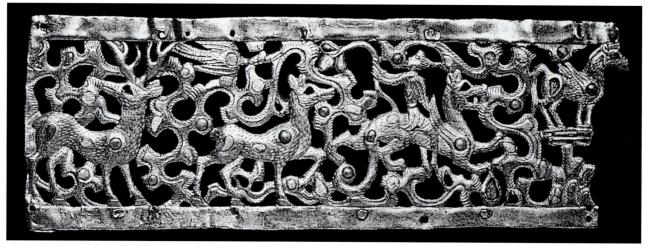

Figure 58. Gold openwork diadem with image of feathered man (see also fig. 63), Kargali Valley, Almaty region. 2nd century B.C.–1st century A.D. (after Arbore-Popescu, Silvi Antonini, and Baitakov 1998, pl. 466)

Figure 59. Jade winged chimera, Western Han. 1st century B.C.–1st century A.D. Arthur M. Sackler Gallery, Smithsonian Institution, Washington, D.C., Gift of Arthur M. Sackler, S1987.26 (after Lawton et al. 1987, pl. 69)

known does not necessarily give primacy of the occurrence of the image to China. It is quite possible that the Chinese adopted the image and gave it a native meaning, something that has happened in other instances. It should perhaps be pointed out, for the purpose of future discussion, that in the Almaty image the rider's head is turned backward and the flow of his hair is in the direction opposite to the movement of the galloping animal, whereas in the Chinese image the rider always looks forward and his hair flows backward, naturally.

Another element in the design pattern of the gold diadem that parallels Chinese decorative schemes of the Western Han is the wavy lines that serve as the ground pattern. A series of diagrams consisting of circular dots amid wavy lines (fig. 60) are painted on the pottery slabs that form the ceiling tiles of a late Western Han tomb in Luoyang. The dots have been interpreted as representations of stellar constellations—the earliest of such known in China.[18] In all discussions of these diagrams, little attention has been paid to the wavy pattern, which consists of two sets of more or less parallel undulating lines of different shades that are presumed to represent clouds. This type of cloud representation, which was to become extremely popular in the decorative arts in the several centuries following the Western Han in China, as seen for example in silk textiles (fig. 61), seems to have made its first appearance at the same time as the feathered man. Indeed, in the same tomb with the constellation diagrams, on the openwork pottery tiles that form the gable of the partition in the middle of the tomb chamber, there is also a representation of a feathered man riding on a dragon not unlike the image on another part of the Almaty diadem, except that the Chinese figure wears a conical hat (fig. 62, and fig. 63 on the left side). Furthermore, in the same Han tomb, on the other side of the openwork pottery tiles, are

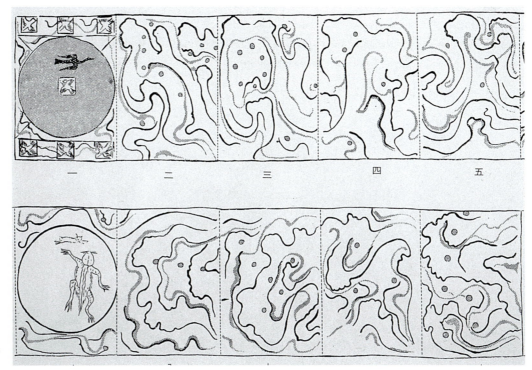

Figure 60. Ceiling tiles with representations of stellar constellations, from a late Western Han tomb, Luoyang, Henan Province. 2nd–1st century B.C. (after *Kaogu xuebao* 1964, no. 2, colorpl. 1)

Figure 61. Silk brocade arm protector with Chinese characters and cloud patterns, from tomb 8, Niya cemetery, Minfeng, Xinjian Province. 3rd century B.C.– 5th century A.D. (after Shanghai 1998, pl. 34)

animals with cloudlike patterns on their bodies (fig. 64) reminiscent of the animals on the saddle covers of applied felt in barrows 1 and 2 at Pazyryk in the Altai (fig. 65), a site dating from the late fourth to the early third century B.C., where Chinese silks and a mirror have been found.[19] This rather unusual manner of ornamenting the bodies of animals, however, soon disappeared from the Chinese repertory.

There are other areas in the arts of the Western Han that would lend themselves to this kind of observation,[20] but the above examples may suffice to make the point that a major aspect in the decorative art of China in the last two centuries B.C. is related to that of the nomads of the steppes from the Altai in southern Siberia to the Tianshan in Central Asia. It is not possible at present to trace the route or the

Figure 62. Openwork pottery tiles with image of feathered man, from a late Western Han tomb, Luoyang, Henan Province. 2nd–1st century B.C. (after *Kaogu xuebao* 1964, no. 2, pl. 8)

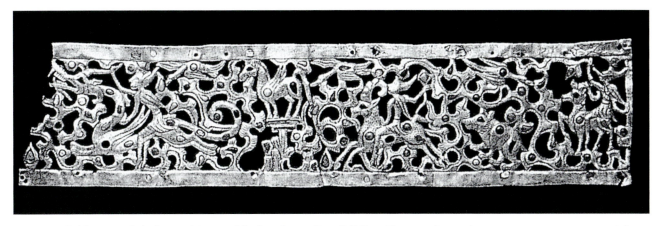

Figure 63. Gold openwork diadem with image of feathered man, Kargali Valley, Almaty region. 2nd century B.C.–1st century A.D. (after Arbore-Popescu, Silvi Antonini, and Baipakov 1998, pl. 468)

mode of transmission of ideas and motifs. The finds of Chinese objects at Pazyryk provide evidence that the actual transfer of objects was involved. The Xiongnu, whose territory extended into the Orkhon River valley, in the Transbaikal, may well have been the intermediary between the Altai and North China, and may possibly have provided the indirect contact between China and the Tianshan region, although there could have been more direct traffic between China and Central Asia via the Gansu corridor in Northwest China.[21]

Toward the end of the first century B.C., both the Han empire and the Xiongnu confederation collapsed.[22] This marked the beginning of another phase in the interaction between the nomadic tribes and the sedentary populations in North China. While there was a restoration of the Han dynasty after a brief interregnum at the beginning of the first

Figure 64. Animal scene, from a late Western Han tomb, Luoyang, Henan Province. 2nd–1st century B.C. (after *Kaogu xuebao* 1964, no. 2, colorpl. 1)

Figure 65. Applied felt saddle covers showing an elk (above) and an eagle-griffin (below), from kurgan 2, Pazyryk, Altai Mountains, southern Siberia. Late 4th–early 3rd century A.D. (after Rudenko 1970, pl. 168)

century, the Xiongnu never completely recovered. Unable to exact large subsidies from the court of the Later (or Eastern) Han (A.D. 25–220) and suffering from a succession of natural disasters and military setbacks, the Xiongnu in the middle of the first century A.D. broke into two factions, one moving westward into Central Asia and the other into North China, settling in several communities in what is now Shanxi Province. At the same time, other nomadic tribes, from the northeastern and western borders of China, also began to migrate into traditional Chinese territory and, by the fourth century, various tribes of nomadic background were able to set themselves up as rulers of small states with a mixed population of Han Chinese and nomads—the so-called Sixteen States.

The fourth and fifth centuries were a period of intense mutual acculturation, but the exchange was more in social institutions and customs than in artistic traditions, as the nomads in China gradually adapted to Chinese material culture. Indeed, pastoral tribes that had established themselves in China, such as the Toba Xianbei, who eventually united North China under the Wei dynasty (A.D. 386–534), were busily keeping other tribes at bay along the traditional frontiers between China and the steppe region. The new artistic and cultural fashions that came into China from the fourth to the sixth century were brought mainly by traders from Central Asia, particularly from Bactria and Sogdiana—

known as the Western Regions in China. But these new styles and fashions were eclectic creations born of a cross-fertilization of Hellenistic, Iranian, Indian, and nomadic elements. The Xianbei rulers in North China were themselves captivated by "Western" culture, not only in the visual arts but in music and dance.[23] Thus, the first cycle of artistic exchange between China and the nomadic world came to an end as a result of the mass settlement of nomadic tribes in the region of North China.

THE LEGACY OF NOMADIC ART IN CENTRAL ASIA

Perhaps the last, and in some ways the most interesting and somewhat unexpected, manifestation of nomadic art, with reverberations in both Europe and China, took place in Central Asia in the thirteenth and fourteenth centuries under the dispensation of the Mongol empire. This very important event in the art history of Central Asia has only recently been pointed out by Anne Wardwell in her study of medieval textiles. In her article "Indigenous Elements in Central Asian Silk Designs of the Mongol Period, and Their Impact on Italian Gothic Silks," Wardwell draws attention to the treatment of animals, dragons, and other motifs in the design of Central Asian silks of the Mongol era that exhibit the same characteristics as those portrayed in the art of the early nomads.[24] She further demonstrates, quite convincingly, that

Figure 66. Central Asian textile of lampas, silk, and gold with design of phoenixes amid floral vines. 13th–mid-14th century (after Wardwell 2000, fig. 9)

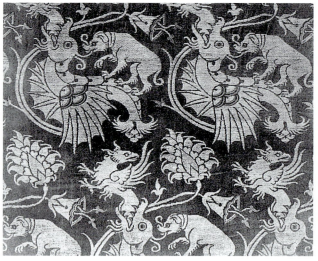

Figure 67. Italian textile of lampas, silk, and gold inspired by Central Asian zoomorphic designs. Late 14th century. Formerly Kunstgewerbemuseum, Berlin (after Wardwell 2000, fig. 11)

206

Figure 68. Wool textile in tapestry weave with design of deer, from Shanpula cemetery, near Khotan, Xinjiang Province. 2nd century B.C.–2nd century A.D. (after Schorta 2001, fig. 80)

early nomads—as manifested in animal images of applied felt from Pazyryk (fig. 65). As noted by Griaznov, the color scheme of the pictorial decoration on the felt hangings is "entirely arbitrary and conventional," bearing no relationship to the natural coloring of the objects represented.[27] The same exuberant use of color is seen in the textile fragments (mostly parts of garments) found at the cemetery site at Shanpula, near Khotan, in Xinjiang Province, Chinese Central Asia, dating from the second century B.C. to the second century A.D. This is particularly evident in the wool textiles in tapestry weave (fig. 68).

As pointed out by Emma C. Bunker, some of the imagery on the Shanpula tapestries recalls that found on felt hangings from Pazyryk dating from the third century B.C.[28] If

the inspiration for the fantastic designs on Italian Gothic silks in the fourteenth century was none other than the silks produced in Central Asia under Mongol administration. In particular, she points to the twist in the body of the animals, which is one of the chief stylistic markers in the art of the early nomads (as seen, for example, in cat. no. 96), and the motif of animal combat, albeit in a modified form but nevertheless retaining the suggestion of spiritedness and energy. The twisted body applies to both animals and birds, such as the phoenix in a thirteenth- to mid-fourteenth-century Central Asian silk (fig. 66). In this design, "the graceful majesty of the Chinese phoenix has been transformed into a scene of aggressive frenzy between the birds in one row with those in the next."[25] The "energy, immediacy and life-threatening drama of Central Asian animal designs" inspired fourteenth-century Italian weavers to produce silks exemplified by a fourteenth-century piece formerly in the Kunstgewerbe-museum, Berlin, in which all the characteristic elements are traceable to early nomadic art (fig. 67).

The Central Asian silks discussed by Wardwell that influenced Italian silk production and design mostly belong to a type sometimes known as "cloth of gold"—a weave of silk and gold threads that maximizes the amount of gold seen on the surface. Within Central Asia, particularly at Beshbaliq (present-day Jimsar, in eastern Xinjiang Province), where weaving workshops were set up in the early years of the Mongol Empire,[26] a class of silks in tapestry weave was produced that reflects yet another characteristic of the art of the

Figure 69. Silk tapestry, Central Asia. 11th–12th century. The Metropolitan Museum of Art, Fletcher Fund, 1987 (87.275)

comparison of the finds from Pazyryk with those from Shanpula demonstrates the spread of a distinctive decorative style over long distances in a relatively short time, the persistence of this style in Central Asia over the span of more than a millennium is attested by silk tapestries from Central Asia in the Mongol period. These were likely to have been made in Bashbaliq by Uygurs, who had a long tradition of wearing silk garments of tapestry weave going back to at least the ninth century, when they were still in Mongolia.[29] A piece of Central Asian silk tapestry in The Metropolitan Museum of Art is a good example (fig. 69). Although the vocabulary of the motifs is what was current at the time, the artistic idiom continues very much in the ancient tradition of nomadic art. Thus, the twisting body of the hybrid dragon (composed of Chinese and Indian elements) is endowed with the dynamic life force of an animal in the wild, and the brilliant use of color for decorative and expressive effect with no regard for the natural coloring of the plants finds no parallel in any artistic tradition in the world outside the Eurasian steppes — until the appearance of Fauvism in Paris in the early twentieth century.

Another aspect of the disjuncture of art and nature is in the treatment of the vegetal pattern. While the various floral sprays suggest the look of real plants, they are actually made up of disparate elements. This is particularly noticeable in the branch that begins above the mane of the lower dragon. Emerging from the same stem are flowers and leaves of different plants, treated as if they occurred that way in nature. One is tempted to draw a parallel between this manner of floral representation and the animal art of the early nomads, in which parts of an animal's body metamorphose into the head of a bird or the body of another creature.

There are thus two distinct aspects to the legacy of the art of the ancient nomads. Certain motifs and decorative styles are absorbed into the artistic traditions of sedentary peoples whose territories border the steppes. Such is the case in China. In Central Asia, the reverse seems to be true. Motifs originating from adjacent areas of "high culture" find expression in an artistic language that has its roots in the art of the early nomads, which, judging from available evidence, seems to have reached the peak of its development in the middle of the first millennium B.C. While it is possible to trace nomadic elements in the arts of China up to the present time, it is, sadly, impossible to do the same in the arts of

Central Asia, owing to the scarcity of material remains from that region in the later historical periods. The reason we have been able to catch a glimpse of Central Asian art in the late Middle Ages is because of the greatly increased production of industrial art in the Mongol Empire, particularly luxury items in gold and silk, the former recovered archaeologically and the latter preserved in the treasuries of Tibetan temples and European churches and a few burial sites. Unless future archaeological work can bring forth material evidence from other periods, there will always be gaps in our knowledge.

The present discussion has been limited to the eastern part of the Eurasian steppes and China, as objects in our exhibition are mostly from the northern borders of China. It is to be hoped that studies along similar lines applied to other areas will one day give us a more complete account of the art of the ancient nomads as a major source of inspiration in the visual arts of the greater continent of Eurasia.

1. A proposed outline of the interaction between the sedentary civilization in China and the inhabitants north of the Great Wall is given in Barfield 1991.

2. See note 2 on page 5 of the Introduction.

3. Paper delivered by Sergei Miniaev at The Metropolitan Museum of Art, January 15, 1999.

4. Waldron 1990, p. 63.

5. Chen Zhengxiang 1983, pp. 93–94.

6. The identification of objects found in the Ordos as being associated with the Xiongnu can be confirmed by comparison with those excavated in the Transbaikal region can be firmly attributed to the Xiongnu. (See note 2 on page 5 of the Introduction.)

7. In Tian and Guo 1986, "Han and Pre-Han Metalware Found in Inner Mongolia," no distinction is made between Xiongnu and Xianbei artifacts. A major step toward differentiating Xiongnu and Xianbei sites and artifacts is made in Wu En 1987, in which sites in the Orkhon River valley and the Ordos are identified as being those of the Xiongnu.

8. *Bei Shi, juan* 49 (Biography of Lei Shao), Zhonghua edition (1974), vol. 6, p. 1807.

9. See Rawson 1995, p. 360, no. 26.5.

10. See Hebei 1995.

11. Li Xueqin 1979, pp. 37–41.

12. Mi Fu, *Hua shi*, Meishu Congshu ed. (Taibei, 1967), p. 9.

13. Watt 1980, no. 20.

14. *Wenwu* 1982, no. 9, pp. 1–17, pls. 1–4. For the dating of the inscribed bronze artifacts, see Yuan 1982, pp. 18–20.

15. Arbore-Popescu, Silvi Antonini, and Baipakov 1998, p. 225, pls. 466–68.

16. Wang Chong (A.D. 27–ca. 97) in his *Lun heng* (*juan* 2, "The Negation of Form") describes the image of the immortal (*xianren*) as having "hair growing on his body, his arms changing into wings, and walking on clouds." In the 1990 Zhonghua Shuju edition of the *Lun heng* (combining the

commentaries compiled by Huang Hui and annotation by Lin Panshui), vol. 1, pp. 66–67, references are given for citations of "feather men" in literature of earlier periods (from the third century B.C. onward).

17. A jade carving of a feathered-man rider on a winged horse on a board with an incised cloud pattern was found near the tomb of Emperor Zhaodi (r. 87–74 B.C.). See *Kaogu,* no. 3 (1973), p. 169, pl. 12. Feathered men with or without winged horses are frequently seen on elaborate bronze and pottery lamps of the Eastern Han period. *Kaogu xuebao* 1964, no. 2, pl. 8.2 (reproduced here as fig. 62).

18. Xia 1965, reprinted in Xia 1979.

19. Rudenko 1970. For the dating of the barrows at Pazyryk and a discussion of the local artistic style in relation to outside contacts, see Rubinson 1992, pp. 68–76.

20. For one of the most interesting questions raised in this connection, see Jacobson 1985.

21. The discovery of Scytho-Siberian timber-type burials at Alagou, south of Urumqi in Xinjiang, with artifact types similar to those found at Issyk-Kul, north of Tianshan in southeastern Kazakhstan, provides evidence of a possible travel route between Tianshan and interior China through Xinjiang and the Gansu Corridor. See Jacobson 1985, pp. 141–42, n. 53.

22. The disintegration of the Xiongnu confederation began as early as 56 B.C. as a result of internal strife arising out of rival claims to the title of *shanyu* (chief or ruler). See Lin Gan 1984, pp. 51–52. However, diplomatic and trading activities were still maintained between the Han court and various Xiongnu factions, while raiding activities by the Xiongnu and alliances with other tribes increased.

23. Chen Yinke (1944) 1994, pp. 125–33 (chapter on music).

24. Wardwell 2000, pp. 86–97.

25. Ibid.

26. Watt and Wardwell 1997, pp. 14–15, 130–31.

27. Griaznov 1969, p. 196.

28. Bunker 2001, pp. 28–29, 39.

29. Watt and Wardwell 1997, pp. 61–62.

BIBLIOGRAPHY OF WORKS CITED

COMPILED BY JEAN WAGNER

For a more extensive bibliography, see Bunker et al. 1997.

Akishev, Kemal' A.

1978   *Kurgan Issyk: Iskusstvo sakov Kazakhstana* (Issyk Mound: The Art of the Saka in Kazakhstan). Moscow: Iskusstvo.

Amandry, Pierre

1966   "À propos du trésor de Ziwiye." *Iranica Antiqua* 6, pp. 109–29.

Andersson, J. G.

1929   "Der Weg über die Steppen." *Bulletin of the Museum of Far Eastern Antiquities,* no. 1, pp. 143–63.

1932   "Hunting Magic in the Animal Style." *Bulletin of the Museum of Far Eastern Antiquities* 4, pp. 221–317.

1933   "Selected Ordos Bronzes." *Bulletin of the Museum of Far Eastern Antiquities* 5, pp. 143–54.

Andrews, Peter A.

1979   "The Mongol Trellis Tent." In *Mongolia, Land of Five Animals,* pp. 10–22. London: Horniman Museum and Library.

Arbore-Popescu, Grigore, Chiara Silvi Antonini, and Karl Baipakov, eds.

1998   *L'uomo d'oro: La cultura delle steppe del Kazakhstan dall'età del bronzo alle grandi migrazioni.* Exh. cat. Mantua: Palazzo Te; Milan: Electa.

1999   *Altyn adam. L'uomo d'oro: La cultura delle steppe del Kazakhstan dall'età del bronzo alle grandi migrazioni.* Exh. cat. Naples: Museo Archeologica Nazionale; Milan: Bagatto Libri.

Ardenne de Tizac, Jean Henri d'

1923   *Animals in Chinese Art: A Collection of Examples Selected and Described by H. d'Ardenne de Tizac.* London: Benn Brothers.

Ariadne Galleries

1998   *Treasures of the Eurasian Steppes: Animal Art from 800 B.C. to 200 A.D.* Text by Tina Pang. Exh. cat. New York: Ariadne Galleries, Inc.

Arnold, Dorothea

1995   "An Egyptian Bestiary." *Metropolitan Museum of Art Bulletin* 52, no. 4 (spring).

Arnold, Dorothea, et al.

1996   *Ancient Art from the Shumei Family Collection.* Exh. cat. New York: The Metropolitan Museum of Art.

Artamonov, Mikhail I.

1969   *The Splendor of Scythian Art: Treasures from Scythian Tombs.* Translated by V. R. Kupriyanova. New York: Praeger.

1973   *Sokrovishcha sakov: Amudar'inskii sklad, altaiskie kurgany, minusinskie bronzy, sibirskoe zoloto* (Saka Treasures: The Oxus Treasure, Altai Mounds, Minusinsk Bronzes, Siberian Gold). Moscow: Iskusstvo.

Aruz, Joan, ed.

2000   *The Golden Deer of Eurasia: Scythian and Sarmatian Treasures from the Eurasian Steppes. The State Hermitage, Saint Petersburg, and the Archaeological Museum, Ufa.* Exh. cat. New York: The Metropolitan Museum of Art.

Asia Society

1970   *Masterpieces of Asian Art in American Collections, II: An Offering of Treasures Celebrating the Tenth Anniversary of Asia House Gallery.* Exh. cat. New York: Asia House Gallery, Asia Society.

Askarov, A., V. Volkov, and N. Ser-Odjav

1992   "Pastoral and Nomadic Tribes at the Beginning of the First Millennium B.C." In Dani and Mason 1992, pp. 459–72.

Azarpay, Guitty

1981   *Sogdian Painting: The Pictorial Epic in Oriental Art.* Contributions by A. M. Belenitskii, B. I. Marshak, and Mark J. Dresden. Berkeley and Los Angeles: University of California Press.

Azoy, G. Whitney

1982   *Buzkashi: Game and Power in Afghanistan.* Philadelphia: University of Pennsylvania Press.

Bacon, Edward, ed.

1963   *Vanished Civilizations: Forgotten Peoples of the Ancient World.* Texts by Henri Lhote et al. London: Thames and Hudson.

Bagley, Robert W.

1987   *Shang Ritual Bronzes in the Arthur M. Sackler Collections.* Washington, D.C.: Arthur M. Sackler Foundation; Cambridge, Mass.: Arthur M. Sackler Museum, Harvard University.

Barbier, Jean Paul

1996   *Art des steppes: Ornements et pièces de mobilier funéraire scytho-sibérien dans les collections du Musée Barbier-Mueller.* Exh. cat. Geneva: Musée Barbier-Mueller.

Barfield, Thomas J.

1991 "Inner Asia and Cycles of Power in China's Imperial Dynastic History." In Seaman and Marks 1991, pp. 21–62.

1993 *The Nomadic Alternative.* Englewood Cliffs, N.J.: Prentice Hall.

Barkova, L. L.

1987 "Obraz orlinogolovogo grifona v iskusstve drevnego altaia" (The Eagle-headed Griffin in the Ancient Art of the Altai). *Arkheologicheskii sbornik* 28, pp. 5–29.

Basilov, Vladimir N., ed.

1989 *Nomads of Eurasia.* Catalogue translated by Mary Fleming Zirin. Exh. cat. Los Angeles: Natural History Museum of Los Angeles County; Seattle: University of Washington Press.

Beijing

1956 Zhongguo Kexueyuan Kaogu Yanjiusuo. *Henan Huixian fajue baogao* (Report on the Excavation at Hui County, Henau Province). Beijing: Kexue Chubanshe.

1959 Zhongguo Kexueyuan Kaogu Yanjiusuo. *Shangcunling Guoguo mudi* (Guo State Cemetery at Shangcunling). Beijing: Kexue Chubanshe.

1980a Zhongguo Shehui Kexueyuan, Kaogu Yanjiusuo, and Hebeisheng Wenwu Guanlichu. *Mancheng Hanmu fajue baogao* (Excavation of the Han Tombs at Mancheng). 2 vols. Beijing: Wenwu Chubanshe.

1980b Hebeisheng Bowuguan Deng (Hebei Provincial Museum). *Hebeisheng chutu wenwu xuanji* (Select Artifacts Excavated in Hebei Province). Beijing: Wenwu Chubanshe.

1980c *Yinxu Fu Hao mu.* Beijing: Wenwu Chubanshe.

1983 *Qin ling er hao tong che ma* (Bronze Chariot and Horses from Qinshihuang's Tomb). Xi'an, Shaanxi Province: Kaogu yu Wenwu Bianji Bu.

1987 See *Yushu Laoheshen.*

1989 Hubeisheng Bowuguan. *Zeng hou yimu* (The Tomb of Yi, Marquis of Zeng). 2 vols. Beijing: Wenwu Chubanshe.

1991 Guangzhou Shi Wenwu Guanli Weiyuanhui et al. *Xi Han Nanyue wang mu* (Tomb of the Prince of Nanyue of the Western Han Dynasty). 2 vols. Beijing: Wenwu Chubanshe.

1992 *Xi'an: Legacies of Ancient Chinese Civilization.* Beijing.

1993 *Houma zhutong yizhi.* 2 vols. Beijing: Wenwu Chubanshe.

1998 *Zhongguo qingtongqi quanji* (Compendium of Chinese Bronzes). Vol. 12, *Qin Han.* Beijing: Wenwu Chubanshe.

2001 *1999 Zhongguo zhongyao kaogu fanxian* (Major Chinese Archaeological Discoveries in 1999). Beijing: Wenwu Chubanshe.

Berdnikova, V. I., V. M. Vetrov, and Yu. P. Lykhin

1991 "Skifo-sibirskii stil' v khudozhestvennoi bronze verkhnei leny" (The Scythian-Siberian Style in the Bronze Art of the Upper Lena). *Sovetskaia arkheologiia*, no. 2, pp. 196–206.

Berti, Roberto, and Edoardo La Porta, eds.

1997 *Glorie de Tracia: L'oro più antico, i tesori, i miti.* Exh. cat. Florence: Basilica di S. Croce, Museo dell'Opera e Cripta.

Bökönyi, Sándor

1974 *The Przevalsky Horse.* Translated from Hungarian by Lili Halápy. London: Souvenir Press.

Bokovenko, N. A.

2000 "The Origins of Horse Riding and the Development of Ancient Central Asian Nomadic Riding Harnesses." In Davis-Kimball et al. 2000, pp. 304–10.

Borovka, Grigorïi I.

1960 *Scythian Art.* Translated from German by V. G. Childe. Reprint of 1928 ed. Kai Khosru Monographs on Eastern Art. New York: Paragon Book Gallery.

von Bothmer, Dietrich, ed.

1990 *Glories of the Past: Ancient Art from the Shelby White and Leon Levy Collection.* Exh. cat. New York: The Metropolitan Museum of Art.

Brinker, Helmut

1975 *Bronzen aus dem alten China.* Exh. cat. Zürich: Haus zum Kiel, Museum Rietberg.

Bulbeck, F. David, and Noel Barnard, eds.

1996 –97 *Ancient Chinese and Southeast Asian Bronze Age Cultures: The Proceedings of a Conference Held at the Edith and Joy London Foundation Property, Kioloa, NSW, 8–12 February 1988. Conference Papers.* 2 vols. Taipei: SMC Publishing.

Bunker, Emma C.

1978a "The Anecdotal Plaques of the Eastern Steppe Regions." In Denwood 1978, pp. 121–42.

1978b "The Long Sword and Scabbard Slide in Asia," a review. *Oriental Art* 24, no. 3 (autumn), pp. 331–32.

1979 "Alligators or Crocodiles in Ancient China." *Oriental Art,* n.s., 25, no. 3, pp. 340–41.

1981 "Ancient Art of Central Asia, Mongolia, and Siberia." In Markoe 1981, pp. 139–85.

1983–85 "The Steppe Connection." *Early China* 9–10, pp. 70–76.

1987 "Two Snakes and a Frog: A Warring States Period Bronze Belt Buckle from Eastern Mongolia in the Asian Art Museum of San Francisco." *Orientations* 18 (January), pp. 42–45.

1988 "Lost Wax and Lost Textile: An Unusual Ancient Technique for Casting Gold Belt Plaques." In *The Beginning of the Use of Metals and Alloys: Papers from the Second International Conference on the Beginning of the Use of Metals and Alloys, Zhengzhou, China, 21–26 October 1986,* edited by Robert Maddin, pp. 222–27. Cambridge, Mass.: MIT Press.

1989 "Dangerous Scholarship: On Citing Unexcavated Artefacts from Inner Mongolia and North China." *Orientations* 20 (June), pp. 52–59.

1990a "Ancient Ordos Bronzes with Tin-Enriched Surfaces." *Orientations* 21 (January), pp. 78–80.

1990b "Bronze Belt Ornaments from North China and Inner Mongolia." In Von Bothmer 1990, pp. 65–72.

1992a "Gold Belt Plaques in the Siberian Treasure of Peter the Great: Dates, Origins, and Iconography." In Seaman 1992, pp. 201–22.

1992b "Significant Changes in Iconography and Technology among Ancient China's Northwestern Pastoral Neighbors from the Fourth to the First Century B.C." *Bulletin of the Asia Institute*, n.s., 6, pp. 99–115.

1993 "Gold in the Ancient Chinese World: A Cultural Puzzle." *Artibus Asiae* 53, no. 1–2, pp. 27–50.

1994a "The Enigmatic Role of Silver in China." *Orientations* 25 (November), pp. 73–78.

1994b "The Metallurgy of Personal Adornment." In White and Bunker 1994, pp. 31–54.

1997 "A Late Eastern Zhou Lamp Stand: Questions of Identity and Gender." *Orientations* 28 (October), pp. 67–71.

1997a with Richard Kimball and Julie Segraves. "Ancient Gold Wire in China." *Orientations* 28 (March), pp. 94–95.

2001 "The Cemetery at Shanpula, Xinjiang: Simple Burials, Complex Textiles." In Keller and Schorta 2001, pp. 15–45.

Bunker, Emma C., et al.

1997 *Ancient Bronzes of the Eastern Eurasian Steppes from the Arthur M. Sackler Collections.* New York: Arthur M. Sackler Foundation.

Bunker, Emma C., Bruce Chatwin, and Ann R. Farkas

1970 *"Animal Style" Art from East to West.* Exh. cat. New York: Asia House Gallery, Asia Society.

Bunker, Emma C., Julia M. White, and Jenny So

1999 *Jin cui liu fang: Mengdiexuan cang Zhongguo gudaishi wu / Adornment for the Body and Soul: Ancient Chinese Ornaments from the Mengdiexuan Collection.* Exh. cat. Hong Kong: University Museum and Art Gallery, University of Hong Kong.

Burkett, Mary E.

1979 *The Art of the Felt Maker.* Kendal, Cumbria: Abbot Hall Art Gallery.

Burney, Charles

1999 "Beyond the Frontiers of Empire: Iranians and Their Ancestors." *Iranica Antiqua* 24, pp. 1–20.

Carter, Martha L.

1993 "A Preliminary Study of Two Indo-Scythian Bronzes in the Nitta Group Collection." In *Proceedings of the Twelfth International Conference of the European Association of South Asian Archaeologists Held in Helsinky University 5–9 July 1993,* edited by Asko Parpola and Petterri Koskikallio, vol. 1, pp. 125–36. Helsinki: Suomalainen, 1994.

Chang, Claudia, and Harold A. Koster

1986 "Beyond Bones: Toward an Archaeology of Pastoralism." In *Advances in Archaeological Method and Theory,* edited by Michael B. Schiffer, vol. 9, pp. 97–148. London and New York: Academic Press.

Chang, Kwang-chih

1986 *The Archaeology of Ancient China.* 4th ed. New Haven: Yale University Press.

Changsha Chu mu

2000 Hunansheng Bowuguan et al. *Changsha Chu mu* (Changsha Chu State Tombs). 2 vols. Beijing: Wenwu Chubanshe.

Chen Fangmei

1995 *Gugong qingtong bingqi tulu / Illustrated Catalogue of Ancient Bronze Weaponry in the National Palace Museum.* Taibei: Guoli Gugong Bowuyuan.

2000 "Tian cangcang, ye mangmang, feng chui cao di xian niu yang. Beifang Caoyuan minzu de tongbing" (Bronze Weapons from the People of the Northern Steppes). *Gugong wenwu yuekan* 211 (October), pp. 4–22.

Chen Yinke

1994 *Sui-Tang Zhidu yuanyuan luelun gao* (Origins of Sui and Tang Institutions). Taipei. First published 1944.

Chen Zhengxiang

1983 *Zhongguo wenhua dili* (The Cultural Geography of China). Beijing.

Cheng Changxin and Zhang Xiande

1982 "Lijin cangsang, chongfang guanghua —Beijingshi jianxuan gudai qingtongqi zanlan jianji" (An Exhibition of Chinese Bronzes Picked in Beijing). *Wenwu,* no. 9, pp. 24–33.

Cheng, Te-k'un

1963 *Chou China.* Cambridge: W. Heffer and Sons; Toronto: University of Toronto Press.

Cherednichenko, N. N., and E. E. Fialko

1988 "Pogrebenie zhritsy iz berdianskogo kurgana" (The Burial of a Priestess in the Berdiansk Mound). *Sovetskaia arkheologiia,* no. 2, pp. 149–66.

Chernykh, Evgenil Nikolaevich

1992 *Ancient Metallurgy in the USSR: The Early Metal Age.* Translated by Sarah Wright. New York: Cambridge University Press.

Chlenova, Nataliia L.

1963 "Le cerf scythe." *Artibus Asiae* 26, pp. 27–70.

1967 *Proiskhozhdenie i ranniaia istoriia plemen tagarskoi kul'tury* (The Origin and Early History of Tribes of the Tagar Culture). Moscow: Nauka.

Clutton-Brock, Juliet

1981 *Domesticated Animals from Early Times.* London: British Museum (Natural History); Austin: University of Texas Press.

Curtis, John E.

1978 "Some Georgian Belt-Clasps." In Denwood 1978, pp. 88–120.

Dai Yingxin and Sun Jiaxiang

1983 "Shaanxi Shenmuxian chutu Xiongnu wenwu" (The Xiongnu Artifacts Excavated at Shenmu County, Shaanxi Province). *Wenwu,* no. 12, pp. 23–30.

Dalley, Stephanie

1985 "Foreign Chariotry and Cavalry in the Armies of Tiglath-Pileser III and Sargon II." *Iraq* 47, pp. 31–48.

Dandamayev, M. A.

1994 "Media and Achaemenid Iran." In Harmatta 1994, pp. 35–65.

David-Weill sale

1972 *Collection D. David-Weill: Bronzes antiques des steppes et de l'Iran; Ordos, Caucase, Asie centrale, Louristan. . . .* Sale cat., edited by Charles Ratton. Paris: Hôtel Drouot, June 28–29.

Davis-Kimball, Jeannine, Vladimir A. Bashilov, and Leonid T. Yablonsky

1995 *Nomads of the Eurasian Steppes in the Early Iron Age.* Berkeley: Zinat Press.

Davis-Kimball, Jeannine, Eileen M. Murphy, Ludmila Koryakova, Leonid T. Yablonsky

2000 *Kurgans, Ritual Sites, and Settlements: Eurasian Bronze and Iron Age.* BAR International Series 890. Oxford: Archaeopress.

Davydova, Antonina Vladimirovna

1971 "K voprosu o khunnskikh khudozhestvennikh bronzakh" (On Bronze Art among the Huns). *Sovetskaia arkheologiia,* no. 1, pp. 93–105.

1995 *Ivolginskii arkheologicheskii kompleks* (Ivolga Archaeological Complex). Vol. 1, *Ivolginskoe gorodizhe* (Ivolga Fortress). Arkheologicheskie pamiatniki Siunnu (Archaeological Sites of the Xiongnu), vol. 1. Saint Petersburg

1996 *Ivolginskii arkheologicheskii kompleks* (Ivolga Archaeological Complex). Vol. 2, *Ivolginskii mogil'nik* (Ivolga Cemetery). Arkheologicheskie pamiatniki Siunnu (Archaeological Sites of the Xiongnu), vol. 2. Saint Petersburg.

Debaine-Francfort, Corinne, and Abduressul Idriss

2001 *Kériya, mémoire d'un fleuve: Archéologie et civilisation des oasis du Taklamakan.* Paris: EDF and Findakly.

Denwood, Philip, ed.

1978 *Arts of the Eurasian Steppelands: A Colloquy Held 27–29 June 1977.* Colloquies on Art and Archaeology in Asia, no. 7. London: University of London School of Oriental and African Art, Percival David Foundation of Chinese Art.

Desroches, Jean-Paul, ed.

2000 *L'Asie des steppes: D'Alexandre le Grand à Gengis Khan.* Exh. cat. Barcelona: Centre Cultural de la Fundació "la Caixa"; Paris: Musée National des Arts Asiatiques-Guimet. Paris: Réunion des Musées Nationaux.

Devlet, Marianna A.

1980 *Sibirskie poiasnye azhurnye plastiny: II v. do n.e.–I v. n.e* (Siberian Openwork Belt Plaques: 2nd Century B.C.–1st Century A.D.). Moscow: Nauka.

Di Cosmo, Nicola

1999 "The Northern Frontier in Pre-Imperial China." In Loewe and Shaughnessy 1999, pp. 885–966.

2002 *Ancient China and Its Enemies: The Rise of Nomadic Power in East Asian History.* Cambridge: Cambridge University Press.

Duan Shu'an, ed.

1995 *Beifang minzu: Zhongguo qingtongqi quanji, 15, Zhongguo meishu fenlei quanji* (Minority Peoples of the North: Compendium of Chinese Bronzes; Categorized Compendium of Chinese Art, no. 15). Beijing: Wenwu Chubanshe.

Egami, Namio, and Seiichi Mizuno

1935 *Uchi Mōko Chōjō chitai: Mōko saisekki bunka, Suien seidōki oyobi Shina Hokkyō Josekimon doki iseki / Inner Mongolia and the Region of the Great Wall.* Tokyo: Tōa Kōko Gakkai.

Eliade, Mircea

1964 *Shamanism: Archaic Techniques of Ecstasy.* Translated from French by Willard R. Trask. Bollingen series, 76. New York: Bollingen Foundation.

Érdy, Miklós

1995 "Hun and Xiongnu Type Cauldron Finds throughout Eurasia." *Eurasian Studies Yearbook* 1995, pp. 5–94.

Eskenazi

1977 *Ancient Chinese Bronze Vessels, Gilt Bronzes, and Sculptures: Two Private Collections, One Formerly Part of the Minkenhof Collection.* Exh. cat. London: Eskenazi Ltd.

1995 *Early Chinese Art: 8th century B.C.–9th Century A.D.* Exh. cat. London: Eskenazi Ltd.

1996 *Sculpture and Ornament in Early Chinese Art.* Exh. cat. London: Eskenazi Ltd.

Feng Zhou

1983 "Kaogu zaji" (Random Notes on Archaeolgy). *Kaogu yu wenwu,* no. 1, pp. 101–5.

Fong, Wen, ed.

1980 *The Great Bronze Age of China: An Exhibition from the People's Republic of China.* Exh. cat. New York: Metropolitan Museum of Art.

Fu Tianqiu, ed.

1985 *Zhongguo meishu quanji, diao su bian.* Vol. 2, *Qin Han diao su* (Sculpture of the Qin and Han Dynasties). Beijing: Renmin Meishu Chubanshe.

Gai Shanlin

1965 "Neimenggu zizhiqu Zhungeerqi Sujigou chutu yipi tongqi" (The Bronze Objects Unearthed at Soujigou, Jungar Banner, Inner Mongolian Autonomous Region). *Wenwu,* no. 2, pp. 44–46.

1989 *Wulanchabu yanhua* (Petroglyphs in the Wulanchabu Grassland). Beijing: Wenwu Chubanshe.

Galanina, Liudmila K.

1994 "K probleme khronologii kelermesskikh kurganov" (On the Kelermes Kurgans' Chronology). *Rossiiskaia arkheologiia,* no. 1, pp. 92–107.

Gale, Esson McDowell, trans.

1931 *Yan tie lun / Discourses on Salt and Iron: A Debate on State Control of Commerce and Industry in Ancient China, Chapters I–XIX.* Translated from the Chinese of Huan Kuan and with notes by Esson McDowell Gale. Leiden: E. J. Brill.

Gao Tianlin

1991 "Huanghe Liuyu Xin Shiqi de Taogu Bianxi" (Analysis of the Neolithic Pottery Beakers in the Yellow River Valley). *Kaogu xuebao,* no. 2, pp. 125–40.

Gimbutas, Marija Alseikaité

1965   *Bronze Age Cultures in Central and Eastern Europe.* The Hague: Mouton.

Godard, André

1950   *Le trésor de Ziwiyè (Kurdistan).* Publications du Service Archéologique de l'Iran. Haarlem: J. Enschedé.

Goldman, Bernard

1974–77   "The Animal Style at Ziwiyeh." *Ipek* 24, pp. 54–67.

Grach, A. D.

1983   "Istoriko-kul'turnaya obshchnost' ranneskifskogo vremeni v tsentral'noi Azii" (The Historical-Cultural Commonality of the Early Scythian Period in Central Asia). *Arkheologicheskii sbornik* 23, pp. 30–35.

Griaznov, Mikhail Petrovich

1969   *The Ancient Civilization of Southern Siberia.* Translated by James Hogarth. Geneva.

1984   *Der Grosskurgan von Arzan in Tuva, Südsibirien.* Translated by A. von Schebek. Materialien zur allgemeinen und vergleichenden Archäologie, vol. 23. Munich: C. H. Beck.

Griessmaier, Viktor

1936   *Sammlung Baron Eduard von der Heydt, Wien: Ordos-Bronzen, Bronzen aus Luristan und dem Kaukasus, Werke chinesischer Kleinkunst aus verschiedenen Perioden.* Vienna: Krystall-Verlag.

Guo Min (Baicheng City Museum)

1997   "Jilin Da'an xian Houbaoshi mudi diaocha" (Excavation of a Cemetery at Houbaoshi in Da'an County, Jilin Province). *Kaogu,* no. 2, pp. 85–86.

Gyllensvärd, Bo

1953   *Chinese Gold and Silver in the Carl Kempe Collection.* Stockholm: Nordisk Rotogravyr.

Hall, Mark E.

1997   "Towards an Absolute Chronology for the Iron Age of Inner Asia." *Antiquity* 71, no. 274 (December), pp. 863–74.

Han Ruben and Emma Bunker

1993   "Biaomian fuxi de E'erduosi qingtong shipin de younjiu" (The Study of Ancient Ordos Bronze with Tin—Enriched Surface in China). *Wenwu,* no. 9, pp. 80–96.

Han Xiang

1982   "Yanqi guodu, Yanqi dudufu zhisuo yu Yanqi zhencheng" (The Capital of the State of Yangi, the Commandery of Yanqi, and the Town of Yanqi). *Wenwu,* no. 4.

Harmatta, János, ed.

1994   *History of Civilizations of Central Asia.* Vol. 2, *The Development of Sedentary and Nomadic Civilizations, 700 B.C. to A.D. 250.* Paris: Unesco.

Haskins, John F.

1988   "China and the Altai." *Bulletin of the Asia Institute* 2, pp. 1–9.

Haussig, Hans Wilhelm

1992   *Archäologie und Kunst der Seidenstrasse.* Darmstadt: Wissenschaftliche Buchgesellschaft.

He Yong and Liu Jianzhong

1993   "Hebei Huailai Ganzibao faxian de Chunqiu muqun" (A Group of Tombs from the Spring and Autumn Period Discovered at Ganzibao in Huailai, Hebei Province). *Wenwu chunqiu,* no. 2, pp. 23–40, 75, figs. 3–16.

Hearn, Maxwell K.

1987   *Ancient Chinese Art: The Ernest Erickson Collection in The Metropolitan Museum of Art.* New York: The Metropolitan Museum of Art.

Hebei

1995   Hebeisheng Wenwu Yanjiusuo. *Cuo mu: Zhan guo Zhongshan guo guo wang zhi mu* (Tomb of Cuo, the King of the Zhongshan State in the Warring States Period). 2 vols. Beijing: Wenwu Chubanshe.

Henan

1959   Henansheng Wenhuaju Wenwu Gongzuodui. *Henan Xinyang Chumu wenwu tulu.* Zhengzhou: Henan Renmin Chubanshe.

Höllmann, Thomas O.

1992   "Social Structure and Political Order as Reflected in the Maoqinggou Burials: A Few Preliminary Remarks." Paper given at International Conference of Archaeological Cultures of the North Chinese Ancient Nations, Huhehot, Inner Mongolia, August 1992.

Höllmann, Thomas O., and George W. Kossack

1992   *Maoqinggou: Ein eisenzeitliches Gräberfeld in der Ordos-Region (Innere Mongolei).* Contributions by Karl Jettmar et al. Materialien zur allgemeinen und vergleichenden Archäologie, vol. 50. Mainz: Philipp von Zabern.

Hôtel Drouot

1996   *Bronzes des steppes.* Sale cat. Paris: Hôtel Drouot, October 18.

1999   *Archéologie: Art des steppes, bassin méditerranéen et Moyen-Orient.* Sale cat. Paris: Hôtel Drouot, November 9, 1999.

Hu Changyu

1983   with Sichuan Wenwu Quanli Weiyuanhui. "Chengdu shuyang Xi Han muguomu." *Kaogu yu wenwu,* no. 2, pp. 26–27.

Huang Xiaofeng and Liang Xiaoqing

1985   "Gansusheng Huachixian faxian toudiao jin daishi" (The Gold Openwork Buckles Unearthed in Huachi County, Gansu Province). *Wenwu,* no. 5, p. 40.

Huang Zhanyue

1996   "Guanyu Liangguang chutu Beifang dongwu wen paishi wenti" (On the Tablet Ornament of the Northern Animal Designs Unearthed in Guangdong and Guangxi). *Kaogu yu wenwu,* no. 2, pp. 55–60.

Humphrey, Caroline, and David Sneath, eds.

1996   *Culture and Environment in Inner Asia.* 2 vols. Cambridge: White Horse Press.

Jacobson, Esther

1983   "Siberian Roots of the Scythian Stag Image." *Journal of Asian History* 17, pp. 68–120.

1984 "The Stag with Bird-Headed Antler Tines: A Study in Image Transformation and Meaning. *Bulletin of the Museum of Far Eastern Antiquities* 56, pp. 113–80.

1985 "Mountains and Nomads: A Reconsideration of the Origins of Chinese Landscape Representation." *Bulletin of the Museum of Far Eastern Antiquities* 57, pp. 133–80.

1988 "Beyond the Frontier: A Reconsideration of Cultural Interchange between China and the Early Nomads." *Early China* 13, pp. 201–40.

1992 "Symbolic Structures as Indicators of the Cultural Ecology of the Early Nomads." In Seaman 1992.

1993 *The Deer Goddess of Ancient Siberia: A Study in the Ecology of Belief.* Studies in the History of Religions, vol. 55. Leiden: E. J. Brill.

1995 *The Art of the Scythians: The Interpenetration of Cultures at the Edge of the Hellenic World.* Handbuch der Orientalistik, ser. 8, Zentralasien, vol. 2. Leiden: E. J. Brill.

1999 "Early Nomadic Sources for Scythian Art." In Reeder 1999.

Janse, Olov

1932 "Tubes et boutons cruciformes trouvés en Eurasie." *Bulletin of the Museum of Far Eastern Antiquities* 4 (1932), pp. 187–209.

Jettmar, Karl

1964 *Die frühen Steppenvölker: Der eurasiatische Tierstil, Entstehung und sozialer Hintergrund.* Kunst der Welt, ser. 1, Die aussereuropäischen Kulturen. Baden-Baden.

1967 *Art of the Steppes.* Translated by Ann E. Keep. Art of the World. New York: Crown Publishers.

Jettmar, Karl, and Volker Thewalt

1987 *Between Gandhara and the Silk Roads: Rock-Carvings along the Karakorum Highway. Discoveries by German-Pakistani Expeditions, 1979–1984.* Exh. cat. London: Pitt Rivers Museum; Mainz: Philipp von Zabern.

Ji Naijun

1989 "Yan'an diqu wenguanhui shoucang de Xiongnu wenwu" (The Xiongnu Artifacts Kept by the Administrative Committee on Cultural Relics in the Yan'an Region). *Wenbo*, no. 4, pp. 72–73.

Jia Zhenguo

1985 "Xi Han Qiwang mu suizang qiwu keng" (The Funerary Pits around the Tomb of Prince Qi of the Western Han Dynasty). *Kaogu xuebao*, no. 2, pp. 223–66, pls. 13–20.

Jin Fengyi

1982 "Lun Zhongguo Dongbei digu hanquren qingtong duanjian de wenhua yicun." *Kaogu xuebao*, no. 4, pp. 387–426.

1990 "Shanrong muzang chenhequan." *Beijing kaogu*, no. 8, pp. 2–7, 32, 35.

Jinan

1997 Ziboshi Bowuguan and Qi Gucheng Bowuguan. *Linzi Shangwang mu di* (Ancient Cemeteries at Shangwang, Linzi). Jinan: Qilu Shushe.

Kaogu

1976 Beijingshi Wenwu Guanlichu. "Beijing diqu de you yi zhongyao kaogu shouhuo Changping Baifu Xizhou mugongmu de xin qishi" (The Wood-Chambered Tombs from the Western Zhou Dynasty at Baifu in Changping County, Beijing Area). *Kaogu*, no. 4, pp. 246–58.

1977 Neimenggu Bowuguan and Neimenggu Wenwu Gongzuodui. "Neimenggu Zhungeerqi Yulongtai de Xiongnu mu" (The Xiongnu Tomb at Yulongtai in Jungar Banner, Inner Mongolia). *Kaogu*, no. 2, pp. 111–14.

1981 Zhongguo Shehuikexueyuan Aksogu Yanjiusuo Dongbei Gongzuodui. "Neimenggu Ningchengxian Nanshan'gen 102 hao shiguomu" (Cist-Tomb No. 102 at Nanshan'gen, Ningcheng County, Inner Mongolia). *Kaogu*, no. 4, pp. 304–8.

1984 Zhongguo Kexueyuan Kaogu Yanjiusuo Neimenggu Gongzuodui. "Neimenggu Aohanqi Zhoujiadi mudi fajue jianbao" (Excavation of a Cemetery at Zhoujiadi, Aohan Banner, Inner Mongolia). *Kaogu*, no. 5, pp. 417–26.

1988 Heilongjiangsheng Bowuguan and Qigihaershi Wenguanzhan. "Qigihaershi Dadaosanjiazi muzang qingli" (Excavation of Tombs at Dadaosanjiazi, Qiqihar). *Kaogu*, no. 12, pp. 1090–98.

1997 Xinjiang Wenwu Kaogu Yanjiusuo, Hami Diqu Wenguansuo. "Xinjiang Hamishi Hanqigou mudi fajue jianbao" (Excavation of a Cemetery at Hanqigou in Hami, Xinjiang Province). *Kaogu*, no. 9, pp. 33–38.

2000 Kaifengshi Wenwu Guanli Chu. "Henan Qixian Xucungang yihao Han mu fajue jianbao" (Excavation of the No. 1 Han Tomb at Xucungang, Qi County, Henan Province). *Kaogu*, no. 1, pp. 38–44.

Kaogu xuebao

1964 Henansheng Wenhua Ju Wenwu Gongzuodui. "Luoyang Xi Han bihua mu fajue baogao" (Excavation of a Western Han Tomb with Wall Paintings at Luoyang) *Kaogu xuebao*, no. 2, pp. 107–24.

1975 Zhongguo Kexueyuan Kaogu Yanjiusuo Neimenggu Gongzuodui. "Ningcheng Nanshan'gen yizhi fajue baogao" (Excavation of Archaeological Sites at Nanshan'gen, Ningcheng County, Liaoning Province). *Kaogu xuebao*, no. 1, pp. 117–56.

1976 Hubeisheng Bowuguan. "Yichang Qianping Zhanguo liang Han mu." *Kaogu xuebao*, no. 2, pp. 115–48.

1986 Hubeisheng Bowuguan. "Yijiuqiba nian Yunmeng Qin Han mu fajue baogao" (Excavation of Qin and Han Dynasty Tombs in Yunmeng, Hubei Province, in 1978). *Kaogu xuebao*, no. 4, pp. 479–525.

1988 Ningxia Wenwu Kaogu Yanjiusuo, Zhongguo Shehui Kexueyuan Kaogusuo Ningxia Kaoguzu, and Tongxinxian Wenwu Guanlisuo. "Ningxia Tongxin Daodunzi Xiongnu mudi" (The Xiongnu Cemetery at Daodunzi in Tongxin County, Ningxia Province). *Kaogu xuebao*, no. 3, pp. 333–56.

1989 Neimenggu Wenwu Kaogu Yanjiusuo. "Liangcheng Chunxian Yaozi mudi." *Kaogu xuebao*, no. 1, pp. 57–81.

1993 Ningxia Wenwu Kaogu Yanjiusuo and Ningxia Guyuan Bowuguan. "Ningxia Guyuan Yanglang qingtong wenhua mudi" (Bronze-Culture Cemetery at Yanglang, Guyuan County, Ningxia). *Kaogu xuebao*, no. 1, pp. 13–56.

1995 Ningxia Wenwu Kaogu Yanjiusuo. "Ningxia Pengbao Yujiazhuang mudi" (The Yujiazhuang Cemetery at Pengbao, Ningxia Province). *Kaogu xuebao*, no. 1, pp. 79–107.

Kaogu yu wenwu

1988 Ningxia Wenwu Kaogu Yangiusuo and Tonxinxian Wenguan-suo. "Ningxia Tongxinxian Lijiataozi Xiongnumu qingli jianbao" (Excavation of a Xiongnu Tomb at Lijiataozi, Tongxin County, Ningxia Province). *Kaogu yu wenwu*, no. 3, pp. 17–20.

Karlbeck, Orvar

1955 "Selected Objects from Ancient Shou-Chou." *Bulletin of the Museum of Far Eastern Antiquities* 27, pp. 41–130.

Keightley, David N., ed.

1983 *The Origins of Chinese Civilization*. Berkeley and Los Angeles: University of California Press.

Keller, Dominik, and Regula Schorta, eds.

2001 *Fabulous Creatures from the Desert Sands—Central Asian Woolen Textiles from the Second Century B.C. to the Second Century A.D.* Riggisberger Berichte 10. Riggisberg: Abegg-Stiftung.

Kenk, Roman

1986 *Grabfunde der Skythenzeit aus Tuva, Süd-Sibirien: Unter Zugrun-delegung der Arbeit von A. D. Grac*. Munich: C. H. Beck.

Kessler, Adam

1993 *Empires beyond the Great Wall: The Heritage of Genghis Khan*. Contributions by Shao Qinglong et al. Exh. cat. Los Angeles: Natural History Museum of Los Angeles County.

Keverne, Roger, ed.

1991 *Jade*. London: Anness Publishing.

Kilunovskaya, Marina, and Vladimir Semenov

1995 *The Land in the Heart of Asia*. Translated from Russian by Yuri Pamfilov. Saint Petersburg: EGO Publishers.

Knauer, Elfriede Regina

1998 *The Camel's Load in Life and Death: Iconography and Ideology of Chinese Pottery Figurines from Han to Tang and Their Relevance to Trade along the Silk Routes*. Zurich: Akanthus.

Kozloff, Arielle P., David Gordon Mitten, and Michel Sguaitamatti

1986 *More Animals in Ancient Art from the Leo Mildenberg Collection*. Mainz: Philipp von Zabern.

Kriukov, Michael V., and Vadim P. Kurylev

1992 "The Origins of the Yurt: Evidence from Chinese Sources of the Third Century B.C. to the Thirteenth Century A.D." In Seaman 1992, pp. 143–56.

Kuzmina, Elena

2000 "The Eurasian Steppes: The Transition from Early Urbanism to Nomadism." In Davis-Kimball et al. 2000, pp. 118–25.

Lally, J. J., & Co.

1986 *Chinese Ceramics and Works of Art: Inaugural Exhibition*. Exh. cat. New York: J. J. Lally & Co.

1998 *Arts of the Han Dynasty*. Exh. cat. New York: J. J. Lally & Co.

Lawergren, Bo

1988 "The Origin of Musical Instruments and Sounds." *Anthropos* 83, pp. 31–45.

1990 "The Ancient Harp from Pazyryk." *Beitrage zur allgemeinen und vergleichenden Archäologie* 9–10, pp. 111–18.

1995 "The Spread of Harps between the Near and Far East
–96 during the First Millennium A D—Evidence of Buddhist Musical Cultures on the Silk Road." *Silk Road Art and Archaeology* 4, pp. 233–75.

1997 "Mesopotamien." In *Die Musik in Geschichte und Gegenwart: Allgemeine Enzyklopädie der Musik*, edited by Ludwig Finscher, vol. 6. 2d ed. Kassel: Bärenreiter.

2000 "Strings." In So 2000, pp. 65–85.

Lawton, Thomas

1982 *Chinese Art of the Warring States Period: Change and Continuity, 480–222 B.C.* Exh. cat. Washington, D.C.: Freer Gallery of Art, Smithsonian Institution.

Lawton, Thomas, et al.

1987 *Asian Art in the Arthur M. Sackler Gallery: The Inaugural Gift*. Washington, D. C.: Arthur M. Sackler Gallery, Smithsonian Institution.

Leth, André

1959 *Kinesisk kunst i Kunstindustri Museet: Catalogue of Selected Objects of Chinese Art in the Museum of Decorative Art, Copenhagen*. Copenhagen: Danske Kunstindustrimuseum.

Lewis, Mark Edward

1990 *Sanctioned Violence in Early China*. Albany: State University of New York Press.

Li Hong, ed.

1995 *Zhongguo qingtongqi quanji* (Compendium of Chinese Bronzes). Vol. 8, *Dong Zhou, 2*. *Zhongguo meishu fenlai quanji*. Beijing: Wenwu Chubanshe.

Li Xiating, Liang Ziming, and Robert Bagley

1996 *Art of the Houma Foundry*. Princeton: Princeton University Press.

Li Xueqin

1979 "Pingshan muzangqun yu Zhongshan guo de wenhua" (The Pingshan Cemetery and the Culture of the State of Zhongshan). *Wenwu*, no. 1, pp. 37–41.

1985a *Eastern Zhou and Qin Civilizations*. Translated by K. C. Chang. New Haven: Yale University Press.

1985b as editor. *Zhongguo meishu quanji, gongyi meishu bian (5), qingtong qi (2)* (Compendium of Chinese Art. Craftwork Section, 5: Bronzes, 2). Beijing: Wenwu Chubanshe.

1991 "Chu Bronzes and Chu Culture." In *New Perspectives in Chu Culture during the Eastern Zhou Period*, edited by Thomas Lawton, pp. 1–22. Princeton: Princeton University Press.

Li Yiyou

1959a "Neimenggu Helin'geerxian chutu de tongqi" (Bronzes Unearthed in Helin'geer County, Inner Mongolia). *Wenwu*, no. 6, p. 79.

1959b "Neimenggu Zhaowuda meng chutu de tongqi diaocha" (Bronzes Unearthed in the Zhaowuda League, Inner Mongolia). *Kaogu*, no. 6, pp. 276–77.

Li Yiyou and Wei Jian, eds.

1994 *Neimenggu wenwu kaogu wenji* (Papers on Inner Mongolian Cultural Relics and Archaeology). 2 vols. Beijing: Zhongguo Dabaike Quanshu Chubanshe.

Lin Gan

1984 *Xiongnu lishi nianbiao* (Chronology of Xiongnu History). Beijing: Zhonghua Shuju.

Lin Yun

1986 "A Reexamination of the Relationship between Bronzes of the Shang Culture and of the Northern Zone." In Chang 1986, pp. 237–73.

1998 "Dui Nanshangen M102 chutu kewen guban de yixie kanfa." In *Lin Yun xueshu wenji* (Scholastic Collection of Lin Yun), pp. 296–301. Beijing: Zhongguo Da Baike Quanshu Chubanshe.

Linduff, Katheryn M.

1997 "An Archaeological Overview." In Bunker et al. 1997, pp. 18–98.

1997a "Here Today and Gone Tomorrow: Bronze-Using Cultures outside the Central Plain." *Lishi Yuyan Yanjiusuo Jikan* (Bulletin of the Institute of History and Philology, Nankang, Academia Sinica, Taipei), pp. 393–428.

2000a "Beyond Essentializing Interpretation: What Archaeological Remains Can Tell Us about Life and Art in the Northern Frontier." Paper delivered at China Institute, April 1, 2000.

2000b "Imaging the Horse in Early China: From the Table to the Stable." Paper delivered at the symposium, *Horses and Humans: The Evolution of Equine/Human Relationships*, Powder Mill Nature Reserve, Pittsburgh, October 17–21, 2000.

Linduff, Katheryn M., and Zhang Zhongpei

2000 "Regional Lifeways and Cultural Remains in the Northern Corridor." Paper delivered at the Society for American Archaeology.

Littauer, M. A., and J. H. Crouwel

1979 *Wheeled Vehicles and Ridden Animals in the Ancient Near East*. Handbuch der Orientalistik, ser. 7, Künst und Archäologie, vol. 1. Leiden: E .J. Brill.

Litvinskii, Boris A.

1984 *Eisenzeitliche Kurgane zwischen Pamir und Aral-See*. Munich: C. H. Beck.

Liu Dezhen and Xu Junchen

1988 "Gansu Qingyang Chunqiu Zhanguo muzang de qingli" (Excavation of a Tomb from the Spring and Autumn and the Warring-States Periods in Qingyang Gansu Province). *Kaogu*, no. 5, pp. 413–24.

Loehr, Max

1949 "Ordos Daggers and Knives: New Material, Classification, and Chronology. First Part: Daggers." *Artibus Asiae* 12, no. 1–2, pp. 23–83.

1951 "Ordos Daggers and Knives: New Material, Classification, and Chronology. Second Part: Knives." *Artibus Asiae* 14, no. 1–2, pp. 77–162.

1956 *Chinese Bronze Age Weapons: The Werner Jannings Collection in the Chinese National Palace Museum, Peking*. Ann Arbor: Michigan University Press; Oxford: Oxford University Press.

Loewe, Michael

1993 "Yen t'ieh lun" (On Salt and Iron, by Huan Kuan). In *Early Chinese Texts: A Bibliographic Guide*, edited by Michael Loewe, pp. 477–82. Berkeley and Los Angeles: University of California Press.

Loewe, Michael, and Edward L. Shaughnessy, eds.

1999 *The Cambridge History of Ancient China: From the Origins of Civilization to 221 B.C.* Cambridge: Cambridge University Press.

Lu Guilan

1988 "Yulin diqu shoucang de bufeng Xiongnu wenwu" (Some Xiongnu Artifacts in the Collections in the Yulin Region). *Wenbo* (Relics and Antiquities), no. 6, pp. 16–19.

Lu Liancheng and Hu Zhisheng

1988 *Baoji Yuguo mudi* (Yu State Cemeteries in Baoji). 2 vols. Beijing: Wenwu Chubanshe.

Luo Feng and Han Kongle

1990 "Ningxia Guyuan jinnian faxian de beifangxi qingtongqi" (Bronzes of the Northern Style Unearthed in Guyuan, Ningxia Province, in Recent Years). *Kaogu*, no. 5, pp. 403–18.

Macdonald, David, ed.

1984 *The Encyclopedia of Mammals*. New York: Facts on File.

Machida, Akira

1987 *Kodai Higashi Ajia no sōshokubo* (Decorated Tombs in Ancient East Asia). Kyōto.

Marazov, Ivan, ed.

1998 *Ancient Gold: The Wealth of the Thracians. Treasures from the Republic of Bulgaria*. Essays by Alexander Fol, Margarita Tacheva, and Ivan Venedikov. Exh. cat., Saint Louis Art Museum and other cities. New York: Harry N. Abrams.

Markoe, Glenn, ed.

1981 *Ancient Bronzes, Ceramics, and Seals: The Nasli M. Heeramaneck Collection of Ancient Near Eastern, Central Asiatic, and European Art, Gift of the Ahmanson Foundation*. Essays by P. R. S. Moorey, Emma C. Bunker, Edith Porada, and Glenn Markoe. Exh. cat. Los Angeles: Los Angeles County Museum of Art.

Masson, V. M., and Timothy Taylor

1989 "Soviet Archaeology in the Steppe Zone. Introduction." *Antiquity* 63, no. 241 (December), pp. 779–83.

Matiushchenko, V. I., and Larisa V. Tataurova

1997 *Mogil'nik Sidorovka v Omskom Priirtysh'e*. Novosibirsk: Nauka.

Mayor, Adrienne

1994 "Guardians of the Gold." *Archaeology* 47 (November–December), pp. 52–58.

McGovern, William Montgomery

1939 *The Early Empires of Central Asia: A Study of the Scythians and the Huns and the Part They Played in World History*. Chapel Hill: University of North Carolina.

Miho Museum

1997 *Miho Museum, South Wing*. [Shigaraki, Shiga Pref.]: Miho Museum.

Milleker, Elizabeth J., ed.

2000 *The Year One: Art of the Ancient World, East and West*. Exh. cat. New York: The Metropolitan Museum of Art.

Miniaev, Sergei S.

1995a "The Excavation of Xiongnu Sites in the Buryatia Republic." *Orientations* 26 (November), pp. 44–45.

1995b "Noveishchie nakhodki khudozhestvennoi bronzi i problema formirovaniia 'geometricheskogo stila' v iskusstve syunnu" (The Newest Bronze Art Discoveries and the Formation of the 'Geometric Style' in the Art of the Xiongnu). *Arkheologicheskii vestnik* 4, pp. 123–36.

1996 "Les Xiongnu." In "Tombes gelées de Siberie," *Les Dossiers d'archéologie*, no. 212, pp. 74–83.

1998 "A Bronze Belt Plaque from the Dyrestuy Burial Ground." *Orientations* 29 (July–August), pp. 34–35.

1998a *Dyrestuiskii mogil'nik* (Dyrestuy Burial Ground). Arkheologicheskie pamiatniki siunnu (Archaeological Monuments of the Xiongnu), vol. 3. Saint Petersburg.

Moorey, P. R. S.

1967 "Some Ancient Metal Belts: Their Antecedents and Relatives." *Iran, Journal of the British Institute of Persian Studies* 5, pp. 83–98.

1971 *Catalogue of the Ancient Persian Bronzes in the Ashmolean Museum*. Oxford: Clarendon Press.

1998 "Material Aspects of Achaemenid Polychrome Decoration and Jewellery." *Iranica Antiqua* 33, no. 1 (1998), pp. 155–71.

Moshkova, Marina G., ed.

1992 *Stepnaia polosa aziatskoi chasti SSSR v skifo-sarmatskoe vremia* (The Steppe Belt of the Asian Area of the USSR during the Scythian-Sarmation Era). Moscow: Nauka.

Mu Shunying, Qi Xiaoshan, and Zhang Ping

1994 *Zhongguo Xinjiang gudai yishu / The Ancient Art in Xinjiang, China*. Ürümqi: Xinjiang Meishu Sheyin Chubanshe.

Munakata, Kiyohiko

1991 *Sacred Mountains in Chinese Art*. Exh. cat. Urbana-Champaign: Krannert Art Museum, University of Illinois at Urbana-Champaign; New York: The Metropolitan Museum of Art.

Murphy, E. M., and J. P. Mallory

2000 "Herodotus and the Cannibals." *Antiquity* 74, no. 284 (June), pp. 388–94.

Muscarella, Oscar White

1977 "Unexcavated Objects and Ancient Near Eastern Art." In *Mountains and Lowlands: Essays in the Archaeology of Greater Mesopotamia*, edited by Louis D. Levine and T. Cuyler Young Jr., pp. 153–207. Malibu, Ca.: Undina Press.

Musée Cernuschi

2001 *L'or des Amazones: Peuples nomades entre Asie et Europe*. Exh. cat. Paris: Musée Cernuschi.

National Museum of India

1981 *Thracian Treasures from Bulgaria*. Exh. cat. New Delhi: National Museum.

Neimenggu wenwu kaogu

1992 Yikezhaomeng Wenwu Gongzuozhan. "Yijinhuoluoqi Shihuigou faxian de E'erduosishi wenwu" (Ordos Artifacts Discovered at Shihuigou, Eijin Horo Banner). *Neimenggu wenwu kaogu*, no. 1–2, pp. 91–96.

Nelson, Sarah Milledge, ed.

1995 *The Archaeology of Northeast China: Beyond the Great Wall*. London: Routledge.

Novgorodova, Eleonora A.

1980 *Alte Kunst der Mongolei*. Translated by Lisa Schirmer. Leipzig: E. A. Seemann.

1989 *Drevniaia Mongoliia* (Ancient Mongolia). Moscow: Akademiia Nauka.

Okladnikov, A. P.

1946 "Novaia 'skifskaia' nakhodka na Verkhnei Lene" (A New "Scythian" Discovery on the Upper Lena River). *Sovetskaia arkheologiia* 8 (1946), pp. 285–88.

Ortiz, George

1994 *In Pursuit of the Absolute: Art of the Ancient World from the George Ortiz Collection*. Exh. cat. London: Royal Academy of Arts; Berne: Benteli-Werd Publishers.

Osaka Municipal Museum

1991 *Chūgoku Sengoku jidai no bijutsu: Kin no kagayaki to seichi no waza* (Art of the Chinese Warring-States Period). Exh. cat. Osaka: Osaka Shiritsu Bijutsukan.

Phillips, E. D.

1961 "The Royal Hordes: The Nomad Peoples of the Steppes." In Piggott 1961, pp. 301–28.

Piggott, Stuart, ed.

1961 *The Dawn of Civilization: The First World Survey of Human Cultures in Early Times*. London: Thames and Hudson.

Piotrovskii, Boris B., ed.

1987 *Tesori d'Eurasia: 2000 anni di storia in 70 anni di archeologia sovietica*. Exh. cat. Venice: Palazzo Ducale; Milan: Mondadori.

Piotrovskii, Boris B., and Klaus Vierneisel

1991   *L'or des Scythes: Trésors de l'Ermitage, Leningrad*. Exh. cat. Brussels: Musée Royaux d'Art et d'Histoire.

Pirazzoli-t'Serstevens, Michèle

1982   *The Han Dynasty*. Translated by Janet Seligman. New York: Rizzoli.

1994   "Pour une archéologie des échanges: Apports étrangers en Chine—transmission, réception, assimilation." *Arts asiatiques* 49, pp. 21–33.

Polosmak, Natalia

1991   "Un nouveau kourgane à 'tombe gelée' de l'Altai (rapport préliminaire)." *Arts asiatiques* 46, pp. 5–12.

Porada, Edith

1965   with R. H. Dyson and Charles K. Wilkinson. *The Art of Ancient Iran: Pre-Islamic Cultures*. New York: Crown Publishers.

Potratz, Johannes A. H.

1963   *Die Skythen in Südrussland: Ein untergegangenes Volk in Südosteuropa*. Basel: Raggi.

Prusek, Jaroslav

1966   "The Steppe Zone in the Period of Early Nomads and China of the 9th–7th Centuries B.C." *Diogenes* 54, pp. 23–46.

1971   *Chinese Statelets and the Northern Barbarians, 1400–300 B.C.* Dordrecht: D. Reidel.

Pulleyblank, E. G.

1983   "The Chinese and Their Neighbors in Prehistoric and Early Historic Times." In Keightley 1983, pp. 411–66.

Qi Dongfang

1999   *Tangdai jin yin qi yanjiu* (Research on Tang Gold and Silver). Beijing: Zhongguo Shehui Kexue Chubanshe.

Qufu Lu guo

1982   *Qufu Lu guo gu cheng* (The Ancient Qufu City of the Kingdom of Lu). Beijing: Wenwu Chubanshe.

Ragué, Beatrix von

1970   *Ausgewählte Werke ostasiatischer Kunst*. 2d ed. Berlin-Dahlem: Museum für Ostasiatische Kunst, Staatliche Museen Preussischer Kulturbesitz.

Rawson, Jessica

1978   "The Transformation and Abstraction of Animal Motifs on Bronzes from Inner Mongolia and North China." In *Arts of the Eurasian Steppelands*, pp. 52–73. London.

1990   *Western Zhou Ritual Bronzes from the Arthur M. Sackler Collections*. 2 vols. Washington, D.C.: Arthur M. Sackler Foundation; Cambridge, Mass.: Arthur M. Sackler Museum, Harvard University.

1995   with the assistance of Carol Michaelson. *Chinese Jade: From the Neolithic to the Qing*. Exh. cat. London: British Museum.

1996   as editor. *Mysteries of Ancient China: New Discoveries from the Early Dynasties*. London: British Museum Press.

1999   "The Eternal Palaces of the Western Han: A New View of the Universe." *Artibus Asiae* 59, no. 1–2, pp. 5–58.

Rawson, Jessica, and Emma C. Bunker

1990   *Ancient Chinese and Ordos Bronzes*. Exh. cat. Hong Kong: Hong Kong Museum of Art.

Reeder, Ellen D., ed.

1999   *Scythian Gold: Treasures from Ancient Ukraine*. Essays by Esther Jacobson et al. Exh. cat. Baltimore: Walters Art Gallery; San Antonio: San Antonio Museum of Art.

Rubinson, Karen S.

1990   "The Textiles from Pazyryk: A Study in the Transfer and Transformation of Artistic Motifs." *Expedition* 32, no. 1, pp. 49–61.

1992   "A Reconsideration of Pazyryk." In Seaman 1992, pp. 68–76.

n.d.   "Helmets and Mirrors: Markers of Social Transformation." Forthcoming in the Papers from the Golden Deer Symposium. New York: The Metropolitan Museum of Art.

Rudenko, Sergei I.

1958   "The Mythological Eagle, the Gryphon, the Winged Lion, and the Wolf in the Art of the Northern Nomads." *Artibus Asiae* 21, no. 2, pp. 101–22.

1962   *Sibirskaia kollektsiia Petra I* (The Siberian Collection of Peter the Great). Moscow: Izdatel'stvo Akademii Nauk SSSR.

1969   *Die Kultur der Hsiung-nu und die Hügelgräber von Noin Ula*. Bonn: Habelt.

1970   *Frozen Tombs of Siberia: The Pazyryk Burials of Iron Age Horsemen*. Translated by M. W. Thompson. Berkeley and Los Angeles: University of California Press.

Salmony, Alfred

1933   *Sino-Siberian Art in the Collection of C. T. Loo*. Translated by Frances Chase Hollis. Paris: C. T. Loo.

Salomon, Richard

1997   "A Unique Inscribed Gandharan Buddhist Reliquary of the Late First Century B.C." *Bulletin of the Miho Museum* (Shumei Culture Foundation), no. 3, pp. 69–86.

Sarianidi, Victor Ivanovich

1985   *The Golden Hoard of Bactria: From the Tillya-tepe Excavations in Northern Afghanistan*. New York: Harry N. Abrams; Leningrad: Aurora Art Publishers.

Schafer, Edward

1950   "The Camel in China down to the Mongol Dynasty." *Sinologia* 2, no. 3, pp. 174–92.

Schiltz, Véronique

1994   *Les Scythes et les Nomades des steppes: VIIIe siècle avant J.-C.—Ier siècle après J.-C. L'univers des formes*, 39. Paris: Gallimard.

1995   as editor. *Entre Asie et Europe: L'or des Sarmates. Nomades des steppes dans l'antiquité*. Exh. cat. Daoulas: Abbaye de Daoulas.

Schorta, Regula

2001   "A Group of Central Asian Woolen Textiles in the Abegg-Stiftung Collection." In Keller and Schorta 2001, pp. 79–114.

Seaman, Gary, ed.

1992　*Foundations of Empire: Archaeology and Art of the Eurasian Steppes.* Proceedings of the Soviet-American Academic Symposia, Los Angeles County Museum of Natural History, February 3–5, 1989; Denver Museum of Natural History, June 8–11, 1989; Museum of Natural History, Smithsonian Institution, Washington, D.C., November 16–17, 1989, in conjunction with the museum exhibit, "Nomads: Masters of the Eurasian Steppe," vol. 3. Los Angeles: Ethnographics Press.

Seaman, Gary, and Daniel Marks, eds.

1991　*Rulers from the Steppe: State Formation on the Eurasian Periphery.* Los Angeles: Ethnographics Press, University of Southern California. Based mainly on papers delivered at the symposium held at the Museum of Natural History, Smithsonian Institution, Washington, D.C., November 16–17, 1989.

Shanghai

1998　*Xinjiang wei wu er Zizhiqu si lu kao qu zhen pin / Archaeological Treasures of the Silk Road in Xinjiang Uygur Autonomous Region.* Edited by Ma Chengyuan. Exh. cat. Shanghai: Shanghai Museum.

2000　*Caoyuan guibao—Neimenggu wenwu kaogu jingpin* (Treasures from the Steppes: Select Cultural and Archaeological Artifacts from Inner Mongolia). Exh. cat. Shanghai: Shanghai Museum.

Shi Yongshi

1980　"Yanguo de hengzi." In *Zhongguo kaoguxuehui de 'erci nianhui lunwenji,* pp. 172–75. Beijing: Wenwu Chubanshe.

Smirnov, Konstantin F.

1961　*Vooruzhenie savromatov* (Weaponry of the Sauromatians). Materialy i issledovaniia po arkheologii SSSR, vol. 101. Moscow: Izd-vo Akademii nauk SSSR.

So, Jenny F.

1980a　"New Departures in Eastern Zhou Bronze Designs: The Spring and Autumn Period." In Fong 1980, pp. 251–301.

1980b　"The Inlaid Bronzes of the Warring States Period." In Fong 1980, pp. 305–20.

1992　"Ordos and Qin: A Northwestern Connection." In *Zhongguo gu dai bei fang min zu kao gu wen hua guo ji xue shu yan tao hui / The International Academic Conference of Archaeological Cultures of the Northern Chinese Ancient Nations.* Huhehaote: Neimenggu Wen Wu Kao Gu Yan Jiu Suo.

1995a　"Bronze Weapons, Harness and Personal Ornaments: Signs of Qin's Contacts with the Northwest." *Orientations* 26 (November), pp. 36–43.

1995b　*Eastern Zhou Ritual Bronzes from the Arthur M. Sackler Collections.* Ancient Chinese Bronzes from the Arthur M. Sackler collections, vol. 3. Washington, D.C.: Arthur M. Sackler Foundation.

1997　"The Ornamented Belt in China." *Orientations* 28 (March), pp. 70–78.

2000　as editor. *Music in the Age of Confucius.* Exh. cat., Arthur M. Sackler Gallery, Washington, D.C. Washington, D.C.: Freer Gallery of Art and Arthur M. Sackler Gallery.

So, Jenny F., and Emma C. Bunker

1995　*Traders and Raiders on China's Northern Frontier.* Exh. cat. Washington, D.C.: Arthur M. Sackler Gallery, Smithsonian Institution; Seattle: University of Washington Press.

Song Xinchao

1997　"Zhongguo zaoqi tongjing jiqi xiangguan wenti" (Early Chinese Bronze Mirrors and Related Problems). *Kaogu xuebao,* no. 2, pp. 147–69.

Su Bai

1977　"Dongbei Neimenggu diqu de Xianbei yiji" (Vestiges of the Xianbei People in Manchuria and Inner Mongolia). *Wenwu,* no. 5, pp. 42–54.

1977a　"Shengle, Pingcheng yidai de Tuoba Xianbei—Bei Wei yizhi." *Wenwu,* no. 11, pp. 38–46.

Sulimirsky, T.

1963　"The Forgotten Sarmatians." In Bacon 1963, pp. 279–99.

Sun Ji

1994　"Xian Qin, Hn, Jin yaodai yong jinyin daikou" (Gold and Silver Belt Buckles of the Pre-Qin, Han, and Jin Periods). *Wenwu,* no. 1, pp. 50–64.

Sun Shoudao

1957　"Xichagou gumuqun beijue shijian de jiaoxun" (The Looting of Ancient Tombs at Xichagou). *Wenwu cankao ziliao,* no. 1, pp. 53–56.

1960　"Xiongnu Xichagou wenhua gumuqun de faxian" (Excavation of a Group of Ancient Tombs Representing the Xichagou Culture of the Xiongnu People). *Wenwu,* no. 8–9, pp. 25–35.

Takahama, Shu

1994　"Chūgoku no Kama." *Sōgen Kōko Tsūshin* 4 (July), pp. 2–9.

Takahama, Shu, and Hatakeyama Tei

1997　*Daisōgen no kiba minzoku: Chūgoku hoppō no seidōki* (Mounted Nomads of the Asian Steppe: Chinese Northern Bronzes). Exh. cat. Tokyo: Tokyo National Museum.

Takahama, Shu, Toshio Hayashi, and Kōichi Yukishima

1992　*Sukitai ogon bijutsu ten: Ukuraina Rekishi Hōmotsu Hakubutsukan hizō* (Scythian Gold: Museum of Historic Treasures of Ukraine). Exh. cat. Shinjuku, Tokyo: Mitsukoshi Bijutsukan; Kyōto Bunka Hakubutsukan; Fukuoka-shi Bijutsukan; Tokyo: Nihon Hōsō Kyokai; NHK Puromōshon.

Tao Zhenggang

1985　"Shanxi chutu de Shangdai tongqi." In *Zhongguo kaogu xuehui disici nianhui lunwenji 1983.* Beijing: Wenwu Chubanshe.

Tate, George H. H.

1947　*Mammals of Eastern Asia.* New York: Macmillan.

Tian Guangjin

1983   "Jinnian lai Neimenggu diqu de Xiongnu Kaogu." *Kaogu xuebao*, no. 1, pp. 7–24.

Tian Guangjin and Guo Suxin, eds.

1986   *E'erduosishi qingtongqi* (Ordos Bronzes). Beijing: Wenwu Chubanshe.

Tokyo

1983   *Chūgoku uchimōko hoppō kiba minzoku bunbutsu ten* (Artifacts of Northern Nomads in Inner Mongolia). Tokyo: Nihon Keizai Shinbunsha.

1986   *Koga bunmei tenran* (Antiquities of the Yellow River Region). Exh. cat. Tokyo: Tokyo Kokuritsu Hakubutsukan.

1988   *Tonkō, Seika Ōkoku ten: Shiruku rōdo no bi to shinpi* (Exhibition of Dunhuang and Xixia Dynasty: The Aesthetics and Mystery of the Silk Road). Exh. cat. Tokyo: Nihon Keizai Shinbunsha

1992   *Dai Mongōru* (Great Mongolia). Tokyo: Kadokawa Shoten.

Toshio Hayashi

2000   "East-West Exchanges as Seen through the Dissemination of the Griffin Motif." In *Kontakte zwischen Iran, Byzanz und der Steppe im 6.–7. Jahrhundert*, edited by Csanád Bálint, pp. 253–65. Varia Archaeologica Hungarica, vol. 10. Budapest: Institut für Archäologie der UAW. Papers from a conference held in Rome, October 25–28, 1993.

Tosi, Maurizio

1992   "Theoretical Consideration on the Origin of Pastoral Nomadism." In Seaman 1992.

Trousdale, William

1975   *The Long Sword and Scabbard Slide in Asia*. Smithsonian Contributions to Anthropology, no. 17. Washington, D.C.: Smithsonian Institution Press.

Tsultem, Niamosoryn

1987   *Dekorativno-prikladnoe iskusstvo mongolii / Mongolian Arts and Crafts / Arts artisanaux de la Mongolie / Arte decorativo aplicado de Mongolia*. Edited by D. Bayarsaikhan. Ulan-Bator: Gosizdatel'stvo.

Tu Cheng-Sheng

1999   "The 'Animal Style' Revisited." In *Exploring China's Past: New Discoveries and Studies in Archaeology and Art*, edited by Roderick Whitfield and Wang Tao, pp. 137–49. London: Saffron Books.

Uldry, Pierre, Helmut Brinker, and François Louis

1994   *Chinesisches Gold und Silber: Die Sammlung Pierre Uldry*. Exh. cat. Zürich: Museum Reitberg Zürich.

Umehara, Sueji

1933   *Shina-kodō seikwa; or, Selected Relics of Ancient Chinese Bronzes from Collections in Europe and America*. Vol. 1, part 3. Osaka: Yamanaka and Co.

1937   *Rakuyō Kin-son kōbo shūei*. Kyōto: Kobayashi Shashin Seihanjo Shuppanbu.

1956   "Two Remarkable Tombs of Wooden Construction Excavated in Pyongyang, Korea." *Archives of the Asian Art Society of America* 10, pp. 18–29.

Vainshtein, Sevyan

1980   *Nomads of South Siberia: The Pastoral Economies of Tuva*. Edited by Caroline Humphrey; translated by Michael Colenso. Cambridge Studies in Social Anthropology, vol. 25. Cambridge: Cambridge University Press.

Waldron, Arthur

1990   *The Great Wall of China: From History to Myth*. Cambridge: Cambridge University Press.

Wang Binghua

1986   "Xinjiang dongbu faxian de jipi tongqi." *Kaogu*, no. 10, pp. 887–90.

1987   "Recherches historiques préliminaires sur les Saka du Xinjiang ancien." *Arts asiatiques* 42, pp. 31–44.

Wang Changqi

1991   "Xi'anshi wenguanhui cang E'erduosishi qingtongqi jiqi tezheng" (Bronzes of the E'erduosi Style Kept in the Xi'an Administrative Committee of Cultural Relics and Their Characteristics). *Kaogu yu wenwu*, no. 4, pp. 6–11.

Wang Renxiang

1986   "Daikou lüelun" (A Study on Hook Buckles). *Kaogu*, no. 1, pp. 65–75.

1990   "Zhongguo gudai jinshiju bi zhu cha yanjiu." *Kaogu xuebao*, no. 3, pp. 267–94.

Wang Weixiang

1994   "Neimenggu Lindong Tazigou chutu de yangshou tongdao." *Beifang wenwu* (Northern Cultural Relics), no. 4, p. 31.

Wang Zhengshu

1999   "Shangbo yudiao jingpin Xianbei tou mingwen bushi" (A Study on the Inscription on a High-Quality Jade Buckle of Xianbei Origin in the Shanghai Museum). *Wenwu*, no. 4, pp. 50–53.

Wardwell, Anne E.

2000   "Indigenous Elements in Central Asian Silk Designs of the Mongol Period and Their Impact on Italian Gothic Silks." *Bulletin du CIETA*, no. 77, pp. 86–98.

Watson, Burton, trans.

1961   *Records of the Grand Historian of China*. Translated from the *Shiji*, by Sima Qian. 2 vols. New York: Columbia University Press.

1993a   *Records of the Grand Historian: Han Dynasty*. 2 vols. Rev. ed. Translated from the *Shiji*, by Sima Qian. Hong Kong and New York: Renditions-Columbia University Press.

1993b   *Records of the Grand Historian: Qin Dynasty*. Translated from the *Shiji*, by Sima Qian. Hong Kong and New York: Renditions-Columbia University Press.

Watson, William

1963   *Handbook to the Collections of Early Chinese Antiquities*. London: Trustees of the British Museum.

1971 *Cultural Frontiers in Ancient East Asia.* Edinburgh: University Press.

Watt, James C. Y.

1980 *Chinese Jades from Han to Ch'ing.* Exh. cat. New York: Asia House Gallery, Asia Society.

1990 *The Arts of Ancient China. Metropolitan Museum of Art Bulletin* 48, no. 1 (summer).

Watt, James C. Y., and Anne E. Wardwell

1997 *When Silk Was Gold: Central Asian and Chinese Textiles.* Exh. cat. New York: The Metropolitan Museum of Art.

Weber, George W., Jr.

1973 *The Ornaments of Late Chou Bronzes: A Method of Analysis.* New Brunswick, N.J.: Rutgers University Press.

Wei Zheng, Li Huren, Zou Houben

1998 "Jiangsu Xuzhoushi Shizishan Xihan mu de fajue yu Shouhuo" (Excavation and Achievements of the Western Han Period Tombs at Shizishan in Xuzhou City, Jiang Su). *Kaogu,* no. 8, pp. 1–20.

Wenwu

1980 Yikezhaomeng Wenwu Gongzuozhan and Neimenggu Wenwu Gongzuodui. "Xigoupan Xiongnu mu" (A Xiongnu Grave at Xigoupan). *Wenwu,* no. 7, pp. 1–10.

1982 Xianyang Diqu Wenguanhui, Maoling Bowuguan. "Shaanxi Maoling yi hao wuming ying chongzang ken de fajue" (Excavation of the Satellite Shaft No. 1 of the Unknown Tomb No. 1 around Maoling Mausoleum in Shaanxi Province). *Wenwu,* no. 9, pp. 1–17.

1983 Linquxian Wenhuaguan and Weifang Diqu Wenwu Guanli Weiyuanhui. "Shandong Linqu faxian Qi Xun Zeng zhuguo tongqi" (Bronzes of the States of Qi, Xun, and Zeng Discovered at Linqu County, Shandong Province). *Wenwu,* no. 12, pp. 1–6.

1988 Shaanxisheng Kaogu Yanjiusuo, Baoji Longzuozhan, and Baojishi Kaogu Gongzuo. "Shaanxi Longxian Bianjiazhuang wuhao Chunqiumu fajue jianbao" (Excavation of Tomb No. 5 from the Spring and Autumn Period at Bianjiazhuang in Long County, Shaanxi Province). *Wenwu,* no. 11, pp. 14–23, 54.

1989 Liaoningsheng Wenwu Kaogu Yanjiusuo. "Liaoning Lingyuanxian Wudaohezi Zhanguomu fajue jianbao" (Excavation of the Tombs from the Warring States Period at Wudaohezi, Lingyuan County, Liaoning Province). *Wenwu,* no. 2, pp. 52–61.

1995 Shanxisheng Kaogu Yanjiusuo Houma Gongzuozhan. "Yijiujiuer nian Houma zhutong yizhi fajue jianbao" (Excavation of a Bronze Casting Site at Houma, Shanxi Province, in 1992). *Wenwu,* no. 2, pp. 29–53.

Wenwu ziliao congkan

1985 Ningchengxian Wenhuaguan and Zhongguo Shehui Kexueyuan Yanjiu Shengwu Kaoguxi Dongbei Kaogu Zhuanye. "Ningchengxian xin faxian de Xiajiadian shang-

ceng wenhua muzang jiqi xiangguan yiwu de yangiu" (A Study on Newly Discovered Funerary Pits in Ningcheng County Representing the Upper Class Culture and Related Artifacts of Xiajiadian). *Wenwu ziliao congkan* 9, pp. 23–58.

White, Julia M., and Emma C. Bunker

1994 *Adornment for Eternity: Status and Rank in Chinese Ornament.* Exh. cat. Denver: Denver Art Museum.

White, William Charles

1934 *Tombs of Old Lo-yang: A Record of the Construction and Contents of a Group of Royal Tombs at Chin-ts'un, Honan, Probably Dating 550 B.C.* Shanghai: Kelly & Walsh, Limited.

Wilkinson, Charles K.

1955 "Assyrian and Persian Art." *Bulletin of The Metropolitan Museum of Art,* n.s., 13 (March), pp. 213–24.

1963 "Treasure from the Mannean Land." *Bulletin of The Metropolitan Museum of Art,* n.s., 21 (April 1963), pp. 274–84.

Wu En

1978 "Guanyu woguo beifang de qingtong duanjian" (Notes on the Bronze Daggers of North China). *Kaogu,* no. 5, pp. 324–33, 360.

1981 "Woguo beifang gudai dongwu wenshi" (Animal Décor of the Northern Frontier Peoples of Ancient China). *Kaogu xuebao,* no. 1, pp. 45–61.

1985 "Yin zhi Zhou chu de beifang qingtongqi" (Bronzes of Northern China from the Late Shang Dynasty to the Early Western Zhou Dynasty). *Kaogu xuebao,* no. 2, pp. 135–56.

1987 "Shilun Handai Xiongnu yu Xianbei yiji de qubie." *Zhongguo kaogu xuehui diliuci nianhui lunwenji,* pp. 136–50. Beijing.

Wu Hung

1984 "A Sanpan Shan Chariot Ornament and the Xiangrui Design in Western Han Art." *Archives of Asian Art* 37, pp. 38–59.

Xia Nai

1965 "Luoyang Xihan bihua mu zhong de Xinxiang tu" (Representations of Constellations in the Western Han Tomb with Murals in Luoyang). *Kaogu,* no. 2. Reprinted in Xia Nai 1979.

1979 *Kaoguxue he keji shi* (Essays on Archaeology of Science and Technology in China). Beijing: Kaoxue Chubanshe.

Xiang Chunsong

1984 "Xiaoheishigou faxian de qingtongqi" (Bronzes Discovered at Xiaoheishigou). *Neimenggu wenwu kaogu,* no. 3, pp. 120–23.

Xiang Chunsong and Li Yi

1995 "Ningcheng Xiaoheishigou shiguomu diaocha qingli baogao" (Excavation of a Stone-Chambered Tomb at Xiaoheishigou, Ningcheng, Inner Mongolia). *Wenwu,* no. 5, pp. 4–22.

Xinjiang wenwu

1998 Xinjiang wenwu kaogu yanjiusuo, Shihezi junken bowuguan. "Shihezi shi wenwu pucha jianbao" (A Summary of the General Examination of the Cultural Relics at the City of Shihezi). *Xinjiang wenwu,* no. 4, pp. 54–64.

Yablonsky, Leonid T.

1990 "Burial Place of a Massagetan Warrior." *Antiquity* 64, pp. 288–96.

1994 as editor. *Kurgany levoberezhnogo Ileka* (Burial Mounds on the Left Bank of the Ilek River). Vol. 2. Moscow: Institute of Archaeology, Russian Academy of Science, 1994.

1995 "The Material Culture of the Saka and Historical Reconstruction." In Davis-Kimball, Bashilov, and Yablonsky 1995, pp. 201–39.

2000 "'Scythian Triad' and 'Scythian World.'" In Davis-Kimball et al. 2000, pp. 3–8.

Yan Jinzhu

1985 "Shanxi Jixian chutu Shang dai qingtongqi" (Shang Bronzes Excavated from the Ji County, Shanxi Province). *Kaogu,* no. 9, pp. 848–49.

Yan Shizhong and Li Huairen

1992 "Ningxia Xiji faxian yizuo qingtong shidai muzang" (A Newly Discovered Tomb from the Bronze Age in Xiji, Ningxia Province). *Kaogu,* no. 6, pp. 573–75.

Yang Boda, ed.

1987 *Jinyin boli falang qi* (Goldwork, Silverwork, Glassware, and Enamel). Vol. 10 of *Zhongguo meishu quanji: Gong yi meishu bian* (The Great Treasury of Chinese Fine Arts: Arts and Crafts). Beijing: Wenwu Chubanshe.

Yang Hong, ed.

1992 *Weapons in Ancient China.* New York: Science Press.

Yang Ninggu and Qi Yuezhang

1999 "Ningxia Pengyang xian Jinnian chutu de Beifangxi Qingtongqi." (Bronzes of the Northern-System Recently Unearthed in Pengyang, Ningxia). *Kaogu,* no. 12, pp. 28–37.

Yang Shaoshun

1981 "Shanxi Shilou Zhujiayu Caojiayuan faxian Shang dai tongqi" (Shang Bronzes Unearthed at Zhujiayu and Caojiayuan in Shilou, Shanxi Province). *Wenwu,* no. 8, pp. 49–53.

Yang Tienan

1997 "Chaoyangshi Bowuguan shoucang de yijian qingtong duan-jian" (A Bronze Dagger in the Collection of the Chaoyang City Museum). *Wenwu,* no. 10, p. 89.

Yü, Ying-shih

1967 *Trade and Expansion in Han China: A Study in the Structure of Sino-barbarian Economic Relations.* Berkeley and Los Angeles: University of California Press.

Yuan Anzhi

1982 "Tan 'Xinyang jia' tongqi" (On the "Xinyang jia" Bronzes). *Wenwu,* no. 2, pp. 18–20.

Yushu Laoheshen

1987 Jilinsheng Wenwu Kaogu Yanjiusuo. *Yushu Laoheshen* (Excavation at Laoheshen in Yushu County). Beijing: Wenwu Chubanshe.

Zavitukhina, Mariia Pavlovna

1983 *Drevnee iskusstvo na Enisee: Skifskoe vremia* (Ancient Art along the Yenisei: The Scythian Era). Leningrad: Iskusstvo.

Zhang Yuzhong and Zhao Derong

1991 "Yili Hegu Xin Faxian de Daxing Tongqi ji Youguan Wenti" (Large Bronzes Newly Unearthed from the Yili River Valley and Related Questions). *Xinjiang wenwu,* no. 2, pp. 42–48.

Zhao Congcang

1991 "Fengxiang chutu yipi Chunqiu Zhangguo wenwu" (The Cultural Relics of the Spring and Autumn Period Unearthed in Fengxiang County). *Kaogu yu wenwu,* no. 2, pp. 2–13.

Zhao, Ji, ed.

1990 *The Natural History of China.* New York: McGraw-Hill.

Zheng Long

1991 *Zhongguo gudai beifang minzu qingtongqi wenshi yishuji* (A Collection of Artistic Designs of Bronze Ware). [Hohhot]: Neimenggu Renmin Chubanshe.

Zheng Shaozong

1991 "Lüelun Zhongguo beibu Changcheng didai faxian de dongwu wen qingtong shipai" (Bronze Tablets with Animal Motifs Discovered along the Great Wall in Northern China). *Wenwu chunqiu,* no. 4, pp. 1–32.

Zhong Kan

1978 "Ningxia Guyuanxian chutu wenwu" (Artifacts Unearthed in Guyuan County, Ningxia Province). *Wenwu,* no. 12, pp. 86–90.

Zhong Kan and Han Kongle

1983 "Ningxia nanbu Chunqiu Zhanguo shiqi de qington wenhua" (The Bronze Culture of the Spring and Autumn and the War-ring States Periods in Southern Ningxia Province). *Zhongguo kaogu xuehui disici nianhui lunwenji,* 1983, pp. 203–13.

Zhongguo wenwu bao

1991 "Anxiang qingli Xi Jin Liu Hong mu" (The Excavation of Liu Hong's Tomb of the Western Jin Dynasty at Anxiang). *Zhongguo wenwu bao,* August 18, 1991, p. 1.

Zhou Xinghua

1989 "Ningxia Zhongweixian Langwozikeng de qingtong duan-jian muqun" (Excavation of Graves of Bronze Daggers at Langwozikeng, Zhongwei County, Ningxia Province). *Kaogu,* no. 11, pp. 971–80.

Zhu Jieyuan and Li Yuzheng

1983 "Xi'an dongjiao Sandiancun Xihan mu" (A Western-Han Tomb at Sandiancun in the Eastern Suburb of Xi'an). *Kaogu yu wenwu,* no. 1, pp. 22–25.

Zimmermann, Jean-Louis

1991 *Ancient Art from the Barbier-Mueller Museum.* Translated by Leonor Michelsen. New York: Harry N. Abrams.

Zou Houben and Wei Zheng

1998 "Xuzhou Shizishan Xihan mu de Jinkou Yaodai" (The Gold Buckles from a Western-Han Tomb at Shizishan, Xuzhou). *Wenwu,* no. 8, pp. 37–43.

INDEX

animal style, 4, 8, 200. *See also* animal representations

Anxiang, Hunan Province, 114

Anyang, Henan Province, 74, 76, 80

Apollonia, Bulgaria, 95

Aral Sea area, 160

archers, mounted, 12, 27

arm protector, *204*; fig. 61

arsenical alloys, 30, 77, 98, 102; nos. 64, 69, 70, 78, 80,
    105, 113

Arzhan, Tuva Republic, southern Siberia, 19

    harness ornament, 24, *25*, 161; fig. 34

    canopy finials, 19, *20*, 58, 60; fig. 24

Assyrians, 11, 25

Avesta, 5

axe heads, 74, 76, 200; no. 42

Bactria, 175, 206; no. 163

Baidi. *See* Xianyu

Baifu, Changping county, outside Beijing, 193

Bashadar, Altai Mountains, 123

    saddle ornaments, 21, *22*; fig. 30

    wooden coffin with animal combat scenes, 23, *23*, 45, 98, 122,
        165, 174; fig. 32

bells, ornament with, 177–78; no. 165. *See also* jingles

belt boss mold, 21, *22*; fig. 28

belt buckles, 94–117; nos. 59–87

belt hooks, 143–54; nos. 118–132

belt plaques, 118–42; nos. 88–117

belts, 15, 22, 23, 94, 155; fig. 31

    small weapons attached to, 19, *20*; fig. 25

Beshbalik, Xinjiang, 207

Beycesultan, Turkey, 178–79

bi (food-scooping instruments), 177

Bianjiazhuang, Long county, Shaanxi Province, 24, 64

Binder Uul, Hentii aimag, Mongolia, 6; fig. 1

Black Sea (Pontic) region, 3, 4, 8, 9, 11, 16, 18, 24, 26, 90, 124,
    160, 161, 162, 180, 183, 195

bone objects, 186

    belt ornaments, 96, 128

    cylinder bead, 45, 98, 131, 172–73; no. 159

    finials, 185–86; no. 175

    plaque, 16, *16*, 56; fig. 17

brass, 117 and n. 5

breast ornaments. *See* harness fittings; pectorals

bridle fittings, 19, 52–53; nos. 17, 19

bridle ornaments, 24, *24*, 27, 45, 49; figs. 33; no. 13

British Museum, London, 128, 129, 138

Bronze Age tombs, 17, *18*; fig. 21

buckles, 106, 174–75; nos. 74, 162. *See also* belt buckles; shoe
    buckles

Buddhism, 179

Bulgaria, 26, 46, 47, 49, 95; nos. 9, 10, 13, 60

burials, 19, 34

    kurgans, 3, 4, 34, *34*; fig. 51

    slab grave, *18*; fig. 21

Buryatia, 30, 110, 111, 132, 137

buzkashi (goat-grabbing), 13

camels, 11, 25, 35, 50, 110, 121

canopies, 34, 111; no. 81. *See also* funeral canopy and cart
    ornaments

canopy finials. *See* finials

carnelian, 113–14, 116; nos. 83, 86

Carpathian Mountains, 8

carts, 16, *16*, 111; fig. 17; no. 81. *See also* chariot fittings; funeral
    canopy, and cart ornaments

Caspian Sea region, 25, 118

casting models, 29–30, 138, *138*; no. 112

Caucasus, 78, 94, 117; no. 87

cauldrons (*fu*), 194–96; nos. 185–87

ceiling tiles, 203; fig. 60

censers. *See* incense burners

Central Plains, 199

ceramic drums, 178

Changsha, Hunan Province, 124

Chaoyang City Museum, 78

chariot fittings and ornaments, 16–17, 26, 162, 181

    fittings, 17, *17*, 52–53, 95; fig. 18

    plaque fragment, 16, *16*, 56; fig. 17

    pole ornament, 72; no. 39

    yoke ornaments, 64–65, *66*–67, 68, 69, 70; nos. 31–35, 37

    See also finials; harness fittings; jingles

chariot-shaped plaques, 16, 56, *57*; no. 23

cheekpieces. *See* harness fittings

Chengdu, Sichuan, 99–100

Chifeng, Inner Mongolia, 102

    plaque, *18*; fig. 22

Chilikta, Kazakhstan, 26, 160

Chinese, 5, 11, 15, 16, 25, 94, 170, 199, 200

    adoption of horseback riding, 8, 12

    ancient authors, 3, 11–12, 16

    landscape representations, 35, 189

    ritual vessels, 18–19, 32, 89, 96, 97, 192

Chongli county, Hebei Province, 161

Chu, state of, 25, 80, 98, 101, 124, 145, 188

Chujiayu, Shilou county, Shanxi Province, 192

cinnabar, 113, 186

clay casting model, 138; no. 112

clothing, 12, 36, 156; fig. 54

cloth of gold, 207

cloudlike patterns, 203–4, *202*, *203*, *204*, *205*; figs. 58, 60,
    61, 64

Xichagou, Xifeng county, Liaoning Province, 100, 102, 103–4, 108, 110, 111, 138n. 1, 139

Xietuncun, Ansai county, Shaanxi Province, 144

Xigoupan, Jungar banner, Inner Mongolia, *28; 30*, 55, 106, 161; figs. 39, 42, 43

Xinjiang Uyghur Autonomous Region, *11*, 16, 29, 113, 132, 183, 193, 196, 209n. 21; fig. 10; no. 171

Xinyang, Henan Province, 145

Xinyangxiang, Guyuan county, Ningxia, 45

Xinzhuangtou, Yi county, Hebei Province, 28, 52, 173

Xiongnu (Hsiung-nu), 4, 5, 11–12, 27, 30–31, 32, 53, 70, 101, 104, 106, 110, 111, 199, 127, 132, 133, 134, 136, 137, 139, 140, 169, 175, 199–200, 205, 208nn. 6, 7
  federation, 4, 27, 29, 30, 168, 199, 202, 205, 209n. 22

Xucungang, Zhulin township, Qi county, Henan Province, 55

yaks, 148

Yan, state of, 28, 52, 173

Yanglong, 186

Yanqi, Xinjiang, 114

Yan tie lun (On Salt and Iron), 12, 35

Yanxiadou, 28–29

Yellow River, 26, 199

Yenisei River, 9, 29

Yeuzhi. *See* Rouzhi

Yinshan Mountains, 19, 199, 200

Yinzhuangtou, Yi county, Hebei Province, ornament, *31*; fig. 44

Yixian, Hebei Province, 28

Yu family cemetery, Rujiahuang, 193

Yuhuangmiao, Yanqing county, Beijing district, 19, 20, *20, 21*, 172; figs. 25, 27

Yuijiazhuang cemetery, Pengpu township, 186

Yulin, Shaanxi Province, 150

Yulongtai, Jungar banner, Inner Mongolia, 24, 69, 70, 72

yurt, 12. See also *ger*

Zeng, marquis of, tomb of, 187

Zhalainoer, Inner Mongolia, 115

Zhangjiakou, Hebei Province, 19, 58

Zhao, state of, 12, 20, 26, 27

Zhaodi, emperor, tomb of, 209n. 17

Zhikaigou, 90

Zhongshan, Hebei Province, 34

Zhongwei county, Ningxia, 96

Zhou, 120, 179. *See also* Eastern Zhou; Spring and Autumn period; Warring States period; Western Zhou

Zhoujiadi, Aohan banner, Inner Mongolia, 94, 96, 156

Zhukaigou, Inner Mongolia, 19, *20*, 74; fig. 26

zithers. See *qin; se*

zither string anchor (*se rui*), 189; no. 180

Ziwiye Treasure, Iran, 18, 162, 172, 180–81; no. 168

zoomorphic motifs. *See* animal representations